CU00703969

Prodigal Daughters

Prodigal Daughters

Stories of South African Women in Exile

Edited by
Lauretta Ngcobo

UNIVERSITY OF KWAZULU-NATAL PRESS

Published in 2012 by University of KwaZulu-Natal Press
Private Bag X01
Scottsville, 3209
South Africa
Email: books@ukzn.ac.za
Website: www.ukznpress.co.za

© 2012 University of KwaZulu-Natal

All rights reserved. No part of this publication may be reproduced or transmitted in any form or by any means, electronic or mechanical, including photocopying, recording, or any information storage and retrieval system, without prior permission in writing from University of KwaZulu-Natal Press.

ISBN: 978-1-86914-234-6

Editors: Jane Argall and Sally Hines
Typesetter: Patricia Comrie
Proofreader: David Kaplin
Cover designer: MDesign
Cover photographs: Drum Social Histories / Baileys African History Archive / Africa Media Online
(top left); Gisele Wulfsohn / South Photographs / African Media Online (top right); handmadepictures / 123RF.COM (bottom).

Printed and bound by Interpak Books, Pietermaritzburg

'If you do not write your history, history will write you off.'

For Thokozile maZulu Chaane who, in her final hours, inspired this collection.

Contents

Acknowledgements

Just hours before she died, I had the privilege of spending time with Thokozile maZulu Chaane when we spoke together of our lives as young girls at Fort Hare College, our long years together in exile and our writing. Her funeral on 29 December 2009 in Johannesburg provided the opportunity for many women from exile to come together to mourn and celebrate the life of an admired and longstanding friend. It was here that we agreed that it was not only important to recall our history in exile, but to capture it for posterity as well.

I volunteered to undertake this responsibility. I undertook it with joy. I had no idea that that happy afternoon I spent with Thokozile was our last because an hour after leaving her house she died. For me this book is a commemoration of her life.

I would like to thank the women who rose to this task and whose stories are recorded in this anthology. Each has contributed because deep down each has believed in the importance and worth of the project. I knew it would mean asking these women to prod old sores and to relive every twinge of pain as they recalled those many years and experiences spent in other people's countries. I have always thought that South African women are worth their salt. This collection demonstrates that.

I want to express my unreserved gratitude to Nonqaba waka Msimang and Busi D. Chaane for their sterling editorial work in assisting with the assembly of the collection. I owe a lot to them. I would also like to thank my son, Luyanda Gwina, who has been a constant support in administration and public relations in this project.

I am grateful for a stipend we received, halfway through the project, from the National Arts Council of South Africa, which assisted greatly in facilitating correspondence and meetings.

Foreword

Prodigal Daughters is not just an academic exercise. As editor, Lauretta Ngcobo has woven together a rich literary tapestry, drawing in the voices of women of various political persuasions, and affording each a brilliant space to stitch together their experiences and memories of the struggle for freedom in South Africa.

These stories from South African women who experienced exile during the years of apartheid remind us of the harsh realities women had to face under these oppressive conditions. Many were arrested, detained, imprisoned and tortured by state forces. Leaving the country of their birth, many were forced to take calculated, though dangerous, risks to cross borders. In exile many experienced discrimination; some experienced persecution in military camps. All lived with the uncertainties and stresses of being 'in the underground' and in the distant yet distinct hope that they would one day be able to return to a liberated homeland. Lauretta has invited just some of these 'prodigal daughters' to express their fears, doubts, anxieties and hopes in telling their stories.

A member of the Pan-Africanist Congress, Lauretta is herself one of this collection's 'prodigal daughters'. She tells the story of her flight into exile to escape imprisonment at home. History recognises Lauretta as an educator, writer, editor, compiler of short stories and a literary critic. Her first novel, *Cross of Gold* (1981), revolves around the turbulence of violence in South Africa from the 1950s. In *And They Didn't Die* (1990) she examines women's struggles against colonialism, racial supremacy, patriarchy, and the untold predicaments of women caught between custom, white law and the migrant system. While in Britain, Lauretta edited a collection of essays by black women writers under the title *Let It Be Told* (1987). Six years later she published a children's book, *Fiki Learns to Like Other People* (1993).

The contributors to this collection tell of experiences that are no longer shared within South Africa. They write believing in the importance of using their voices to reach a wide audience. Through their stories a dialectical framework is set up, allowing us to observe the constant motion, development and transformation of each writer as she charts the passage of leaving her country of birth to return again – for some, to an unsure present and fear of an unknown future. Each depicts an oppositional situation that is both confining and liberatory. Each looks at the causes of her exile and the ways she survived it. Each attempts to recuperate from the past and at the same time re-imagine and relive it. Their experiences transcend regionalism, move towards nationalism and encompass the dynamics of globalism.

The tensions in *Prodigal Daughters* move across various trajectories. One of these is evident in the diverse forms of social and cultural alienation that exile brings. Another is in the deep sense of loss – of land, family, job, friends – and the attendant feelings of isolation and estrangement. Some speak of being assimilated into 'foreign cultures' and being influenced by international communities of intellectuals. Some talk of developing a sense of 'fragmented self', of non-belonging, and, with it, a longing to return home and become part of the 'struggle' within South Africa. All continued to believe that while in exile they still had a personal stake in a future liberated South Africa.

The narratives in this collection therefore suggest that, for these women, there was never a moment of detachment or disconnection from the home country and of being outside the history of the struggle for liberation. Certainly there were frustrations between moments of flux, but their inner strength and courage predicated their hopes and dreams for their return. From the shores of exile we are able to witness the challenges of the 'politics of memory' with each writer refusing to be caught in the 'politics of oblivion'.

Lauretta has pulled together stories of an intensely personal nature, inviting these South African women who experienced exile to expose their vulnerabilities. The successful outcome is testament to her dedication, commitment and sensitivity.

Prodigal Daughters is a thoughtful and diverse collection of stories with a distinct literary bent. It makes for compelling reading.

Sumboornam (Sam) Moodley
Co-ordinator of Women in Action South Africa

Introduction

'Something is so final about being in exile, like a door banged shut in your face. Exile is a vast desert, a call on unconscious inner resources for survival. You live through exile, survive and grow through it.' – Baleka Mbete

The close of the nineteenth century put an end to the wars of dispossession in our part of the continent, South Africa. The English and the Afrikaner ended their feud and began settling the agenda of joint control of their newly acquired booty of manpower and land. So began a century that was to be like no other in our history.

From beginning to end, the twentieth century was marked by sharply divided, racist and oppressive policies that brought untold suffering to those who were of non-European descent, in particular, to black Africans who are the original inhabitants of the continent.

By the end of 1912, a clear delineation had been laid out for the future of what life would be like for all racial groups in the country for the rest of the century. The Natives Land Act of 1913 effectively zoned Africans, who constituted eighty per cent of the population, to thirteen per cent of the land. As a result of this Act, there was simply not enough land for the African population.

African men became landless and were forced to work for wages on what had become white farms when the white government usurped African-owned land. Some had to move to work on the mines and to supply labour in industrial areas.

To execute this vast movement of people from all rural corners of the country, a Pass system was devised to control all African male movements. Going hand in hand with this was a system of taxation that would force African men out of their traditional homes, away from their families, to find money in urban areas to pay for the various taxes that were imposed on them. One could only be and work where one's Pass designated one to be, or one would fall foul of the law.

But the people who were hardest hit by the new laws were the African women who were left to fend for themselves in the reserves. The same laws prohibited women from working in the cities or following their husbands. In one stroke the white government broke the livelihood of rural people and the basic structure of their family life.

1

Women in the pre-conquest days in South Africa had enjoyed a clearly defined economic and social role that gave them independence and bestowed a high sense of self. Under white rule this was lost. In 1927, the government passed the Native Administration Act which consolidated a uniform approach to all the black peoples of African descent. Under this new law women were deemed perpetual minors and relegated to the guardianship of their fathers, husbands, sons or any male relation.

There was clearly a conflict in the practical application of the law itself. The same women who had lost their legal status and were losing their social authority were expected to take on greater responsibility as men vacated the reserves, no longer able to provide for their families. So women were not only oppressed and burdened with more responsibility, they were also disabled as the authority and power to run societies was, in the same Act, filched away and preserved for the benefit of those absent men.

What was even more paradoxical was that when African communities finally woke up to the need to form political organisations, they did so to the exclusion of their women. Women were not immediately and automatically granted membership in the African political organisations. Only as late as the 1940s were they given a universal suffrage in their organisations. And, throughout this period, even the emerging political organisations regarded it as 'unnatural' for women to participate in political work.

Stranger still, in the intervening years African women themselves were not drawn to political issues, but rather concerned themselves with domestic and social issues like Passes, rents, the cost of living and other community matters. A case of severe conditioning, I assume.

It is no surprise that there should have been such a reaction on the part of the women, for these restrictions affected their capacity to free themselves from both traditional bonds and newly imposed restrictions under the new white code of law.

Nevertheless, African males were spurred on to form their own political organisations. Party politics was a new phenomenon as a system of organising society. But the aggressive approach of the new government left them no choice but to adapt to new ways.

From the beginning, the women of the oppressed saw themselves as part of the resistance. They soon formed their own organisation to fight for their own rights. In the newly formed Bantu Women's League, they were led by the fearless Charlotte Maxeke, a Wilberforce University graduate from Ohio in the United States. On 23 September 1913, women of the Orange Free State burnt their Passes in front of the municipal offices in Bloemfontein. The skirmishes between the women and the authorities, including Indian women, went on until 1918 when the anti-Pass campaign finally ended in triumph for the women. In spite of a relaxation of the rule, the Pass issue continued to fester, bringing more and more suffering to African families throughout the twentieth century.

The Bantu Women's League had been formed under the African National Congress (ANC). But the ANC constitution of 1919 indicated clearly that women could not become full members; instead they were accorded the status of 'auxiliary membership', without voting rights. Women were to provide the catering and organise the entertainment at meetings for male politicians.

In the meantime, the arrival of the white Communist Party in 1921 had brought new ideas that had the effect of splitting African views. The Communist Party had come from Europe, aiming to attract Africans to their philosophy. The exclusive white parliament that had been formed in 1910 had created a political vacuum and the newly arrived white communists had a sympathetic outlook towards the excluded Africans. They were, therefore, seen as the convenient representatives of the African majority in the South African parliament. They were designated as the Native Representative Council, intended to represent African interests in the white parliament. As a result of this fractured view, a new African organisation was formed which held differing views from the Communist Party of South Africa (CPSA). It was called the All African Convention.

The CPSA, which changed its name in 1953 to the South African Communist Party, was expelled from the white parliament when the National Party came to power in 1948. After its expulsion, the party sought refuge in African organisations such as the ANC. This led to the subsequent split between the ANC and the Pan-Africanist Congress (PAC) in 1959.

Around 1935, Charlotte Maxeke was honoured at the All African Convention conference as a speaker. It was at this convention that a resolution was passed to establish the National Council of African Women. But, sad to say, this organisation, too, did not live up to expectations. And so for many years there was a kind of stagnation.

The Native Administration Act of 1927 imposed further conservative strictures on the position of women, which was already codified under the Natal Code. Under Customary Law, women were always deemed perpetual minors, forever assigned to the guardianship of their men folk, no matter their age or educational level. As time went on women found this inferior legal status a real handicap, exacerbated further if the man should die on the mines or away from home or should simply never return home. There was clearly a conflict of a practical nature, if nothing else.

But in the early 1940s, the ANC itself, under Dr A.B. Xuma, began to undergo changes and lay the basis for a more radical mass movement. The organisation began to push for a policy of universal adult franchise that included women. So, for the first time, the word 'adult' was advanced in a way that included women. This, in effect, introduced the idea of majority rule. This definition replaced the earlier demand of a racially segregated electoral roll that the Hertzog government had introduced in 1936.

In 1943, the Congress Youth League was formed, introducing a more radical group of young leaders in the ANC. They acted as a pressure group from within the ANC.

The Pass system went hand in hand with the deteriorating conditions of black miners on the gold and diamond mines. In 1919, against their pig-level living conditions and low wages, 70 000 miners went on strike. The troops and police and armed white civilians attacked a meeting of the striking miners, killing eight and wounding eighty. The vicious labour conditions went on without relenting.

Late in 1959, the New Native Labour Regulations were published. They drew women deeply into the system of labour control. From this time on, all women who were in employment were obliged to register with the bureaus which had been set up to control and distribute the African labour force.

Over many years women had operated separately according to the social and political position that the white government had allocated to them. White women enjoyed what privileges the government bestowed on them. Indian women suffered the disabilities that were allocated to all Indians. But, as time went on, it became clear that many enlightened women from these different sectors wished it otherwise.

It was not until April 1954 that their dream was realised when they met in the Trades Hall in Johannesburg and constructed the framework for a national organisation 'uniting all women in common action for the removal of all political, legal, economic and social disabilities'. White women were in the forefront of this organisation, but the executive included powerful African women like Ida Mtwana, Lilian Ngoyi, Bertha Mkhize and others.

The formation of the Women's Charter galvanised women to be more aware of their political strength and stimulated women of all races into action. It was the first comprehensive statement of principles backed by all women from all the racial groups of South Africa.

On 9 August 1956, about 20 000 women marched to the seat of government, the Union Buildings in Pretoria, to present a petition against the carrying of Passes by women to the Prime Minister, J.G. Strijdom. Strijdom chose to avoid meeting the women and disappeared. The petition was handed over to his secretary.

For thirty minutes the women stood in front of the Union Buildings. Then they broke into song, singing 'Nkosi Sikelel' iAfrika' (God Bless Africa) and the issuing of the thunderous shout of 'wathint' abafazi, wathin' 'imbokodo' (you strike a woman, you strike a rock). We, who were standing in the crowds, felt the wave of the voices in front and carried it in another wave further down. (At the time, I was carrying my six-month-old son.) It was the most moving demonstration of dignity, unity and determination and has come to represent the courage and strength of South African women.

The Women's Charter and the women's anti-Pass campaign, which culminated in the famous women's march to Pretoria, became benchmarks in the struggle and continued to inspire decades of women until democracy was finally realised in 1994. Since 1995, the women's march of 1956 is celebrated as Women's Day on 9 August each year.

It was in 1960 that the PAC, under the leadership of Robert Mangaliso Sobukwe, launched a nationwide protest against the Pass laws. The PAC simply invited people, in an act of peaceful civil disobedience, to present themselves on 21 March 1960 to every police station, without their Pass books, thus courting arrest. That taunt was enough for the police to start shooting at the unarmed demonstrators. The assault led to the now historic events known as the Sharpeville massacre.

Within a few minutes sixty-nine people were shot dead. More were killed in Langa, Cape Town, and in other parts of the country when police opened fire on similar gatherings of peaceful demonstrators. The news of this massacre spread across the world like wildfire, prompting a storm of condemnation against the apartheid government of South Africa.

In reaction, the government moved swiftly to crack down on the political liberation movements. The PAC, ANC and other organisations were banned immediately and a state of emergency was declared. Hundreds of active and not-so-active politicians were arrested.

Many chose to leave the country altogether, not just to escape the state's ferocious treatment of people in jails, but also to seek military solutions for the unspeakable suffering of black people under white rule in South Africa at the time.

In this way, many people 'skipped' the country and went into exile, often living in three or more countries during their stateless sojourn. Some of those people were women whose experiences are recounted in the following pages – in stories that weave a pattern of racial, cultural and political criss-crossing of the South African landscape.

There were as many paths to the solitary, perilous journey into exile as there are contributors to this collection. From a life of privilege or severe hardship, from unintentional exclusion or conscious escape from the land of one's birth, to a simple decision to support a husband – here you will encounter the whole gamut of life circumstances that precipitated the flight into exile for many South African women.

In this collection, life away from home is depicted with understated brevity by the contributors who are lifelong, politically active octogenarians. Alongside them are the more personal contributions from women born in exile. All are vivid and authentic recollections of a life lived apart from the comfort and support of family or community, dislocated from certainty and place – and from belonging. Busi Chaanes put it this way:

It was at this point that I first felt what it was really like not to belong, to be different, and irrevocably so, and for my difference to be made obvious and problematic. This was when I realised that I missed 'home' and I pined after a life that was more accepting of me as I was, dark skin, big backside, poor academic skills . . . and all.

Issues of identity plague the 'born-in-exile' more than most. But, even this has an upside, as Liepollo Pheko notes, bestowing multiple identities on those who find themselves in this situation. 'In Zambia I didn't know I was in exile', she says, and that 'belonging was something . . . to fight for'.

And yet, as Brigalia Bam puts it, exiled life 'contributed so much to my personal growth and maturity that I do not even know how to count my blessings . . . It was in exile that I discovered, fell in love with and was loved by the African continent. Many fellow South Africans who did not have my experience have yet to understand why the continent matters to our country.'

The obvious and chief theme in the pieces is the individual: always agonising in isolation over whether or not to go into exile, and the deeply personal consequences of that state of mind. My own story illustrates the dilemma:

> Neither could I resolve what my next move would be the following day. I was expecting my husband, A.B. Ngcobo, to come out of jail in the next few weeks after serving his three years' prison sentence in Pretoria. He had been into different prisons ever since the Sharpeville massacre of 1960. Then, what malicious fate would throw me into jail just as he was getting out? What spiteful plot would conspire to have me leave my children and my husband into timeless exile? It was unthinkable.

Some contributors show that they were drawn into such decisions through defiance of the apartheid security apparatus. Most inevitably faced harassment, arrest, torture, imprisonment and/or solitary confinement. Some recount first-hand their experiences of bombings, raids, assassinations and more.

Since this is an anthology of women's writing, childbearing, motherhood and child-rearing challenges naturally feature prominently, as the writers detail their attempts to manage the roles of mother, wife, daughter, sister, activist and friend under difficult conditions. Baleka Mbete summaries this experience: 'I would have to leave two babies behind – a seventeen-month-old daughter and a son who was just over five months old.'

Another common theme is a growing realisation, while living in exile, that apartheid was but one facet of oppression in the world. The reality of women's oppression, both at home and elsewhere, galvanises many to champion the cause of women's emancipation. As Barbara Bell puts it: '. . . this convinced me even more that the struggle was not only against apartheid, it was against a system of oppression and exploitation of which apartheid was only one aspect.' It was and remains, in the end, an interconnected struggle for justice and human rights.

Adjusting to the minutiae of daily life in exile was a full-time and often precarious occupation, even for those born into it. Accounts of the varying degrees of acceptance or rejection faced in the host countries – in neighbouring, frontline states such as Swaziland, Tanzania, Zimbabwe or Zambia, or further north, to Algeria, Britain, Canada and Cuba – read like bittersweet memories of survival and intrigue, with the ever-present spectre of the South African secret police, and 'turned' spies in the mix. 'In spite of being so versed in my knowledge of English culture, I was really not a part of it and remained always an outsider to a certain extent,' AnnMarie Wolpe observed. Judith Mkhwanazi had a contrasting experience: 'I was received by the British people with warmth, as cold as the country was.'

For reasons not easy to understand, there is evidence of the abuse of power by the leadership over those under their control, especially of young women who suffered sexual abuses despite belonging to the same struggle. In private, young women would confide of the abuses perpetrated both by the leadership and the so-called 'comrades'.

Other abuses of equality are evident. It is hard to believe that in that barren landscape of exile, there were times when white exiles enjoyed special privileges. Barbara Bell dwells on this theme: 'There was also a difference on apartheid lines. Without exception, to my knowledge, the whites were part of the staff elite, had passports and homes and connections in countries such as England and Canada and were given separate and preferential rations.'

The significance of food and the primacy of shelter are also recurring themes in this anthology. The constant challenge of locating, preparing, consuming and sharing sustenance often provides conscious and unconscious remembrances of and connections to home. The story of shelter deserves a separate mention, for it is through securing somewhere to sleep that many lasting alliances were forged with other people, refugees and migrants among them. The search for shelter leads to interactions with the most unlikely sympathisers and detractors – and offers salutary lessons in the resilience of the human spirit.

Ultimately, this is a contribution to the body of work on South Africa's turbulent history and recent past. Some may feel the exile experience is outdated; others may feel that an examination of the exile's life holds little of lasting value in a free and democratic nation that is almost twenty years old. Mbete, however, suggests that South Africa has yet to fully appreciate the memories and records of life in exile. The journey across that 'desert of exile has helped society to become what it is today; has helped to formulate that space which can truly be called home'.

Lessons from exile

Brigalia Hlophe Bam

Brigalia Ntombemhlophe Bam was born on 21 April 1933 at Tsolo in the Eastern Cape. After her schooling, she went to Lovedale College, qualifying as a teacher. It was while she was at Lovedale that she joined the African National Congress in 1952. Later, at the Jan Hofmeyr School of Social Work, she qualified as a social worker. She went on to work for the Young Women's Christian Association in Durban where she was involved in political activities in a clandestine way. At the YWCA she learnt to organise, work with people and inspire the youth and this led to her accepting a job in 1967 with the World Council of Churches in Geneva, Switzerland. Here, too, she was involved with the International Food and Allied Workers' Association. In 1969 she was rendered stateless when the South African government refused to renew her passport. She stayed in exile for another nineteen years.

Brigalia Bam has been awarded numerous honorary doctoral degrees by South African and other universities for her visionary leadership skills. She currently lives in Pretoria and has recently retired from her position as chairperson of the Electoral Commission of South Africa.

I could not believe my eyes. There she was, a dark-haired, white woman, asking if she could come in and make up my room. I even looked backwards into my room to check if she was talking to someone else. I just kept staring at her. She was also confused by my stunned stare. Where I came from white people did not work. White men, yes, sometimes did manual work. But mostly they were supervisors, watching over black men digging a road, commanding them to lay a pipe here or pick up that brick over there. I had never ever seen white women cleaning. Not in South Africa. For the first time I saw white people doing menial jobs. They were picking up rubbish on the streets, cleaning windows, filling up cars at petrol stations. These whites were different from the whites in apartheid South Africa.

I also did not know there were different kinds of white people and that there was discrimination among whites, against one another; nor did I know that white Italians were regarded as a lower class in Switzerland. Back home all whites were the same. They were all important and superior to blacks. I had never known that discrimination could also be based on class and ethnicity. I was soon to discover that even the colour of white people's hair was different: blonde, auburn, and honey blonde. It seemed to matter a lot in Europe.

Stepping stones

It had taken me two whole years to get a passport to travel to Geneva. I was offered a job by the World Council of Churches (WCC) in 1965. Like many black South Africans, I had been refused a passport by the South African government. I was recruited by the WCC to go and work in its head office in Geneva, as the Program Director in the department called Co-operation of Women and Men in Family, Church and Society. I had been very fortunate to work for the Young Women's Christian Association (YWCA) in South Africa, also an ecumenical organisation.

The world-affiliated YWCA in apartheid South Africa had given me organisational skills in a very difficult working environment. The membership and the bosses were women, very supportive and affirming. What a contrast in the WCC! Most of the directors were white males. One felt alienated being watched in a patronising, friendly way by these men.

It was the YWCA that had first given me an opportunity to travel to the Mindolo Ecumenical Centre in Zambia to participate in a youth work camp. This was a wonderful experience of working with young people from all over the world. On my return from Zambia a fellow camper, John Osmers from New Zealand, visited me in South Africa. He was so shocked by this country that he became active in the anti-apartheid movement. In 1979 he lost his arm through a parcel bomb sent to him by an unknown person.

The second ecumenical experience was the All Africa Youth Conference organised by the WCC in Nairobi in 1962. The theme of the conference was 'Freedom under the crisis'. This was an historical event, an inaugural conference of churches in Africa. The youth delegates represented many African countries. I had no idea that the continent had fifty-three countries of people who, like us, mostly spoke the languages of their French, Portuguese and English colonial masters. This conference was a stepping stone in my life. At the end of the conference, the delegates chose ten of us to represent youth in the All Africa Conference of Churches in Uganda. Dr Francis Wilson and I were among the ten. Little did I know that my working life thereafter would be in the ecumenical and international fields.

Leaving home

I was eventually granted a passport after three years of hard lobbying by Dr Eugene Carson Blake, the American general secretary of the WCC, through his contacts within the United States. He had left no stone unturned to get me this document. When the passport eventually came unexpectedly, it was with mixed emotions that I received it: joy, that I could finally travel; sadness, that I was leaving my son and my brother in prison at Robben Island where he was serving a ten-year sentence; embarrassment, because anyone granted a passport those days was viewed with great suspicion both at home and in the exile community. You were regarded as either a spy or a sell-out and everyone would wonder why the apartheid government was doing you this 'favour' of giving you a passport. The perception during those years was that you had to struggle to be trusted.

I was not the first in my family to go overseas. My sister, Jane, was the first. She had gone to England in 1963 after getting a scholarship through the Anglican church to read neurology for eighteen months at Oxford University. However, I was gone for a longer period of twenty-one years and into exile, for that matter.

I missed my plane on the day of my departure to Geneva in September 1967. After all the preparations, the excitement and anxiety, I could not believe myself, and, to this day, I still find it difficult to do so. I checked in on time and went and sat inside the airport. However, I did not realise that the airport staff were calling my plane's boarding time. I was not used to this and I did not know that they wanted me to board. By the time I stood up to go to the gate it was closed. Imagine the confusion and pain. I suspect the confusion was that there were no seats for non-Europeans in the plane.

Switzerland

I had done little reading to prepare myself for working in Switzerland. I arrived in Geneva the following day on 10 September 1967. All I knew was that Switzerland was a country of many banks and bankers! I did not know how breathtakingly beautiful this quiet country was: the alps and the beautiful lakes. Clichéd as this may sound, I was even more shocked by just how cold Switzerland was, in all senses of that word. The biting, snowy winters went straight to one's soul, not just the outer body. Sometimes I felt as if the chill was penetrating my skin and every part of my being. Although the winters could be quite cold in the Eastern Cape, we had warm fires to sit around in the evenings, and the winter season was not very long. In Switzerland it lasted up to seven months of the year. But I eventually acclimatised. One eagerly waited for the beautiful summer months when the whole country was suddenly transformed. People came out of their shells. They took walks around the lakes. They wore nice skimpy clothes as if they had thrown away those huge coats, scarves and hats that they wore in winter. I loved those summers and they were so beautiful. Each passing year the winters got more bearable, but the summers were always something to look forward to.

Patriarchy is global

Living outside South Africa was a huge learning curve for me. Each day I learnt and discovered something new. The most significant of these lessons, which has continued throughout the years, was finding out just how global, deep-seated and entrenched patriarchy was. Through my work with women in South Africa at the YWCA, I had gradually observed how negatively women were treated in my own community, family and the church that I came from. However, I had assumed that what we went through in South Africa was now history in Switzerland and in the so-called developed world in general.

Several examples stand out in this respect. First, women in Switzerland were only granted the federal vote in 1971. The last Swiss canton to allow women to vote in local elections did so in 1991. Ironically, just as we were disenfranchised in South Africa so were (white) women in a very developed, modern country like Switzerland.

Second, in the WCC itself senior positions were held only by men. For a very long time this continued to be the trend. This was also reflected in the leadership of the WCC member churches where the ordination of women was then a controversial issue. Each time delegates came to the WCC meetings, I was consistently taken aback that there would not be a single woman on most, if any, of the delegations.

Dr Madeline Barot, my predecessor, had a strategy of organising a women's seminar prior to any major conference of the WCC, which I found very useful. These meetings would overlap so that women could participate in the main conference as well since they were there anyway. Most of the member churches' delegations would be predominantly male.

Sex tourism was my next shock. I had never even heard of the concept or the practice before. This is the practice whereby groups of men ostensibly go on business tours to certain countries but specifically for the purpose of buying and enjoying sex with women (sex workers) in that country. In some cases, the men travel in small groups and a package is organised for them by travel agents. On arrival, these men are literally allocated rooms in the hotel and allocated women of their choice. In those days they chose them from photographs sent through by the agents or from a line-up of women on arrival. Nowadays the Internet is used. Without sounding moralistic, sex tourism was, and remains, an indicator of the low status of women in a society. When I became aware of these demeaning practices, I organised resources from the WCC's Department on Women and supported the church women's groups in Thailand that were exposing such practices. In addition, I also supported the Japanese church women who had established a rehabilitation centre for the young women victimised by sex tourism.

Furthermore, as if this was not enough, I was absolutely stunned to discover that baby girls were baptised at a different font from boys in some of the churches. Apparently, in what was clearly a discriminatory practice against girls at a young age, boys were baptised at what was seen as the main baptismal font while girls had to be at the bottom one. Naturally, I was horrified by such blatant discrimination in the church itself. It greatly affected me and made me more determined to fight for the liberation of women, not only in my own country but all over the world. In some churches and countries I was also not allowed to go to the altar. This, too, greatly affected me. I began to see parallels between this practice and how Christianity had been (mis)used by the apartheid state to deny black people their rights. To this day, I am still completely shocked at how the discrimination of women in many countries is still heavily based on justifications of culture and religion.

Over the years, I was to become aware of and meet women from all over the world whose rights had been violated in such vicious ways. For instance, the practice of female genital mutilation, which is still practised in many countries, especially in Africa, affected me deeply. The innumerable stories of women whose property rights had been violated in the name of culture at the death of their spouses was yet another practice that made me feel so powerless, yet determined to continue advocating women's rights. The fact that in some countries there were laws and policies that actually denied women their rights was also depressing. It was this experience that made me call the first workshop on racism, classism and sexism in Mexico.

Intersections

It was these similarities that made my work in the WCC so much easier and rewarding on the one hand, and, on the other hand, enabled me to find sisterhood and solidarity everywhere I went. It was this sisterhood that sustained me not only in Geneva but in my travels – particularly after my passport was taken away by the South African government and I could not return home. Following the WCC's adoption of a resolution against racism and the setting up of the Program to Combat Racism, the South African government declared the WCC, its employees and anyone associated with it *personae non gratae*. They invalidated my passport as well in 1969. Overnight I had become stateless and could no longer return home.

The fourth assembly of the WCC, which was the first one that I attended, gave birth to the programme against racism. The assembly was held in 1968 at Uppsala in Sweden. The African American writer, James Baldwin, was one of the key speakers. He made a statement I will never forget: 'I address you as one of God's creatures whom the Christian Church has most betrayed.' He went on to say: 'I wonder if there is left in the Christian civilisations the moral energy, the spiritual daring, to atone, to repent, to be born again.' It was statements like Baldwin's that led to the establishment of the WCC's Program to Combat Racism. Further, it was the work I did and my travels while in exile that expanded my horizons and made me understand the struggles of poor and excluded people all over the world. Through my work, I became painfully conscious of the many ways in which policies such as apartheid worked, got entrenched, and how, in fact, there were so many variations of the same theme globally.

I travelled to Australia and saw at first hand how the First People of this country (Aborigines) were not only discriminated against but actively brutalised and ill-treated.

In 1972 I was tasked with a mission to India where I witnessed tiny kids, some as young as five years old from the so-called 'untouchable' caste, being made to wash their hands at a different water faucet. This alarming practice happened in our very own Christian schools.

Moreover, it was after I visited factories and sweatshops in Thailand that I fully understood the struggle for workers' rights waged by trade unions like those in South Africa. I also saw very young women working for hours on end, with no food, water or breaks, doing repetitive, nerve-numbing work, assembling electronic parts. These slave labourers – which is what they were essentially – got a mere pittance, were sexually harassed and/or fired for the smallest infractions.

Disappointments

In 1969, I was all set to go home for my vacation at the end of my three-year contract. One of the benefits of WCC policy was to pay for an employee's return trip to his or her country of origin. This was to make sure that staff members keep contact with their countries. The news that I could not return home was communicated to me while I was in Hong Kong attending an ecumenical seminar I had organised for church women of East Asia. I received a telegram from the general secretary of the WCC, Dr Eugene Carson Blake, that the South African government had banned all the WCC staff members in South Africa because of the WCC Central Committee's decision to support the armed struggle against apartheid. The WCC pointed out that many western governments supported the South African white minority regime.

I was very fortunate to have an aunt, Margaret Mazonke Mei, who lived in Botswana in Mochudi village. Her home became our second home. My mother, brother, son, sisters and nieces would cross over to Botswana. But still I missed being part of family gatherings and family celebrations like weddings. I never thought I would miss funerals and opportunities to mourn and grieve with friends and family. I even missed family disagreements over choices of schools for children. It is moments like those that connect us to one another and strengthen relationships.

My son

I had thought that I was leaving my son, Khwezi, with my mother for only a short time. After all, she had raised him and I had thought that it was best to let him finish school in South Africa since he was already in secondary school. However, I eventually brought him overseas after he had completed his matriculation. He was coming to do his A level studies because he could not enter English universities with a South African matriculation certificate. He was later to move to Germany and the United States, but his health deteriorated.

Sadly, Khwezi passed away in December 1985 after a long battle with bipolar disorder. I was far away from him when he died. I blamed myself for never having mothered him. I always found it hard to merely put the blame on exile because I felt that I had never really been a mother to him. It is in this regard that I still carry this guilt, this emptiness of not mothering my son, every day.

Keeping in touch

I kept in touch with my family through letters. I received a few from my son, but many from my mother, sisters, brothers and my friend, Joyce Piliso-Seroke. The letters were delivered to my office address. Nevertheless, I never read them in the office. I would wait until I got home. Then I would have a small ritual. First, I would perch on my favourite seat, settle down comfortably and then read each letter slowly. Not once, not twice, but thrice. I would savour each morsel of news and carefully make each observation. I always looked forward to all these letters. Joyce, my mum and my sister, Jane (with her sense of humour), were all prolific letter-writers. Letters from my brother, Fikile, from Robben Island were shared with me by my mother. I still cannot believe that today we are free and happy human beings after this ordeal.

It was so difficult to phone those days. We had an arrangement that my son would go to the house of someone who had a phone on a particular day. Then I would call. During the holidays it was better because my mother had a phone in the clinic where she worked. So I could speak with my mother and my son. These phone calls were all made from the little town of Bulwer in KwaZulu-Natal. Even the telephone exchange operator recognised my voice. Then there was the anxiety over my nephew, Mawethu, an activist who had to go underground. I thought any day the police would arrest him. What of my younger brother whose business, home and transport were fully used for the struggle?

Geneva was not a hub of struggle activity. Neither were there many South Africans either leaving or even coming through for anything. Much later, as the anti-apartheid movement grew and established connections with churches, and through United Nations agencies and some trade unions or organisations based in Geneva, I got many visitors. I happily accommodated many South Africans and other southern African liberation movement activists in my apartment and this gave me a sense of connection to people from home. People like Emma Mashinini, who was a trade unionist, came to stay with me during the period after I had moved from the WCC to work for the International Union of Food and Allied Workers.

London was the closest hub for me to go and see more South Africans. I made sure that I travelled to or through the United Kingdom just so I could spend time with my sister, Jane, who had returned to come and work in London as a theatre nurse. I also spent a lot of time with Mazisi Kunene who was living in London. It was to London that I escaped for holidays like Christmas and others in between. London was also the hub for exile gossip.

Food, glorious food!

And it was to Mazisi's house and London that I went whenever I needed to eat South African food. The foods that I had taken for granted at home also took major significance in my life. It was hard to get African food in those days in Geneva and there were not that many people coming through to bring me biltong, *mngqusho* (crushed maizemeal), nice beef and sausages. A few days before going to London, I would call Mazisi and ask him to make me *amasi* (sour milk). He would do so and hide it in his wardrobe! This was intended to protect it from other 'marauding' South Africans who could pass through any minute and devour *amasi wami* (my sour milk). I learnt to make my own *amasi* in summer. The only downside was I could not share it with anyone in Geneva as they would have never understood what this strange-tasting yoghurt was.

I also discovered Kenya as a source of good food that was close enough to my own South African comfort food. I would return from trips there laden with vacuum-packed sausages and beef. Fortunately, the Swiss were very tolerant of our strange idiosyncrasies. West Africa certainly had more of them. The only drawback was that I had to sit for an hour or more while they X-rayed the packages, just to make sure that the foodstuffs were not contaminated. I did not mind this minor inconvenience.

Involvement in the struggle

Working in the WCC provided me with vast opportunities to connect with the anti-apartheid struggle at home, to contribute to and be informed about events and developments. In this, I consider myself to have been luckier than other people whose jobs did not afford them these opportunities. Once the WCC took the decision to establish the Program to Combat Racism, my work intersected in so many ways with the anti-apartheid struggle.

I found myself travelling to many parts of the world, speaking about the evils of apartheid. I would always show audiences my identity document or Pass book (the *dompas*, as it was called). I would speak to many anti-apartheid groups and encourage others to join the struggle. For example, in the German Protestant church, which is Lutheran, women had mobilised themselves on anti-apartheid campaigns. They picketed each month for many years outside the South African embassy in Bonn. These women also organised the boycott of South African products such as flowers, fresh and canned fruit. In these indirect ways I felt part of the struggle. These women were very much part of my own network in the work I was doing with women through the WCC. In addition, when I went to Fiji to run the first women's conference of its kind, bringing together church women of the Pacific, I ended up spending extra days there with speaking engagements – once they discovered I was South African. It was the same in Australia, the Netherlands and Nordic countries, just to name a few.

Exile and some of my work broadened my understanding of what was going on in South Africa, on the policies of the apartheid government, as well as on the international connections. I got access to information, for example, on how the government was busting sanctions. Later, when I moved from the WCC to the trade union movement, I was able to gather and disseminate information on the role of businesses that were involved in South Africa, the role of international capital and what trade union movements were doing to end apartheid. Over the years, I got to meet unionists like Emma Mashinini and others and was able to support them and their work. The contact with young women exiles of 1976 was a wonderful experience. A number of us assisted in securing two houses for refugees. The young women had a special place in my heart. Lauretta Ngcobo and I organised two seminars with these young women.

Yet, the small roles one played in the struggle were not always appreciated by others – even by those on the same side as oneself. Granted, the anti-apartheid struggle was complicated, and one could not expect everyone to be always on the same page. Suspicions, rumours and competition were the order of the day and these were all big problems and often played a part in so many nasty ways. Some of us were seen as more genuine freedom fighters or leaders than others. One's legitimacy was questioned many a time, and it was easy for one's motives or good intentions to be misunderstood or misrepresented.

One incident stands out. I had been greatly inspired by Dorothy Height, leader of the US-based National Council of Negro Women, who had set up an organisation for black women, bringing them together to talk about the gender and racism issues they faced, even as they were part of the black/Negro movements. So I wanted to copy this model and create an organisation of South African women in exile. Prior to this, I had contacted other women in exile to form a black women's federation.

This is the organisation that had tried to operate from within South Africa, but was subsequently banned. So the vision was to create a black women's organisation abroad, to link us in exile, as well as to support women living at home. The idea seemed to have been well received by many South African women and it was meant to be inclusive of all women, not just those in political parties. I recruited many South Africans from Germany, Botswana, Switzerland and London, which had the largest number of South Africans then.

Detentions and deportations

When you are in exile, do not have a country to return to and carry a United Nations refugee document or whatever documentation, you are always regarded as suspect. Those receiving you do not have the experience of statelessness, so they often do not understand why you want to come into their country if you have no country to go back to eventually. I went through several humiliating and degrading experiences during those dark years. They were afraid you might be seeking asylum and live off their taxes.

Once you said you were born in South Africa, even if you had a United Nations refugee travel document, the immigration authorities of the country concerned would not welcome you – either because of the sanctions that they had imposed against South Africa, or because they were afraid you would enter and become a refugee. In some of these countries, there were policies based on boycotting apartheid. The irony was that I was the black person, oppressed by the apartheid regime, yet I had to struggle to get support and acceptance!

My first trauma was on a visit to Uruguay. I was still carrying a South African passport then. I did not have a visa, but Uruguay had a policy of not allowing South Africans in because of sanctions against apartheid. I arrived at midnight and immigration refused to let me in. They had no idea of what to do with me in the middle of the night and left me to sleep on a chair at the airport. The people meeting me did not know what to do. I was not familiar with this because I had never experienced such treatment. It took Dr Emilio Castro, then the head of the Methodist Church of Uruguay, to negotiate for me to enter. It took him the whole day to arrange this. In the later years, when he became the general secretary of the WCC, he said that I made him famous. I was meant to proceed to Chile from here, but I never did as I was told that they, too, would not let me in.

In 1975, I was part of a delegation to Russia to brief the Russian Orthodox Church about the forthcoming WCC assembly in Kenya. I was carrying a United Nations travel document. I had two Bibles in my luggage and I was scared the authorities would discover them. This was in the days when religion was banned by the state. But it was not the Bibles that caused a problem. The Russians refused to let me in when they discovered that I was South African. We had a British, a German, a Swiss, a Jamaican and me in the team. They were all met by their ambassadors and consulates, but I had no one to plead for or meet me. We pleaded with the Russians for over four hours. Finally, the head of the delegation decided that if I was not let in then all of us must leave in solidarity. The head of the delegation told this to the Russians and asked if we could do a press conference before we left! In a matter of minutes we were out of the airport. It was 21 April, my birthday. When we sat down to dinner that evening, the Russians, as a gesture of apology, gave me gifts. I have kept them to this day.

Deportation from Trinidad

The most humiliating and unexpected incident occurred in Trinidad. I was travelling during the women's decade (1976–85), talking to churches, encouraging them to adopt programmes and policies to promote the rights of women. My journey took me first to Jamaica, then to Guyana. I was to fly from Barbados on to Trinidad and afterwards to Canada. I arrived in Barbados where Nita Barrow, my friend and colleague, took care of me. I was fêted, given space on radio, in newspapers, etc.

Buoyed by this experience I flew to Trinidad, but was denied entry. The people who were to meet me waited in vain and left, having been told that I had been sent back on the flight to Barbados. I had arrived at about 8 a.m. and been told to take the next flight back to Barbados. I refused and put up a real fight. I was assuming and hoping that my hosts were going to assist.

Around 5 p.m. on that day, a police person arrived with a deportation order. I kept this order for years afterwards. The Commissioner of Police arrived at the airport to see for himself who this cantankerous South African woman was who was refusing to leave. He had, of course, assumed I was white. At the same time, the African and Indian Trinidadians were debating among themselves. The Africans were saying it would be a shame if a black South African woman was sent to prison. Finally, I was put on the plane by police who had to lift me from my seat in the airport. The journalists who were watching never took photographs of me in this very humiliating state. The captain of the plane met me at the door and later offered me a rum and Coke.

The kindness of others

In Kenya, it was one of the women in the immigration department who, after going off shift and coming back to find me still detained, ordered me to be released and allowed me to freely enter Nairobi after having been at the airport for two days. So, too, when I arrived in Togo on one trip, it was close to midnight. The immigration officer drove me to the Minister of the Interior's home to get permission to allow me entry. Although the policy was to ban all South Africans from entering, the minister gave orders for me to get a visa.

The most amazing experience was being given a passport by Liberia. I carried that passport for many years until I returned to South Africa and eventually got a new passport in my free country. When the then president of Liberia, President Tolbert, heard of my plight, he immediately organised for me to be given Liberian citizenship, complete with a passport. It was after I had made a speech on apartheid and how the system had enslaved our people.

What I learnt in exile

Looking back, the twenty-one years of life in Switzerland taught me many lessons and contributed so much to my personal growth and maturity such that I do not even know how to count my blessings. Had I never left South Africa I do not think I would have been where I am today. The first major lesson was about the connections between apartheid and other forms of oppression that I experienced. At the same time, people are struggling against these injustices and each victory, in every corner, matters. Among these struggles stands out the struggle for gender equality and women's rights. All over the world I have friends, sisters, movements that I still connect with and share solidarity with, even as I enjoy post-apartheid South Africa.

I have therefore learnt that one cannot live without others. As human beings we need that touch, that connection. It is that connection, physical or spiritual, that sustains you. It is also others that give you hope for change. In all of my years in Geneva I never gave up hope of returning to South Africa. I even wrote a will which said that I wanted to be buried back home. But I never did actually think that I would die in exile.

It was in exile that I discovered, fell in love with and was loved by the African continent. Many fellow South Africans who did not have my experience have yet to understand why the continent matters to our country. Had it not been for the dozens of African brothers and sisters who adopted me, I would never have coped with being outside South Africa. From big acts of generosity like the Liberians giving me a passport, to my friend, Annie Jiagge, a Ghanaian judge who taught me how to dress like an African, to several families who made me godmother to their children, and even the woman at immigration in Kenya – all performed acts of absolute love and kindness I will forever hold dear.

That was why in my work as the chairperson of the Electoral Commission of South Africa I felt a great deal of responsibility towards all African countries and the need to provide mutual support and solidarity to our peoples.

An elephant is
never burdened by its trunk

Barbara Bell

Barbara Bell was born in 1939 and attended school and college in Johannesburg, graduating as a pre-school teacher. She left for England in 1965 where she worked for the Anti-Apartheid Movement, joined the African National Congress Youth and married fellow exile, Terry Bell. She spent time in Zambia, Botswana and New Zealand before moving to help establish the primary division of the ANC school in Tanzania. A further nine activist years in England followed before she returned home in 1992.

Apartheid's distortions, based on privileges linked to skin colour – to 'racial classification' – followed us into exile. We, both the privileged and the greater majority drawn from disadvantaged communities, were all damaged, although, for the privileged, it was a lot easier to live with that damage.

Through all the years and distances travelled, this is the impression that remains strongest with me because when I left South Africa in 1965 I left with a skill, a good matriculation pass, tertiary qualifications and a background that enabled me to choose, to a large extent, where I would go into exile. It ensured that I would find a good job and a reasonably comfortable lifestyle.

Similar conditions applied – certainly in the 1960s or earlier – to those wealthier, professionally qualified or politically well-connected families not classified 'white' whose sons and daughters had little problem in obtaining scholarships to universities abroad. However, they were very few in number.

For most exiles from the racially persecuted communities, there was no choice. Like all exiles, they left, fearing arrest, imprisonment or worse – or merely because they were tired of the tension and harassment. But they could only flee across the land borders, either to end up in camps of the exiled political movements or to have to eke out precarious existences as strangers or illegal aliens in a foreign land. And for women, it was particularly hard, a fact I became very aware of within my first few years of exile.

The differences began in South Africa and, because of apartheid where that rigid racial pecking order also had its gender component, black women were at the bottom of the pile. Interviews and published material in later years also revealed to me an ironic patriarchal and racist twist because among political prisoners, it was white women, privileged and generally patronised by men, who were best treated, while their black sisters were least considered.

I avoided prison and my upbringing was probably little different from the majority of white females of my generation. In my case, I began my schooling at the Leicester Road state primary school in Kensington, Johannesburg, where all my books and stationery were free and where every morning every student received – free – a small bottle of milk before lunch break. Even if the curriculum, especially in history, was distorted, we became literate, numerate and fairly confident of our abilities. But a few of us, too, began to question.

My family, as racist as any white, middle-class family of the time, were devout members of the Anglican church and were quite horrified by the anti-apartheid utterances of the likes of Bishop Ambrose Reeves and Father Trevor Huddleston. I was instructed by my mother: 'When they speak about God, listen to them, but when they talk about South Africa, they know nothing. They're English.'

Even in my early teens, this did not seem to make too much sense. And to top it off, my parents sent me to a Roman Catholic convent for my secondary schooling, where the Irish nuns talked about oppression and linked what had happened in Ireland to what was happening in South Africa. By the time I got to teacher training college and joined the National Union of South African Students and met fellow delegates from Fort Hare at conferences, I was, at least intellectually, committed to oppose the apartheid system.

It was only a short step from there to being more involved after meeting a couple of African National Congress (ANC) supporters. Those were terrible times. The Rivonia trialists had been jailed for life and the police had launched another crackdown, detaining hundreds of activists under the then notorious General Laws Amendment Act that allowed successive periods of ninety-day detention without trial.

After the arrest, trial and sentencing of comrades I had been involved with, but who had not, apparently, revealed my name, I decided to leave, at least until everything calmed down. But I was only given a passport for one year and, then, only after lengthy interviews with the security police.

In England I found a teaching job and became involved in 1966 with the newly launched ANC Youth. When I went to renew my passport shortly before it expired, this was refused. The message was clear: I was in exile, along with comrades who had fled without papers, with 'acquired' documents or on exit permits that allowed them to leave on condition that they never return. One of those exiles, who had 'skipped' to Zambia and then been deported 'for your own personal' safety to England by President Kenneth Kaunda, was Terry Bell, a journalist and former ninety-day detainee I had known in Johannesburg. We met again and married in September 1966 in England where Terry had managed to obtain a passport.

For both of us there was work in the Anti-Apartheid Movement. I had a good job. Terry had a university scholarship and was part of the ANC cultural group. But we could not settle. We longed for home, for familiar places, faces – and for better weather. In this we seemed to differ from a number of other exiles classified 'white' by the apartheid system. They seemed to find it easy to adapt to England where we all could, I suppose, blend in, being regarded largely as colonial kith and kin.

Most of such exiles, along with a few from other South African communities, were also professional people, lawyers, academics, journalists and doctors, and many soon bought houses, began building careers – and, in some cases, fortunes. I started to realise that skin pigmentation – 'colour' or 'race' – was less important than class.

So we began to save as much money as we could, not to settle down, but to get out, to go back to Africa, back to as close as we could to 'home'. We packed up once again, I gave up my job and Terry turned down a post-graduate scholarship and we set off south, arriving in Zambia in October 1968. It was not a good time for the ANC. Although we were in Ndola, away from the Lusaka headquarters, we heard of the problems and the disgruntlement within Umkhonto we Sizwe (MK), the ANC's armed wing as, over the months, comrades passed through, stopping for a meal or an overnight stay.

This was the time, in 1969, that Chris Hani and other comrades drafted a protest letter referring to 'the rot in the ANC'. It was also the time that the apartheid state seemed all-powerful and was making diplomatic moves into Africa. One of these resulted in the détente between apartheid's John Vorster and President Kaunda that saw the Zambian government refusing to renew work permits of ANC members working in the country. By that time, I had a young child and we planned to stay on in the country until we could finally return home. But we were given notice that our work permits would not be renewed and that we had to leave Zambia in December 1970. In a last-ditch attempt to stay, we drove to Lusaka to see if the movement could not intervene.

ANC President O.R. Tambo and Jack Simons, a senior South African Communist Party (SACP) member who was professor of sociology at the University of Zambia, met us. There was nothing they could do, they said, and we should try to relocate to Botswana and set up a safe house there. If that proved impossible, we should take the other alternative that had been offered to Terry: a job in New Zealand where we could help to establish an anti-apartheid movement. In a borrowed Land Rover, we drove to Gaborone, but although there was a job available, the government, citing 'security reasons', refused to grant a work permit. And so, in early 1971, I ended up, with husband and daughter, in New Zealand where our son was born in 1972, the same year that the New Zealand Anti-Apartheid Movement was launched.

If anything, New Zealand provided, if not a more comfortable, certainly a more relaxed, lifestyle and we felt we were making a positive contribution. Perhaps the

ANC forgot about us because we were left to our own devices, in much the same way the Pan-Africanist Congress (PAC) seemed to forget that their representative, Henry Isaacs, was in New Zealand. In contrast to what we heard later about other parts of the world, the ANC and PAC, comprising one family and one individual, got on perfectly well together.

With no contrary instructions coming from headquarters, we also involved ourselves – as South African ANC members – in solidarity with the Maori land rights campaigns and in blockading nuclear-powered and armed warships as part of the nuclear-free campaign. In addition, Terry and I became heavily involved in education, teaching in and helping to run an experimental primary school.

But things were happening in southern Africa and, after 1976, in South Africa. By 1979, we felt we had done as much as we could in New Zealand. Besides, our children, then aged ten and seven, were, we thought, old enough to move. We wrote to O.R. Tambo asking if there was any posting 'closer to home'. He replied promptly: the ANC was starting a school for the 'Soweto generation', but it had been realised there was a need for a primary division, would we come to Tanzania to start one?

Would we? There was no question. Here seemed to be the prospect of helping to build the sort of education for liberation so many pedagogues had dreamed of over so many years. We could eventually go home, hopefully having built something positive that would serve the interests of a truly democratic and egalitarian society. From ANC statements it also appeared that the movement had finally managed to throw off the corruption, nepotism and chaos of the past. In the Tanzanian bush it was perhaps trying to establish a model of the sort of society we had all talked about and sung about for so many years.

But our arrival in Dar es Salaam was certainly not auspicious. The chaotic lack of organisation that had existed in the past was still evident from the minute we landed. There was no one to meet us and we were stranded in a near-deserted airport for six hours until a friendly Tanzanian official helped us contact a comrade we knew who lived in the city.

The following morning, the promised transport to take us to catch the bus to Morogoro, the town nearest the school, based on a former sisal plantation known as Mazimbu, failed to arrive. However, we managed to beg a lift from a local accountant and caught up to the bus as it was leaving Dar. But in Morogoro, there was nobody to meet us and nobody at the ANC office. By nightfall, we managed to find a taxi driver who knew where Mazimbu was and who agreed to take us there.

So began a period of my exile that I think has affected me more deeply than any other. Despite the chaotic start, we remained quite fiercely optimistic. We had, after all, sold everything to pay our fares as a family and to ship more than a ton of equipment, ranging from books and chalk boards, paper and pencils to start the primary school. It was 1980 and we were sure this would be our last move before going home to a liberated South Africa.

It was not to be. At the Mazimbu complex that housed the Solomon Mahlangu Freedom College (SOMAFCO) we had what I now think of as the post-1994 South Africa in microcosm, a de-racialised hierarchy where the leadership enjoyed a relatively privileged lifestyle down to being provided with four times more toilet paper than the rank and file, and where black women, again, were at the bottom of the pile. A situation of 'haves' and 'have-nots' among South African exiles was still firmly in place.

It was a rude awakening, but we thought, naively, that the Mazimbu community could still become the sort of democratic model of the South Africa of our dreams and hopes: anti-racist, anti-sexist and egalitarian. The rhetoric and the published policies held out this hope, but the practice was vastly different.

There was also a difference on apartheid lines. Without exception, to my knowledge, the whites were part of the staff elite and, almost without exception, had passports and homes and connections in countries such as England and Canada. Some, being members of the SACP, had contacts with East European embassies and were able, from time to time, to secure various luxuries for their households.

I was uncomfortable with this situation, especially the fact that Terry, myself and our children – along with others in 'staff' positions – were given separate and preferential rations. We also had fridges and electric stoves (courtesy of Sweden and Electrolux) while, in those first years that we were there, meals for the secondary school students were prepared over open fires and all too often comprised only *pap* (soft cornmeal) and boiled cabbage.

We also felt that it was wrong that we should be given preferential housing that was of a much higher standard than the homes from which our students came. Many were the children of *mgwenya*, older MK members (some had left in 1962) who had married local women. But our requests that we be relocated to what the hierarchy referred to as 'the locations', where these children lived, or to the school premises in an old sisal plantation house, were rejected.

At least, we argued, there should be equality in the cooking and food rations area. It seemed to us a waste of valuable time to cook individually and, besides, since we were all in exile together, we felt we should all share the same food. So we asked that our rations be sent to the communal kitchen where we would go on the kitchen duty roster.

That, too, failed and we were accused of being elitist for 'not cooking your own meals' and told that we should not compare our situation to that of students 'since nowhere are students and staff equal'. Until we capitulated, food to us was stopped, even for our children, then aged eleven and eight. But although we had to give in on that score, I am proud to say that we refused throughout our stay in Mazimbu to attend the occasional and well-catered for 'staff only' *braais* (barbeques).

All of this convinced me even more that the struggle was not only against apartheid; it was against a system of oppression and exploitation of which apartheid was only one aspect. This was highlighted by the levels of sexism and the harassment and abuse suffered by many of the young women in Mazimbu, often at the hands of visiting leaders or male staff members. I talked with many of these young women, trying to encourage them to make an issue of their abuse, but they never complained openly, pointing out that if they did, there might be no hope of them ever getting out of Mazimbu on scholarship.

Particularly galling was the fact that women students who fell pregnant were effectively punished by being removed from studies and made to look after babies in the Charlotte Maxeke Crèche. The male students responsible for the pregnancies were sent for brief periods of punishment working in the fields before carrying on as before.

A similar situation applied with women from MK who fell pregnant and who arrived at the crèche. As James Ngculu notes in his 2009 book, *The Honour to Serve*: 'This was generally viewed as a form of punishment for getting pregnant. Nothing was done to the man who impregnated the woman, who would, in most cases, simply move on to another woman to satisfy his sexual needs.'

Quite apart from the horrendous sexism, it seemed to me one of the more idiotic aspects of education in exile that child-rearing and food production should be associated with punishment. Another was the refusal by the SOMAFCO administration to allow any form of sex education at Mazimbu.

However, it was the deliberate violence, the beatings and torture that brought matters to a head for me. A group of young men, suspected of having smoked dagga (marijuana), were dragged from their beds one night, taken to the most remote classroom, tied over desks which were then upended, and beaten with a rubber hose on the soles of their bare feet. Their screams echoed throughout the complex.

Terry and I launched an official protest, only to be told by the then national commissar, Andrew Masondo: 'I have seen the police in Moscow beat suspects – and if it's good enough for them, it's good enough for me.'

The final straw came when three women, who had been seen in Morogoro town talking with PAC men who were students at a nearby medical facility, were dragged before a night-time 'court' and sentenced to a sjamboking. This was carried out by a male comrade known for his brutality to his wife and children and was so severe that two of the women required hospital treatment. That 'court' included male teachers from the secondary school, black and white.

I think I was sadder and angrier then than at any time in my years of exile. What I had hoped would be a home from home had turned into a nightmare. So we resigned from SOMAFCO and, perhaps because a senior national executive member of the movement had referred to my husband as 'the conscience of the ANC', we were not expelled. We were given tickets to London where we began what I think of as our exile within exile because there, with very few notable exceptions, we were shunned by ANC members, and even requested at one stage to 'do the decent thing and resign' from the movement.

In the circumstances, I felt I was, for the first time, in a position to really understand that old Nguni dictum quoted by black women exiles: an elephant is never burdened by its trunk. In other words, we will make do with what we have been given – and have no choice about.

The ANC office also put out a statement to members alleging that we had called the ANC leadership stupid and barbaric. What we had in fact written in a letter to headquarters in Lusaka and to the SOMAFCO hierarchy was that in the punishment meted out to the three women 'the barbarity was exceeded only by the stupidity'; that loyalty could not be beaten into people.

But loyalty, blind loyalty, was the demand. If you are not wholly for us, you must be against us, was the rule. Principles, including those laid down in ANC policy documents, often acted as nothing more than public relations sops handed out for the benefit of the donor community.

I felt quite isolated and angry in those first months back in England, but things were moving on the home front, as the new trade union movement began flexing its muscles. Unionists from the radical Metal and Allied Workers Union (MAWU) visited, and we made contact with them. Rain Chiya, the first woman crane drive and a MAWU member, was a notable guest as were a number of others, headed by Moses Mayekiso. Our exile links were replaced by fewer, but, we thought, more meaningful contacts; in our exile from exile we felt closer to home than at any time in the previous twenty years.

When Mayekiso was detained on 28 June 1985 and, especially after he and four other activists from Alexandra township – the 'Alex Five' – were charged more than twenty-two months later, on 13 April 1987, with the capital offence of treason, we liaised with the newly formed National Union of Metalworkers (NUMSA) that incorporated MAWU, and with the International Metalworkers Federation. It was they who encouraged us to co-ordinate what developed into probably the biggest ever trade union, anti-apartheid campaign. But, because Mayekiso was at that stage labelled a 'workerist', being one of the group that supported the idea of establishing a workers' party and democratic, worker control of the economy, the ANC and the SACP-run Congress of South African Trade Unions opposed the campaign.

To me, this was disappointing but not surprising and I remained nominally an ANC member as we co-ordinated the campaign that also linked to the support system for the 970 MAWU/NUMSA strikers at the British-owned BTR-Sarmcol rubber plant in Edendale in KwaZulu-Natal. They downed tools for union recognition and held out against incredible odds, with the survivors of this longest strike in our history winning recognition and compensation in a final court battle thirteen years later.

By 1988, we were sure, for the first time, that we would be going home within a few years. I had mixed feelings about this. Right to the end, I was a reluctant returnee, largely because of my experiences within the movement and especially in Tanzania. I recalled a comment made years earlier by a comrade who said, 'We'll be in real trouble if the *amaBhunu* (Boers) and the ANC ever get together.' By 1990, they were getting together and a negotiated settlement was already on the cards.

There was also the fact that I had made close friends with comrades in Britain and elsewhere. In addition, I had decided that nationalism was a reactionary concept and the experience over the Alex Five campaign had shown me clearly what a global village it is that we live in.

As secretary to the Alex Five campaign, I dealt with the thousands of messages of solidarity that poured in from trade unionists, unions and federations representing more than thirty million workers around the world. This made me realise, as never before, the identity of interest workers everywhere share and the power that united workers can have. It was this unity in action on the ground in South Africa that I felt had pushed international business and financiers into sanctions.

But those contacts with people from home also strengthened my desire to return to the place I grew up in and that had been so much my focus, no matter in which country or on what continent I happened to be living. It was still home in a sense that nowhere else could ever really be. However, I had no illusions that there would be any immediate transformation into the sort of country I had dreamed of in my younger years. Some form of deal would have to be struck between a government that could no longer control the population and the major exiled liberation movement that did not have the power to seize control.

I was sure that apartheid in the formal sense would go, but that the effects would continue until those same masses that had rebelled, especially in the 1980s, started to put in place a truly democratic alternative. And so, when the talks about talks and the talks about a new dispensation got underway, we packed up yet again, emotionally armed with the one sense that I think sustains most exiles: hope. In my case, however, the hope was tinged with doubt, although, once again, I committed myself.

Now, with hindsight, I realise quite how naive I was, before, during and after the years of exile. Like so many of my comrades, I reacted against that regime without realising that it was only one aspect of a system of oppression and exploitation; that sexism and other forms of exploitation and oppression would not simply fall away just because apartheid had been defeated.

The only consolation is that we are never too old to learn. And there is also the hope that younger generations, learning from our mistakes and naivety, will continue the fight.

On behalf of us all

Nomvo Booi

Nomvo Booi was born on 16 May 1929 in Butterworth in the Eastern Cape. She was a founding member of the Pan-Africanist Congress in 1959 and acted as its regional secretary. During the state of emergency that was declared after the Sharpeville massacre in 1960, Nomvo was arrested in Queenstown and detained for four months. Her detention was the first of many. On her release she continued her involvement in underground activities for the PAC. From August 1962 she was detained for eleven months and constantly subjected to interrogation and held in solitary confinement. During this time she was found guilty under the Suppression of Communism Act and sentenced to three years' imprisonment. After her release she was banned to the remote area of Willowvale in the former Transkei. Upon the release of her banning order, she continued to live in the Eastern Cape. She also worked to develop her professional sewing skills as a means by which to help people help themselves. Throughout this period she was subjected to continuous police harassment, intimidation and many periods of detention.

In 1982 Nomvo fled into exile in Lesotho, Tanzania and beyond where she continued to further the work of the PAC. She served on the Central Committee of the organisation for many years in exile and on her return to South Africa in the early 1990s. In 2009 she suffered a stroke and now lives in East London in the Eastern Cape.

My parents, Nkumbikazi and James Booi, named me 'Nomvo' because I was the eleventh of thirteen children. I was born at a place called Ezagwityi in Butterworth in the former Transkei. I went to Zagwityi Primary School under Mr Theophilus Pamla. When no one knew the answer to a question, the teacher, Mr Pamla, often said, 'Tell them, Nomvo'. When I left Ezagwityi, I went and did my Standard 6 at Fort Malan in Idutywa.

One may suppose that I was spoilt as a child, but my parents did not see it that way. My father believed that all his children should learn to work with their hands. As a result, his children became carpenters, weavers, dressmakers and so on. In spite of many thinking that my intelligence was not fully utilised, I went on to Clarkebury College, a Methodist missionary school at Engcobo, to learn dressmaking and design.

Upon completion, I returned to Butterworth and opened a dressmaking business that became very successful. In addition to other items of clothing, I designed wedding gowns. I became the 'go to' person for the best wedding gowns in the region. Among the people whom I designed gowns for was the wife of Thembu chief, Kaiser Matanzima, Mrs Nozuko Matanzima, and other Thembu royalty.

It was while conducting business in Butterworth that I met Mr Strauss. He was a businessman from Queenstown who was impressed with the skill with which I ran the business and thought that if we partnered up we could expand. We agreed to work together and, in addition to designing clothing, I would teach the rest of his staff. I later moved to Queenstown where I worked with Strauss for many years.

At a young age I joined the African National Congress (ANC). I was involved in the successful Defiance Campaign in 1952. At this time I was a member of the ANC Youth League. The Youth League held the opinion that the ANC leadership stopped the campaign too quickly and without much effort. As I will explain, this Youth League was instrumental in the foundation of the Pan-Africanist Congress (PAC) in 1959, under the leadership of Robert Mangaliso Sobukwe. I was closely involved in the founding of the PAC and became the regional secretary in the Transkei.

Joining the PAC

One may wonder why and how I joined the PAC. In 1948 the Afrikaners, led by the National Party, took power from the government which had been under the English for a long time. The National Party's policies were aggressive and racist. It did not want anything to do with the members of the Communist Party of South Africa (CPSA) from early on. The previous English government had agreed to work with the CPSA and had created the Native Representative Council to talk on behalf of African affairs. When the National Party came to power, the first thing they did was to remove the communist members from parliament. The CPSA found a home among black organisations such as the ANC and the Unity Movement.

In 1949, with the initiative of the Youth League, the ANC adopted the 'Programme of Action' as its policy document to fight the new government's racist policies. The programme adopted a more militant position and called for an end to compliance with the racist National Party policies.

From then on several campaigns were launched. Africanists within the Youth League, which later broke away from the ANC to form the PAC, adopted new militant positions known then as the 'Status Campaign' and the 'Positive Action Campaign'. These policies were aimed at the African mind itself – to improve self-respect, dignity and the ability to stand up for their rights. Years of oppression had undermined the African personality. Africans were losing the fight against the assault of white supremacy and seemed unable to resist the new government's aim of destroying their well-being. The assertive Africanist approach in the Youth League had great appeal among African people and attracted great numbers.

By 1952 the ANC adopted the Defiance Campaign, also aimed at persuading the African people to defy the laws of segregation that separated social spaces like entrances to public places, parks, beaches, housing, even graveyards, among other things. For Africanists, however, the call to self-dignity was so much more challenging than protesting over having to swim at a separate beach or be seated on a separate bus.

Many Africanists in the Youth League felt that the white people who had been forced out of parliament for being communist members were putting pressure on the ANC mother body to change policies. Indeed, ANC policy was being influenced by their new-found friends of the CPSA. However, the majority of Africanists seemed to be drawn to the call of the Status Campaign and Positive Action Campaign, which affected the African mind more deeply. Many argued that the Defiance Campaign was more of an idea from the CPSA members. Africanists did not like that the Programme of Action was being taken over by white communists. Some saw little difference between white Afrikaners and white communists.

On 6 April 1959, the Africanist group in the Youth League formed the PAC under the leadership of Robert Sobukwe – one of the Youth League members who piloted the Programme of Action in 1949. He was a born leader and his friends called him 'Prof'.

The PAC held its first national meeting in the Orlando Community Hall in Soweto, Johannesburg. Delegates from across the country attended. The meeting started with slogans such as 'Africa for the Africans', 'From Cape to Cairo, Morocco to Madagascar', '*Izwe lethu i-Africa*' (Africa our land). After that the PAC leadership travelled around the country opening our eyes to the humiliation and the need for us to take action.

That is how the PAC broke away from the ANC and I was drawn away from the ANC and joined the PAC.

The PAC organised the Positive Action Campaign of 1960, which led to the Sharpeville massacre. As a response to the campaign, a state of emergency was declared. While in Queenstown, I was arrested during the state of emergency. I was imprisoned for four months. After this imprisonment, I went underground, working for Poqo, the original name for the military wing of the PAC. The name was later changed to the Azanian People's Liberation Army (APLA).

The Sharpeville massacre

In jail I heard a lot about what had happened in Sharpeville on 21 March 1960. One has plenty of time to kill in jail and, since I was in Queenstown when it happened, I wanted to know more. We shared a lot of stories with other prisoners, especially those from the PAC.

As part of the Positive Action Campaign, our president, Sobukwe, called a press conference to announce that the organisation had organised anti-Pass marches for Monday, 21 March 1960, throughout the country. His instruction to all PAC branches was: 'Our people must be taught now and continuously to observe absolute non-violence.'

Sobukwe's anti-Pass campaign made a call on the people to leave their Passes at home on 21 March and march to police stations around the country and make themselves available for arrest by the police. Under the Pass laws, an African over sixteen years of age had to carry a Pass book (or *dompas*, meaning, in Afrikaans, 'dumb pass') wherever they went, day or night, and any policeman had the right to arrest the individual if found without one. 'No bail! No defence! No fine!' was their slogan. The PAC leadership said that if many people were arrested, the jails would be full and the country would come to a standstill.

Sobukwe's call carried the spirit of the Africans all round, echoing and re-echoing in songs like Masiza's song which questioned the African mind:

Koze kube nini Nkosi,
Koze kube nini?
Zonke izizwe zisibeka phansi konyawo.
('Until when? Oh Lord!
How long? Oh Lord!
All nations are putting us under their feet.')

From the stories I heard, the PAC leaders in Sharpeville in the East Rand gathered in a field joined by a crowd of people. The crowd proceeded to the police station – singing freedom songs and calling out the campaign slogans '*Izwe lethu*' (Our land); '*Awaphele amapasi*' (Down with passes); '*Sobukwe Sikhokhele*' (Lead us, Sobukwe); 'Forward to Independence! Tomorrow the United States of Africa'. The songs of freedom were picking up and the slogans were being repeated with louder voices.

When the marchers reached Sharpeville's police station, many policemen were there waiting outside. The PAC leaders continued to go forward – the PAC motto is 'Leaders in Front' – and asked the white policeman in charge to let them in so that they could give themselves up to be arrested for not carrying Passes.

Without any warning one of the policemen panicked and opened fire. His colleagues followed suit. The firing lasted for a short time, leaving sixty-nine people dead and 180 people seriously wounded. The police claimed that the protesters had begun to stone them. The policemen were apparently scared after a recent event in Durban where nine policemen had been shot a few months earlier.

The police used live ammunition. The people were given no warning to disperse. A large number of people were shot in the back as they were fleeing the scene. This was a needless provocation, especially as the crowd was unarmed and determined to stage a non-violent protest.

According to Humphrey Tyler, the assistant editor at *Drum Magazine*:

The police have claimed they were in desperate danger because the crowd
was stoning them. Yet only three policemen were reported to have been hit
by stones – and more than 200 Africans were shot down. The police also
have said that the crowd was armed with 'ferocious weapons', which littered
the compound after they fled.

I saw no weapons, although I looked very carefully, and afterwards studied
the photographs of the death scene. While I was there I saw only shoes, hats
and a few bicycles left among the bodies. The crowd gave me no reason to
feel scared, though I moved among them without any distinguishing mark to
protect me, quite obvious with my white skin. I think the police were scared
though, and I think the crowd knew it.

The news of the Sharpeville massacre spread quickly in the country and was flashed
around the world. The news was received with horror from every country. The
international conscience was deeply moved by the police action.

When the news of the Sharpeville massacre reached Cape Town, a group of
protestors gathered at Langa township. The police ordered the crowd to disperse.
When protesters reconvened in defiance, the police charged at them with batons, tear
gas and guns. Three people were killed and twenty-six others were injured.

Robert Sobukwe and other leaders were arrested and detained after the Sharpeville
massacre. Mass funerals were held for the victims.

The Minister of Justice suspended Passes throughout the country. Chief Albert
Luthuli and Professor Z.K. Matthews, ANC leaders, called on all South Africans to
mark a national day of mourning for the victims. Phillip Kgosana led a PAC march of
protestors from Langa and Nyanga to the police headquarters in the centre of Cape
Town. The protesters offered themselves up for arrest for not carrying their Passes.
Police were temporarily paralysed with indecision. The event has been seen by some
as a turning point in South African history.

The government responded by declaring a state of emergency and banning all
public meetings. The police and army arrested thousands of Africans who were
imprisoned with their leaders, but still the mass action continued.

A week after the state of emergency was declared, the ANC and the PAC were
banned under the Unlawful Organisations Act of 8 April 1960.

The Sharpeville massacre, the imposition of a state of emergency, the arrest of
thousands of African people and the banning of the ANC and PAC convinced the
leadership that non-violent action was not going to bring about change without armed
action. The PAC and ANC were forced underground and both parties started military
wings of their organisations in 1961.

The PAC had a legal existence of eleven to twelve months after its formation. Because it was banned, its members were monitored by the state security agencies day in and day out; it was important for me to find ways to communicate and operate underground.

On my return to Queenstown after serving four months in prison, I found out that I had lost my job at Strauss's. Mr Strauss bowed to police pressure and terminated my contract on the grounds that I was 'a dangerous person'. The challenges did not end there as I was soon to learn that under what was commonly known as Section 10 of the Suppression of Communism Act, No. 44 of 1950, I had been banned from Queenstown which, until then, had been my home for thirteen years.

Uprooted and jobless, I was forced to appeal to relatives to look after my first child, who was two years old at the time, while I established a sewing career in Clarkebury at Engcobo. My brother was a boarding master at Clarkebury College. The family support base helped me get back on my feet and I was able to continue with my sewing career.

In July 1962, in a midnight raid on my house in Engcobo, I was beaten by the arresting officers and suffered numerous bruises on my back and twisted my neck. I was detained at Engcobo police station over the possession of a letter from a friend in exile. I was refused medical attention for many hours. Eventually when the police relented, the visiting doctor paid little attention to my complaints and said that I was 'fussy'.

I was constantly moved between prisons, got no medical attention and at times got no food. The moves were designed to disorientate and isolate me from friends and family. No members of my family were allowed to visit and were often turned away at the prison gates by officers who claimed to have no knowledge of my whereabouts.

After ten months in prison, where I was constantly interrogated and isolated from other prisoners, I was charged for 'furthering the aims of a banned organisation'. In the eleventh month of my incarceration I was finally taken to court where I was given a three-year sentence in accordance with the Suppression of Communism Act. The initial part of this sentence was served in the East London women's prison. While in prison, I was told that further charges were going to be levelled against me for addressing a gathering in Mqanduli. The charge did not stick since the witnesses failed to appear in court. During the three-year sentence, I was moved from East London to Kroonstad and later to Nylstroom. The latter two were nowhere near familiar faces, food or language.

Although I finished serving my prison sentence in 1966, I could not lead the life of a free person. I was given a two-year banishment order to Idutywa and told to report monthly to a local police station. Once that expired, I was spied upon and my house often raided for no reason at all.

While in prison, my first daughter was raised by my aunt in Tsolo. My second and third daughters were born while I lived in Idutywa. My political responsibilities as a courier called on me to be away from home often. The children were frequently left in the care of neighbours and family. During my last incarceration, my last two were in boarding schools and my first-born lived and worked in Butterworth.

Meanwhile, the injury I incurred during the 1962 arrest was giving me constant problems. A visit to Durban's King Edward VIII Hospital revealed that I had indeed cracked some vertebrae and that the bones had healed badly as a result of the lack of medical attention. Belated treatment helped very little and the pain still persists today.

Police attention only helped to strengthen my political conviction and determination to do my little bit to bring a rapid end to the ways of the National Party government. While my resolve increased, so did that of the police as they continued to raid my house whenever they felt the whim.

In 1972 I began to work for some churches as a sewing instructor. In a project first located in Sada, near Queenstown, I taught sewing to women who had been thrown out of their homes on farms in the area. The project was such a success that they were soon moved to bigger premises at a mission in Shiloh, also near Queenstown. In 1975 I was given the broader responsibility of being an instructor for the Border Council of Churches based in Alice in the former Ciskei and was responsible for a larger group of women, as well as for Zikhulise Home Industries. At Zikhulise, as it was commonly known, I led women who designed and created traditional clothing which was very popular.

My political work was not forgotten as I continued to act as a courier for groups in Lesotho and Botswana.

The biggest task that I had to perform concerned unveiling the tombstone of the late founding president of the PAC, Robert Sobukwe, who died in 1978. This arduous task was organised in complete secrecy. My contact in exile was the late APLA commander, Sabelo Phama. We met in Lesotho to discuss the logistics of the exercise. The organising team was made up of three other comrades, one of whom was Comrade Siwisa, a close friend to Sobukwe. Unknown to the authorities, we organised a well-attended unveiling ceremony in Graaff-Reinet in 1981, well befitting the respect we felt for Sobukwe.

The police, humiliated by the fact that an event of such magnitude could have taken place on their watch, wanted to find out who the organisers were. Numerous arrests were made. The majority of the comrades who were with me on the organising committee were arrested. I was called to Lesotho by the organisation for an urgent meeting. Lesotho had become a vital outpost of the PAC since the banning of political organisations in 1960. In the light of all the arrests, I was advised to stay in Lesotho and not return home, as I was sure to be arrested. There was also the risk that if any of the comrades cracked under interrogation, I would be a target.

It was difficult for me not to return to South Africa because I had left my three children unprepared for the new situation. So, I started my journey back home. I got a lift from a friend who was also travelling to South Africa. Due to the delicate nature of my trip, they decided that I would travel in the boot (trunk) of his car to avoid being found out by the authorities at the Lesotho border. We were successful on the Lesotho side of the border, but I was discovered in a routine check on the South African side. We were both arrested and detained in Lady Grey and from there, we were sent to Umtata where I was interrogated, chiefly about an APLA comrade detained in Lesotho. After spending some weeks in prison, the security police brought my file from Fort Beaufort (the office that oversaw Alice), which, they said, would help them add more weight in achieving a conviction. Fortunately, this did not work. I was tried and convicted for illegal entry into South Africa. We were then fined and both released.

Soon after, one of the organisers of the Robert Sobukwe memorial was released from prison. He advised me that the authorities were well aware of my involvement in the organisation of the memorial. It is important to note that during my imprisonments the Bureau for State Security, the South African intelligence organisation, tried to buy me, asking me if I would work for them. I refused all the time.

At this point, I decided that I had had enough and that it was time I left South Africa. I departed for Lesotho in 1982 and soon travelled on to Tanzania where I joined the freedom fighters in exile. I became a mother figure there and held the Health and Welfare portfolio.

My last two children had followed me to Lesotho where they lived and studied in boarding school under the care of Mr and Mrs Gwintsa, a South African family. To get to there, they had travelled by road with family friends. One family friend drove them to Johannesburg in an overnight trip, and a second group of friends drove the children over the border.

The children were registered as refugees in that country, and under the United Nations High Commissioner for Refugees their school fees were paid and they received a stipend. It was great when my PAC business took me back to Lesotho and I was able to visit my children. This happened twice during the four-year period that it took the last-born to finish high school. Before we left South Africa, I had sat my children down and told them that at sixteen and fourteen they were grown up and I needed them to allow me to fight my cause and indirectly fight for their future. I told them that I had taught them everything that they needed to know to be upstanding young adults and that they should continue to abide by my teachings. When they followed me to Lesotho, I told them that I would soon be leaving for Tanzania and that we should remember the discussion we had had in South Africa, to focus on their studies and recognise that we would not be a family living in the same house any longer.

I assisted my two youngest daughters to get scholarship programmes. My eldest daughter, Khanyisa, remained in the country and qualified as a teacher with a B.A. Honours degree in human ecology and an honours degree in education. Sibongile, the youngest, went to Canada where she qualified as a civil engineer. Mpho went to England where she qualified as a dietician and also holds a master's degree in health sciences.

Exile

Having taken the decision to leave South Africa, I soon found myself drawn to the demands of the organisation. The leadership of the PAC in exile had heard about the work I was doing in the country. They had met my children in Lesotho and had assisted me to arrange for their scholarships to study abroad.

No sooner had I arrived in Tanzania than a call came from the Zimbabwe African National Union – Patriotic Front (ZANU-PF) requesting the PAC to provide a woman to go to Zimbabwe to assist in creating a women's league for them. In exile, certain organisations found it easier to work jointly with those organisations from other countries with similar views on most issues. From a long time ago, ZANU-PF shared a lot in common with the PAC. No sooner had this request arrived than the PAC released me to assist ZANU-PF form their women's league.

After completing my work in Zimbabwe, I returned to Tanzania to continue as head of Health and Social Welfare – to manage food distribution and attend to newborn babies with other PAC women. When Tanzania was first liberated in the 1960s, some women (like Finasse Mama Waki, a nurse) were among the earliest to be dispatched by the political leaders from South Africa, upon President Nyerere's request for such trained women. She has remained in that country, in her position, to this day.

I continued with my political work, advising young people and counselling newly married couples – some of our young men married Tanzanian girls and vice versa – as well as South African couples entering marriage. It was necessary for them to understand each other's culture, such as the *lobola* (dowry) system, where it was necessary. My main role was to bring stability, build family values from each side and change unAfrican behaviour patterns where they occurred. I presided over several weddings, among them Sabelo Phama's, Gqwetha's , Dudu's, Lindela Madondo's and Fezile's.

I was called to assist in creating support structures for the young people – some were as young as ten years old – who had left their parents in South Africa after the Soweto uprising of 1976. There were no social structures, cultural norms and moral values to build a viable community.

I then became an active member of the staff component of the PAC in exile, sitting on the Central Committee. I attended various international women's conferences in places like Vienna in Austria, representing the struggling women of South Africa. As head of Health and Social Welfare in the PAC, together with Mfanasekhaya Pearce Lindi Gqobose, I travelled all over the world to raise funds for the organisation.

Coming back home

In my early years, I realised the incongruity of life under apartheid. It infuriated me and before I knew it I was right in the middle of the struggle against apartheid. The story of my exile is long and began when I was quite young. Prison life is the story of my life. Prison life is in itself a form of exile. But, much later in life, I was finally forced out of South Africa to experience real exile in countries like Lesotho and Tanzania. Yet, to be honest, this variation was more acceptable to me.

I returned to South Africa in 1992 after the unbanning of the PAC, ANC and other political organisations in February 1990 in order to pave a way to negotiate a new dispensation for South Africa, that is, the official end of apartheid as we knew it. For all the toil, sweat and pains over the years, I now felt vindicated. The struggle and sacrifice had not been in vain.

I settled in East London in the Eastern Cape, which had always been my home from the beginning. I continued to be active in politics as a member of the National Executive of the PAC. I continued my social responsibility in assisting the returning exiles or the returnees to connect with their families and homes. Indeed, some of the returnees had lost relatives and family who had been moved from their original homes under apartheid policies.

Many acknowledged me on my return as a leader, a strong follower, friendly and unselfish. To many I was known as 'Mama', who sacrificed her youth and her children and served the people.

Even though I have now been silenced by a stroke that affected my speech in 2009, throughout my adult life I have been very outspoken and never minced my words. My commitment to the PAC has remained with me throughout. One trait that continues in my old age is the stubbornness I displayed in my early life. Once I resolve that an action is justified, nothing else will sway my mind.

On a one-way ticket

Ruth Carneson

Ruth Carneson was born in Cape Town in 1953. At the age of fourteen she travelled to exile in London on her own, following her brother and sister who were already in the United Kingdom. Her mother followed later and her father, who served time in prison on political charges arising from his membership of the South African Communist Party, joined the family when he was released from prison. She lived in the United Kingdom for twenty-four years and developed a career as a visual artist. She returned to South Africa in 1991. From 1997–2007 she worked on Robben Island, first as an artist-in-residence and later as principal of the pre-school. She was short-listed for the Penguin Prize for African Writing and has published poems and short stories in Woman Flashing and Writing the Self, compilations of women's writing. She has also done illustrations for book covers. Today she lives in Cape Town where she manages the South African Sendinggestig Museum, also known as the Slave Church Museum.

Exile
In London I expected to find bright colours and parties
Instead I found the colour grey and endless rain
And a maze of buildings and cold, bad weather
I seem to be going round in circles

I found the colour grey and endless rain
I kept going in the wrong direction
I seem to be going round in circles
I want my Mum and Dad

I keep going in the wrong direction
How can I cry like this? I am not a baby
I want my Mum and Dad
But I am old enough to look after myself

How can I cry like this? I am not a baby
All I see is a maze of buildings and cold, bad weather

I am old enough to look after myself
In London I expected to find bright colours and parties.

My family don't cry
My sister's suitcases are packed
Loved ones wave from the quayside
As streamers precariously connect people
Tears as balloons float into the sky

Balloons are let up into the air
Streamers precariously connect people
Tears as balloons float into the sky
Tugboats steer the ship out of the harbour

People blow kisses and throw streamers
Tears as balloons float into the sky
Tug boats steer the ship out of the harbour
My family don't cry

Loved ones wave from the quayside
Tug boats steer the ship out of the harbour
My family don't cry
My sister's suitcases are packed

I do not remember my brother leaving
He leaves to go over seas
My mind goes blank
I am alone with my mother

He leaves to go over seas
To escape being conscripted
I am alone with my mother
A family in London adopt him

He escapes being conscripted
He has left on the boat
A family in London adopt him
I know he has gone

He has left on the boat
My mind goes blank
I know he has gone
But I do not remember him leaving

On a one-way ticket
I must leave as soon as possible
Under one arm I carry a roll of pictures
In my other arm I hold my teddy bear

I must leave as soon as possible
I wave goodbye as I cross the tarmac
In my arms I hold my teddy bear
I board the plane and my mother disappears

I wave goodbye as I cross the tarmac
I cannot guess the consequences
I board the plane and my mother disappears
BANG my life splits in two

I cannot guess the consequences
Under one arm I carry a roll of pictures
BANG my life splits in two
On a one-way ticket

Looking a gift horse in the mouth

Busi Chaane

Busisiwe D. Chaane was born in 1963 of South African parents in London. She grew up in Lusaka, Zambia, and later moved to the United Kingdom where she confronted some of the hard realities of being a South African in exile. In the United Kingdom she attained a B.A. Honours in communications studies from Coventry University and an M.A. in international journalism from City University. She has since cultivated a successful career as a writer, journalist and editor, publishing many features, editorials, short stories and a book for new readers entitled Ma Lulu's Place. She returned to South Africa in 1993. Today she lives with her family in Johannesburg where she continues to work as a writer and journalist in the print, radio and television industries. She is currently co-writing a book on myths and legends in South Africa.

Growing up as I did, in the post-independence idyll that was Zambia, my life circumstances – a child born in exile to exiled parents – held no special meaning for me beyond the fact that many of my childhood friends and their parents frequently made reference to '*ekhaya*', and that my grandparents were always at a distance, at this 'home'.

So, until my mid-teens, at the point that my parents – my father actually – decided I should continue my English-language education in the European motherland itself, I was blissfully oblivious to the harsh realities of life as an African female.

June 1976 passed me by. Not because I didn't know or care about it, but because 1976 was the year I turned thirteen in Lusaka, and the events that unfolded that particular South African winter coincided with the horrifying realisation that my above-the-knee convent girl's school uniform did nothing to hide what I alone perceived to be my major physical deformities. This calamity absorbed my whole being – there was simply no room for more emotional reaction – even to the momentous events taking place in townships across South Africa.

In the next year, I was prised from the oddly bloodless clutches of the Dominican nuns and deposited in a different secondary school, still in Zambia. This other school had no uniform and admitted boys, throwing the enormity of my physical faults into stark relief.

41

I sought refuge in home-made trousers and calf-length dresses or skirts, long-sleeved tops and a cardigan, year-round, even in the searing heat of Lusaka in October. In vain, I tried to grow my stubbornly not-quite-black hair that hung like a grey-brown, wispy cobweb about my head, leaving what I was certain was my most obvious deformity still plainly exposed. My large, protruding ears, dimpled knees and the constantly goose-pimpled skin on my arms would continue to cause me considerable angst in the years to come.

Come 1979 and I was thrust into the lower sixth form (post-matric) class at an all-girls' Church of England school, nestled in a remote and frequently snow-bound village in the heart of the British Midlands. In the space of ten short hours, in one knee-chafing, economy-class plane journey, everyone and everything I had ever known, loved or taken for granted, was swept away.

June 1979 turned out to be the beginning of my personal introduction to apartheid education – in England. My rebellion against that education would not turn out to be as eloquent or forceful – in fact, I imploded – but it was every bit as life-changing as the tumultuous events that began at Morris Isaacson Secondary.

Suddenly, I was terribly homesick and reading R.D. Laing's *The Oncology of Self*. I battled with feelings of complete despair and failure as I returned again and again to the same English teacher for yet more pointers on how to improve my work in a subject that, for as long as I had been able to write, I had scored no less than eighty-five per cent. As the months wore on, and the days darkened at 3 p.m. in the afternoon, I struggled to retain some semblance of self-respect and dignity in the face of plummeting grades and the singular lack – eventually I sensed complete unwillingness on the part of the said English teacher and her department – of effective remedial measures for my marks.

I made a few friends – rank outsiders like myself: a trio of welcoming sisters from Nigeria (confident, clever and well-off) and a local girl (plain – frumpy would be the word used to describe her).

My chief solace soon became what was to be found on top of the plywood cupboards that lined the vast sixth form common rooms. The generous packets of thickly sliced white bread, the catering-size containers of butter, jam and coffee, milk and sugar, delivered at the same time every two days, became my psychological mainstay. Until this point in my life, I had lived up to my nickname, skinny bones (*sikini mabonzo*, actually); now just a few months into life in true exile, that moniker could no longer apply to me.

It was at this point that I first felt what it was really like not to belong, to be different, and irrevocably so, and for my difference to be made obvious and problematic. This was when I realised that I missed 'home' and I pined after a life that was more accepting of me as I was – dark skin, big backside, poor academic skills (it suddenly appeared) and all.

Still, I thought of this as my bad luck, my misfortune and lack of brains rather than as the predictable outcome of coming face-to-face with institutionalised racism, prejudice, severe culture shock and neglect.

It was only with the arrival one cold spring morning of a television crew from Birmingham, with a dapper, dreadlocked and rather vocal, black British cameraman in its midst, that I awoke from my inner turmoil and realised the truth – I was an outsider and would always be; but he showed that an alternative life existed for outsiders beyond the school fence.

My experiences as an African girl from Zambia surviving perilously in middle England had firmly established this as my future reality. I could not recall feeling this unwanted before now – but, from then on, the only way for me to survive was to accept my status as 'other'. To do this would perhaps hasten my liberation from the internal dislocation I was enduring and from the psychologically crushed state I was now in.

I still don't know how I managed to survive those initial, grim years. Or perhaps I do. It was only through the love and care of like-minded people, outsiders like me, that I escaped knowing the intricate patterns in an outpatient ward. My circle of salvation was a small and ultimately precious one – a boisterous and loving 'parallel' family that I soon discovered nurtured relationships not only with refugees from our homeland, but those from other parts of Africa and further afield who were also fleeing persecution.

From this marginalised yet vibrant unit, I gradually learnt to see beyond my own pain and bewilderment. From them, I later understood the concept of unconditional love. These are the intangible gifts that, in retrospect, lifted me from my cesspit of inner doubt and turmoil and made me realise my situation was not unique. Mine was the life lived by every other outsider like myself – black, female, young, African, in a world that saw no virtue in these things – the very and only things of which I was made. Later, I realised that the South African exile network extended through southern, central, western and northern Africa and spread its tentacles into Europe, the Caribbean and North America. Though our individual stories might seem at first to be unique, there is always a point of convergence, and that point, I believe, is the powerful idea we each harbour within ourselves: the promise of one day returning to that place we call home, a place of unconditional acceptance and belonging.

It has always seemed to me that there are several varieties of exile. Here is the person who went into exile, who was pushed by political circumstances and personal conviction to leave the country of their birth. An adult, they made their choice and stuck with it, often to live out their days in one or other of their adopted homelands, even after things changed back home. Their internal, personal concept of the land of their birth is strong, certain and steeped in real events and happenstance. They are able to transfer their patriotic fervour very strongly to younger generations, to fellow exiles and others with an interest in their lives. Mostly men, there were also women who left their homes, many in support of these principled men and with their families.

Then, there was the person who was similarly moved to leave their home in response to growing state militarisation and repression and their corresponding politicisation and determination to forge a different reality. These are largely the post-1976 exile generation, usually in their mid-twenties or younger when they left, who joined a liberation movement in order to receive military training and instruction in guerrilla warfare, with the view of returning home to take charge of it by any means necessary. Many took the opportunity to study in Europe and the Caribbean, although the majority of these fierce idealists lived their lives in the camps and settlements set aside for exiles from South Africa. Their focus was much more on their exile being a necessary, but temporary, sojourn. Home was always a place remembered through the perspective of the pubescent tumult of longing mixed with ideological conviction and militancy. Such perceptions of home were shared often and passionately, particularly with those who had gone through similar experiences.

Then there was the 'exile-extra' variety, a sort of mutated exile. They are at once resilient, resistant and questioning of the body politic, and yet still dreaming of home. This category of the exile-extra is where I place myself. Born outside South Africa, they are without the collective memory of the raw injustice of the apartheid state. This mutated exile is someone who has never, or has only briefly, lived in the homeland, and who may even be born to one parent who is not even from the homeland. It is certainly a person who has grown up entirely away from the place everyone refers to as home, and consequently this variety of exile has no intrinsic or inbuilt recollection or memory card of the 'home' that others make frequent reference to and to which they all aspire to return.

These exiles, by their very nature, cannot truly relate to those whose memories hold such a strong sense of that place and space. Exile-extras are in some way exiled even from other exiles. They frequently struggle to communicate with their own compatriots in something other than a foreign tongue. Their assumptions, aspirations and anxieties are light years away from those who are closest to them – other exiles. Their perceptions and experiences are totally different from those who have lived past the age of ten in the mother country. For them, the term 'global citizen' is very real. They see their world quite differently from the other variety of exile and, yet, they are unquestionably imbued with a revolutionary fervour and commitment to the homeland of others' dreams. They, too, like the other exiles, yearn 'to return home when things are right'.

And, I believe, there is another category of exile that exists. Called 'insiles', I prefer to regard the large numbers of people who remained within South Africa's borders throughout the period of political turmoil as a category of exile, too. After all, those who remained were disenfranchised and systematically discriminated against and denied decent housing, education, employment opportunities or decent quality of life. They, too, were 'the other' by virtue of something they could never alter – their hair and skin tone. They found a way of surviving on the periphery of 'real life' – never being able to be part of it. Inside-exiles suffered the same alienation and dislocation, sense of loss and dignity, feeling beholden to political parties and ideologies and not belonging to the only life you know as home, as those in physical exile.

For, what is home, after all, except the place where you can be yourself, are accepted, warts and all, for who you are, without exception? Home is the place, the space where you are born, raised and grown into your fullest potential as a person. It is where you belong because you were born there, because it is your right and you are expected to live well in that space. It is the place where your family and friends come from, your grandparents, your ancestors; the community is the one in which you grew up and there are many who have guided you through your rites of passage.

Home is a safe, nurturing, wholesome and bountiful place, a place where you and others live together in harmony and joy, drinking in the pleasures and challenges of life in equal measure. It is the place where who you are is never questioned; it is assumed you belong and you are always welcome. Your right to be, to exist, is sacrosanct. It is engraved in the weathered bark of the tree under which your umbilical cord is buried.

If, however, the exile experience is really the search for belonging and meaning, then I wonder if that shouldn't be every person's chosen journey through life? Doesn't the experience of exile simply sharpen – bring into sharp relief – the human quest for that place within yourself that you recognise never questions your inalienable right to exist and thrive?

I don't mean to sound deeply mysterious here, but looking back on my life, the circumstances and the experience of exile that once seemed set to condemn me to a life of insignificance on the periphery was actually a unique crash course that has enabled me to instinctively recognise, appreciate and treasure humanity wherever I find it. Being an exile offers a gateway to the hidden gifts and value of living on this planet, despite the shape or form in which this gift of insight appears.

Where once I felt envious of those who could boldly claim to belong to a particular people and place they called home, and in which they were unambiguously accepted, today I can say, in all honesty, that while I am part of my people through the values and cultural traditions passed down to me through my parents and society, I am nevertheless also aware that there is more to being human than belonging exclusively to one or two small-bounded, tribal or national groupings.

It isn't enough for me – it never has been – to call myself Tswana or South African. I am these things, but I am also so much more. I am an African, I am a woman; my mother was Zulu, my father Tswana, and I have lived with others with whom I have often found very much in common. These people have been from other countries in

Africa, Asia, Latin and North America, the Caribbean, the Middle East, the Indian sub-continent, even Europe.

If exile was a political act that banished and deracinated those who were forced into that state of existence, its effect, unintended I am sure, was to grant immediate and lifelong citizenship (and all that that state implies) to a far more challenging and life-affirming world than I might otherwise have experienced.

So, does having the history of being an exile mean anything special now, almost twenty years since I returned 'home' to that especially icy welcome reserved for 'have-beens', or to those who apparently had it so good, away from the sickly sight and sound of burning flesh in the townships?

I find I don't think very much at all like the people around me. Judgement and conformity comes less hastily and stays for shorter periods than for my compatriots. And just when I think it must be something to do with the fact that I was born elsewhere, I meet a fellow traveller who left 'home' as an adult, who has also struggled to fit back into what was left behind so long ago. The exiles' return home, indeed, even their presence, has been met with a mixture of consternation and confusion by our compatriots, the insiles. It is as though we have returned from another planet, Saturn perhaps, and have undergone some subtle (or not so subtle) permanent genetic mutation that is manifestly alien in character.

I remember soon after my return how our small gatherings would fall silent as we heard one after another tale of depression, sudden illness and swift death of someone who had returned from exile. The shock of rejection and unending joblessness felled many at home whom we had known in our exile days as tenacious fighters possessed of numerous talents. We shook our heads sadly as we learnt of compromises and climb-downs as these battle-weary idealists succumbed to the prevailing mode of personal liberation at 'home' and climbed on the train to a better life.

Somewhere we also mourned the loss of the heated evening debates and discussions that shaped many a mind in exile, making us see just how many sides there are to every story, how many layers of rhetoric and muddled thinking need to be peeled away to arrive at the truth of any situation.

It seems, at home, that liberation had taken away the right of the common man or woman to a free-thinking attitude, to incisive public analysis and debate over important issues of the day, to rowdy but enlightening arguments in pubs and sitting rooms and community centres everywhere.

Where once we learnt how the world turned, and saw the underbelly of our own world back home, it seems now as though the agenda is set from out there somewhere. Spurious arguments and political gerrymandering gains credence or at least receives more attention than the real issues. Yet, as with the Sunday afternoon debates in Hornsey Green and Brooklyn, talk is cheap at home, too. But, whereas in exile there was still the opportunity to march, speak, petition and support an alternative or expanded world-view on a particular matter, at home these actions seem to have dwindled to emasculated laments around the dinner table, that peter out with a collective sigh of resignation. 'What can you do?' many are heard to ask rhetorically, as they reach for something to drink.

All these years later, it appears that having been in exile is of very little significance, at least to those to whom we have returned. Our voices seem powerless against the scourge of xenophobia that pervades the black community or the fantastic racism that pervades the white community. We have an insular preoccupation with our own survival, rather than a passion for life.

The lot of the exile seems now to be to harbour fond thoughts of the days when the myth of 'going home' still existed as a future possibility. For me exiles are not so much fringe-dwellers as people able to spot other people whose life script also contains kinks, diversions and flooded embankments – whether they have lived the exile life or not – and to pause, smile and acknowledge those crooked paths we all do our best to conceal.

And talking of concealment, there is something I feel I should mention about the lives of women in exile. I can speak personally and recount more incidents than the fingers on one hand, when I had to extricate myself from the unwanted advances forced upon me by someone I previously held in high esteem, someone who had proved over time to be like a family member. This is someone whom I had addressed or regarded as '*bhuti*' ('uncle' or 'older brother'), who, for an appreciable time before this change of behaviour, had been the very picture of brotherly or fatherly attention and possessed of a caring demeanour.

Sometimes it happened after the carefully orchestrated thinning out of a group of people, leaving you almost tipsy and suddenly alone with *ubhuti*. Other times it was a lift offered back home that went wrong – and needing you to collect your wits about you and plan a quick getaway. At yet other times, it was as irritating as a drunken grope as you washed dishes, or as unnerving as a forceful turn of a key in a door, blocking your exit as a previously depressed and on-edge man seems bent on recovery through more than just moral support.

Does this sound fanciful, made up or imagined? I wish it were, but this did happen to me and I managed to make good my escape each time. But to how many others has this also happened? And a more sobering thought: how many didn't manage to extricate themselves from an innocent social situation as it turned invasive? It must be said that these were isolated examples of the line crossed, but I think you would agree that even one instance is already too much. These are some of the things we would prefer not to talk about when we reminisce about our time in exile.

Occasionally, I find myself wondering if my exile existence wasn't just a different phase of exile to the one I'm living now. For, even though I have family and friends and have lived at 'home' for more than fifteen years, I now know that the actual geographical space I am legally entitled to call my home and the place I envisaged it would be, are two completely different places.

I almost want to say it doesn't exist, the *ekhaya* (home) I once heard of, but I don't think that's entirely true. In today's reality the values and ideals, the customs and traditions and way of life that I cherish as making me who I am, float intangibly above the cut-and-thrust of a young nation in mortal conflict with itself. The visualisations of thousands of exiled souls, determined not to forget their homeland or their essential, special humanity, seem like fragile wisps of morning fog against the exigencies of a relentless and fast-changing modern society. Yet, I was raised and grew up on just such intangible intentions and courageous idealism. Today, though, it is hard to locate resonances of these ideals in my homeland. Instead, there seems to be plenty of fear and self-loathing, both in equal measure.

I cherish a felt understanding of belonging to an extended family of loving, principled people who knew who they were, what they stood for and who were proud to be exactly who they were. That strong sense of self did not diminish another's sense of being in the world – on the contrary, it made for deep and lasting bonds between all kinds of exiled souls. Yet, this could also be transitory, it turns out, and, for many, the politics of survival and of expediency has allowed differences to become chasms of hate and dismissal.

Perhaps exile gave us the chance to live in a world that opened up all sorts of possibilities and, most importantly, made us realise the choice to recognise and try to conquer fear. These things, though, are not unique to those who were once forced to live outside their homelands, but it is easier to imagine another way to exist having once actually lived a different reality.

So, have I survived the experience of exile? I believe I have and that mine and thousands of others' experiences must alter the way South African society develops in the future – especially if our myriad experiences can be shared with one another. Where first I saw it as a curse, a blight, on my life's CV to have been an exile – not to speak or write my parents' languages; not to have grown up observing all the customs and traditions; to totally miss the aptness of proverbs – I now no longer see any need to be apologetic about it.

I always do the best I can to learn and understand the ways of my peoples; after that, I can do no more. In fact, I would go as far as to recommend the exile life if experiencing it would mean becoming a person sensitised to injustice and able to discern the truth and what makes us truly human. This is not to imply that the loneliness, suffering and unwelcome status is bearable, but, then, all of South Africa was staggering under the weight of the apartheid dragon, so that is nothing special.

I see the experience of exile as a gift given to me as a means for me to traverse this life with grace. I don't look back at my exile history with gloom or despair, as one might at the sight of several rotten teeth in the mouth of a horse you've been given to ride.

No. Instead, I insert the bit carefully between the teeth, both rotten and good, saddle up that horse and swing myself easily onto its back. Then I take up the reigns, pat the horse fondly and ride on towards the imposing Drakensberg mountains.

A brief reflection on exile

Carmel Chetty

Carmel Chetty was born on 18 August 1954 in Black River, Cape Town. She became involved with the Black Consciousness Movement while a primary school teacher at Wittebome. She was part of the group that started the Black People's Convention in Cape Town and became involved in a series of campaigns and demonstrations against the apartheid regime. In 1975, the security police crackdown on Black Consciousness activists led her to flee the country to Botswana, together with her husband, Roy Chetty, her sister, Gonda Perez, and former brother-in-law, Jaya Josie. Gonda's story is recorded elsewhere in this collection.

In Botswana, Carmel joined exiled members of the Unity Movement, linked to the Non-European Unity Movement, which had been founded in 1943 by militant groupings of teachers, other professionals and students as a non-racial, non-collaborationist, liberationist movement. During their fifteen years' exile in Botswana, Carmel was able to complete her secondary schooling and begin tertiary studies in education through the University of South Africa. Since her return from exile in 1990, she has worked as a teacher in the state sector. Currently, she lives in Durban where she continues to be a social justice activist as part of the broad socialist left. She is also completing work on a Ph.D. in education.

It was 5 May 1975 and we had already travelled up to Johannesburg from Durban. Our journey to Botswana could well be our last in South Africa for a long while. Already some thousand kilometres from our homes, the four of us were to confront several challenges on the way: a puncture just before Zeerust; being followed by what must have been a police reservist on a scrambler bike on the dirt road to Botswana's Lobatse border; our vehicle getting stuck in marshy ground; losing our meagre provisions; being pursued by a Land Rover equipped with searchlights and dogs; and, finally, being searched for by a spotter plane. All this before scrambling over barbed-wire farm and border fences.

As we raced for the Botswana border, Charles (our comrade and assistant), took out the topographical map he had secured and explained the route we would take once he had dropped us off. We spoke very little and listened, munching on some fried chicken. With the aid of only a tiny torch light, we desperately tried to memorise the topographical route in the darkness of the moving car. At Zeerust, while Charles got the puncture fixed, we blacked out some of the number-plate lettering with insulation tape. This was to help against the over-zealous reservist on the scrambler.

Shortly after we had set off on the gravel road from Zeerust, we realised (from the bright lights beaming on us) that we were being followed. Every now and again, the motor cyclist would come up close with his lights off, then beam his bright lights, overtake us and turn back to follow again with his lights switched off. This happened a few times and, needless to say, all of us in the car were extremely scared. After a while, we noticed that the motor cyclist was no longer following us and assumed that he had gone back to Zeerust for reinforcements. (There were five of us, including Charles, and he was on his own.)

Charles' plan was for us to take the side road into Gopane village which adjoined the border. On the bumpy road towards the hills we opened and closed a number of farm gates and drove until we could literally drive no further. The car was stuck in marshy ground – it had rained the day before. It was about 1 a.m. and pitch-black as Charles pointed out to the far-off hills that we were to climb. But first we had to free the car from the marsh. Twigs and leaves under the tyres, together with desperate pushing, eventually moved the car and we urged Charles to drive the hell out of there. It was to be another seventeen or so years before we would meet Charles again, and learn that, on that night, he had found a little churchyard in the village and had parked off for the night before making his way back safely to Johannesburg the following day.

Botswana was not what we had expected. Instead of being welcomed, we were interrogated and photographed like criminals. We had broken the law by crossing the border illegally. The police were extremely officious and quite inefficient – making us write and rewrite our statements until they were satisfied. We were asked why we had come to Botswana rather than go to the newly independent Transkei. Once all the paperwork was done, we were instructed to report to the police three times a week and inform them about our whereabouts at all times. We were not allowed to leave Gaborone without their permission.

While the police treated us like criminals, ordinary people treated us quite well. On arrival in Botswana, we had decided that we would not align ourselves with either of the two Black Consciousness factions there – we knew the members of both factions from home – and opted for an independent position instead. In this way, we think we remained friends with all. However, this also meant that we could not expect the communal assistance of the comrades in securing accommodation and general support.

By the third day, we had to survive on our own with no money and shelter. Fortunately, oranges were in season, plentiful and cheap at R2.50 a pocket. We had our fill of citrus and fat cakes (bought from Uncle Boyce's shop in the African mall). Since Gonda and I had grown up as Catholics, we approached the Catholic cathedral for permission to cook a meal in the kitchen. Bishop Urban Charles Joseph Murphy (a very prominent figure in the small capital) denied us permission to prepare a meal (of tinned fish) in his kitchen, sending word that we had to wait until after the long weekend when the Botswana Christian Council would provide the necessary assistance. He was a member of that council. Fat lot of good that did us as we desperately needed a place to sleep. He had that huge empty cathedral, but would offer no shelter.

That night (and the following), we stayed with a Zimbabwean refugee teacher who was sharing a government prefab house at the local secondary school. Thereafter, we were back on the streets at nightfall. Fortunately for us, as we were preparing to settle for the night in the garden of the Trinity Church, we noticed that a meeting of the church elders was in progress. On hearing of our plight, they readily and very generously gave us the use of the Anglican bishop's guest house for two weeks. We spent that time recuperating. Roy got some medical treatment at the local hospital for his reaction to bush-lice bites sustained while on the border hills. We were also graciously treated by the bishop's wife to a sumptuous Sunday lunch which the four of us greedily devoured.

Soon, too soon, it was time to go, and once again we went to the Reverend Ndebele of the Christian Council. While as guests at his house, Vis (Ivan) Pillay had arrived from home in search of us. He had not heard from us and our contacts in Durban had not informed him that we were safe. He hurriedly boarded a train and made his way to Gaborone. He enquired about us at the police station, spending the night there, before locating us the following morning. Vis returned home to inform the family that we were safe. Vis would soon thereafter excel to become a senior Umkhonto underground operative.

Meanwhile, we were taken by the Botswana Christian Council (BCC) to a dilapidated, windowless, mud hut, with earth as flooring, situated on the shore of the Gaborone Dam. It was isolated and had no facilities whatsoever. Having been supplied with only four thin blankets made of material normally used as under-felt for carpets, the BCC was condemning us to an insecure bush-camp life not two kilometres from where Ongopotso Tiro had been parcel-bombed about eighteen months previously.

The BCC treated us with little sympathy. There were just so many refugees to be issued with the prescribed dole – a remittance from the United Nations that was used to sustain individual refugees. Single persons were issued R20 each per month, and couples R35 as they reckoned that couples could live cheaper than single persons. We asked for assistance as we had lost all our belongings when we crossed the border. Gonda and I desperately needed panties. Gonda needed shoes as hers had shrunk while crossing the river. They refused and Mrs Rogers informed us that we had to share panties. We had three pairs of panties between the two of us. The Refugee Council and the Christian Council were provided with clothes from overseas donors but, to my knowledge and the general word among refugees at the time, very few refugees ever got to see these donations, save for two thin 'dog' blankets each.

We refused to stay at the desolate hut at the Gaborone Dam as we felt it threatened our safety, and they then dropped us off at the refugee house in Broadhurst. It was a dilapidated old farmhouse occupied by male Zimbabwean refugees. The place was very dirty and in need of repair. I remember vividly the huge ant-heap in the middle of the bedroom. The Zimbabwean men were very kind and tried to be helpful. There was no sleeping space for anyone let alone two couples. They cooked over an open fire outside. We decided to walk back to town to try to find something else.

We called on Iyavar Chetty, a known South African refugee who taught at the University of Botswana. We were desperate. We had heard of him because we had been asked if we were related since we shared the same surname. We unashamedly imposed on Iyavar and his family and begged them to accommodate Gonda and me for a while. Iyavar and his wife agreed to put us up, and the two men returned to the Broadhurst house for the night.

Late that same night, our first relief arrived from home. Through Vis, our families had heard of our plight and they immediately packed Roy's uncle's car with food and clothes and dispatched Roy's brother, Sonny, and his close friend, Logan, to drive down to find us. Sonny was able to trace Roy to the Broadhurst house and Roy and Jaya brought them to see us. When Sonny left, Iyavar did not have the heart to tell Roy and Jaya to go back to Broadhurst once they described the appalling conditions they had encountered. They stayed the night and we imposed on Iyavar and his family's hospitality for a while longer.

Lobatse

Then we heard from the BCC that a German couple in Lobatse was offering accommodation for a South African couple. We stretched their generosity by invading their space and budget as *two* couples. But those were desperate times for us. By the time Solveig and Klaus, the German volunteer couple, agreed to take us in we had lived in about ten or more different places. They shared a huge house with Lark, an American Peace Corps volunteer. They offered us their pantry as a bedroom and, after what we had been through, it was real luxury. The house was a huge colonial house that had been built for the former British District Commissioner. The pantry, our living quarters for the next few months, was fairly large and comfortable, though it lacked any privacy. Iyavar, who had driven us the eighty kilometres to Lobatse, took one look at it and said, 'Well . . . it's not exactly the Hilton'. We were given steel divans by our Danish neighbours and Solveig and Klaus were very generous with providing us with an excellent diet. Each couple paid R20 of our R35 monthly dole as our contribution towards the food. We knew that our contribution was nominal as it did not match the contribution of our kind German benefactors.

Our lives settled down to a more normal pace as our primary activity was no longer finding food and shelter. We could now listen to the news on the South African radio and read all the South African newspapers. Klaus had a very keen interest in South African politics and we spent many nights debating the South African situation and political upheavals in the rest of the world. Klaus spent many hours typing and whenever he wasn't around, we started teaching ourselves typing skills using books from the library as learning aids. We had time to read extensively. We used the local libraries and sourced as many Marxist and other political books as we could lay our hands on. We read voraciously and understood more clearly the kind of society we wanted for South Africa.

We continued to report to the police three times a week until it was relaxed to once a week, and this continued well into the 1980s. Our lives were regulated by visitors' permits, work permits and the Special Branch.

While living with Solveig and Klaus we were visited by Sisa Mvambo, a fellow South African refugee who was the principal of Itereleng Secondary School which was staffed by Zimbabwean and South African refugees. Sisa offered Jaya and me jobs as teachers at the school. Roy also taught there a few months later.

Lawrence Notha, another exile and a close friend of Sisa's, also came to visit. He had a clear political message and left us some money (R40) as train fare to visit him at his Serowe home, 400 kilometres north of Lobatse. He was a maths and science teacher at the Swaneng Hill Secondary School. Roy and I took up his offer and went to Serowe. That was the beginning of a deep comradeship, which was sadly cut short by Lawrence's untimely death in January 1985.

In addition to discussions with Sisa Mvambo and Lawrence Notha, we deepened our relationship with other refugees, including those we met during our first days in Botswana. Lenny Martin was one of these.

In late September 1975, when Solveig and Klaus's contract came to an end, we, too, had to vacate the property and find alternate accommodation. Roy had befriended a fellow refugee, Mani Pillay, in the village of Peleng near to where we were staying. Mani had been a member of the Anti-Segregation Council, and of the African People's Democratic Union of South Africa (APDUSA). He ran a shop and occupied the house that had for many years housed mainly the APDUSA leadership who had passed through Lobatse. He remained in Lobatse long after everybody had left and made a home for himself there. As I write, Mani continues to live in Lobatse – quite old now and suffering from Parkinson's disease. Sadly, though, in the post-1990 period, the old historic refugee house, the base for many underground operations into South Africa, was demolished by the owner.

While staying with Mani, Lenny Martin approached us to assist him because the Botswana police were looking for him. A number of South African refugees had been arrested for beating up two suspected South African spies. The spies had escaped and reported their ordeal to the police. Lenny was implicated in that case. Roy went out in search of safer accommodation for the three of us.

Jimmy Chew III, a Maoist American Peace Corps volunteer working as a social worker in the Peleng village, took us in. Jimmy offered us his servant's quarters – the only condition was that we keep the grass in his yard cut. The servant's quarters were opposite the Lobatse Prison and consisted of one room with a toilet and cold shower. We had no furniture and scoured the local dump for anything that we could use. We salvaged a steel shelf (which we hung from the rafters) and a steel dirt bin (for storage). We also sourced an old Joko tea box which became our side table. For our beds we used old home-made eiderdowns that had been brought to us by my mother-in-law. After months we now had a room with a door we could lock.

Lenny remained in hiding and was soon given room in the main building. We successfully hid Lenny for many months and once those who had been arrested had the case thrown out, Lenny felt safe to emerge from hiding and started visiting his friends again.

In early 1976, Roy and I, as members of the Unity Movement, contacted the African National Congress (ANC) representative in Gaborone and enquired about meeting the ANC in exile, but were brushed off then with a few copies of the ANC publication, *Sechaba*, to read. We did not pursue the ANC thereafter. We saw our struggle as one for socialism rather than for petit-bourgeois nationalism. Our next interaction with the ANC was when our friends, Vis and Krish, arrived in Gaborone as members of the ANC, and Roy had to negotiate with the ANC for them to visit us in Serowe. Vis made contact with us again after Lawrence Notha died. Vis was a leading underground worker for the ANC and used our home in Gaborone as a safe haven. Roy was involved in assisting him. In exile it was normal to assist all comrades, irrespective of party affiliation, as our safety depended on maintaining camaraderie with all South African exiles.

On one of his visits that winter of 1976, Lark noticed our makeshift bed on the floor and immediately scolded Jimmy for not noticing. Lark thereupon arranged for a bed to be brought into our tiny room.

We conditioned ourselves to live on as little as possible. Although I was teaching at Itereleng Secondary School, I earned very little money. I took home about R60 a month. We did not have electricity. Our expenses were in paraffin for cooking and lighting, food and travel. We put aside some money every month and continued to live on the same amount of money we had earned as refugees – R35 a month. We chose to live in conditions similar to those forced on the people in Dimbaza. The mini-film, *Last Grave at Dimbaza*, was in the news then and it haunted our conscience.

Life was tough. Bread was a luxury and our daily diet consisted of maizemeal with beans and, when we really splashed out, pilchards. We picked leaves from pumpkin plants that grew wild along the roads after good rains that year. At the vegetable shop we collected the beetroot leaves that they were going to discard. Pumpkin leaves and beetroot leaves were excellent substitutes for veggies that we could not afford. Roy went to a sale at the Lobatse railway station and bought a twenty-five kilogram drum of peanut butter (for R3). We bought bread once a week and thoroughly enjoyed the luxury of peanut butter for some time. The large quantity of peanut butter came in handy when later Mlonzi, Mashobane, Poenkie, his pregnant wife, child and a young man came to stay with us on their arrival into exile. Jimmy was on holiday in Maun when they arrived and they settled with us in Jimmy's house. Soon Roy was hauled before the district commissioner to explain the sudden influx of refugees in that house as well as his own presence there. On Jimmy's return he had some explaining to do. But Jimmy was 'cool', and a committed Maoist comrade.

The money we saved we used for travel, mostly to Serowe and to buy books from the Botswana Book Centre. We saved on taxi fares by hitch-hiking. In Botswana hitch-hiking was not a common practice and most vehicles that stopped expected some payment. If we were unable to negotiate a free ride we would let the vehicle go. This meant long hours standing alongside the road. During this time we undertook long hitch-hiking trips to Serowe and further north to Francistown. We met many interesting people on these trips but never encountered any real problems. On one memorable hitch-hiking trip to Serowe, we hitched a lift on a truck loaded with logs. We sat at the top of the pile of rolling creosote treated logs and were extremely grateful when we finally arrived safely at our destination covered from head to foot in white dust from the long gravel road.

Lawrence Notha and Sisa Mvambo were both former members of the Cape African Teachers Association, affiliated to the Non-European Unity Movement. They were solid Marxists. Sisa had been an underground worker of the newly formed APDUSA since about 1960 until his cover was blown, forcing him into exile. He also ran a bookkeeping business in town with Dan Tloome, one of the leaders of the South African Communist Party.

Lawrence Notha was one of the foremost socialist thinkers and organisers of the Unity Movement. He renounced his position as chief of his tribe because of his political convictions. The chieftainship then passed on to his brother. He worked in the laboratory at the Wits University Medical School before he went into exile in 1965. Lawrence recruited us into Marxist politics. Together with Sisa Mvambo, Lenny Martin and other refugees from Mochudi, we formed the beginnings of an international Marxist movement. We spent many long nights and days discussing and debating, and working out strategies and underground tactics for the South African revolution. We also made links with like-minded groups in Europe and the United Kingdom.

Many comrades from the Unity Movement structures throughout the country went into political exile in and around 1965. Lawrence Notha, Sefton Vutela and Pumi Giyose engaged in political discussions with almost all the revolutionaries who fled into Botswana. Marxist politics took root in Botswana. Sefton Vutela ensured that classical Marxist literature from the Soviet Union and China was available cheaply at the Botswana Book Centre where he worked. In the final months of his exile, Roy also worked there.

Both Lawrence and Sisa were primarily Marxist freedom fighters and prioritised that in their lives. They worked tirelessly for the South African revolution and everything else in their lives took second place.

When Jimmy left Botswana, we once again struggled to find suitable accommodation. We inherited Jimmy's dog, 'Mao', and the pet pig, 'Vorster'. Sisa found us a small house in Peleng village. It had no plumbing or electricity. There were three rooms – two bedrooms and a sitting room-cum-kitchen. Sadly, we had to slaughter Vorster as we had no space to keep him. Mao remained our close companion and security guard dog for many years thereafter.

The police never forgot that Lenny was the one that got away and soon they were hounding him again. Through a source we found out that a prohibited immigrant document had been issued for him. Fortunately when the police came, Mao alerted Lenny of their presence. Lenny recognised their Land Rover and escaped through a small window in the back while Mao kept the Special Branch at bay.

Sisa, who had extensive experience in underground work, assisted us. He suggested Lenny trek up the hills that surrounded Lobatse. Lenny, Roy and Sisa would rendezvous every evening to provide Lenny with food and plot a strategy for his escape. After a few weeks of cloak-and-dagger activity with the police, it was agreed that Lenny would approach the Danish embassy. To our dismay, what we thought was an embassy was just a consulate and they could not accommodate a refugee. Lenny was forced to leave and went back to Mochudi to hide in his girlfriend's room at the nurses' quarters.

Needless to say, a man living in nurses' quarters could not go unnoticed for long and soon Lenny got arrested. However, by this time the Danish government was aware of his predicament and they arranged for his evacuation to Denmark.

Some months after Lenny's deportation, in February 1977, Sisa was stabbed several times while in his bed by a person unknown. Though mortally wounded he stumbled across the main Lobatse road and sought help from a fellow refugee, Wesley Seleka, who took him to hospital. Sisa never recovered and friends blamed his death on poor nursing and medical care as the post-mortem revealed blood clots in his lung. Sisa's death remains a mystery to this day.

This event turned our world upside down. We knew we lived in a dangerous area – just five kilometres on the main road that led to the South African border post. (Our little house was diagonally opposite Sisa's). An event like this was the first of its kind and sent ripples of fear through the refugee community. Sisa's body was laid to rest at the Lobatse cemetery amid the wails and cries of hundreds of fainting children from the school. He was given a hero's funeral at the new school he had been instrumental in building.

It was my first experience of brutal death at such close quarters. Lawrence then arranged jobs for us at the Serowe brigades and we agreed to go. We no longer felt safe in Lobatse and needed a place where we could work closely with Lawrence on the ideas we were developing for the South African revolution.

Serowe

Serowe was a new experience. Lawrence insisted that we stay with him in the new home he had just built having left his teaching job at Swaneng Hill Secondary School. We were allocated a large rondavel and were completely integrated into his home life. During our stay there, Roy developed a bout of tick-bite fever and I was terrified because I thought he would die. Queen, Lawrence's wife, a nursing sister, successfully nursed Roy back to health. We started working at the brigades and were allocated a house at the local teacher training college, but Lawrence insisted that we stay with them. On our return from work, Queen would have a hot meal prepared and we continued our discussions and plans until late into the night every night.

Working at the brigades was a unique experience. It was staffed by largely left-wing people from various parts of the world. Patrick van Rensburg was the larger-than-life co-ordinator. Having so many strong personalities in one organisation led to many disputes and meetings were often very intense. Since our classrooms were widely distributed across Serowe, the academic teachers were given bicycles to use. In Lobatse, Roy had purchased a bicycle from our savings and taught me to ride it while we stayed with Jimmy. I was issued with a bicycle. This gave us the leverage we needed to convince Lawrence that we could move into our own house. He reluctantly agreed.

Shortly after we moved into our house we heard that our close friends Vis Pillay and Krishna Rabilal were in Gaborone. They had been working underground for the ANC for some time but their covers had been blown and they had come to Botswana. Roy immediately borrowed a car from Cas Kikia (a fellow refugee from the Anti-Segregation Council) and left for Gaborone to meet with them. He finally convinced the ANC leadership to grant them a visit to Serowe of two nights. We spent an entire day and night trying to convince them to stay. Neither of them could be persuaded as they were already part of an underground ANC mission in South Africa. We said our goodbyes in the early hours of the morning as they boarded the train back to Gaborone. That was the last time we saw Krish alive. He was killed in Matola in a raid by the South African Defence Force (SADF) on 30 January 1981.

We got to know a number of refugees in Serowe. Cas Kikia was Lawrence's close comrade. Mani Pillay and Cas had been members of the Anti-Segregation Council, and members of APDUSA. They were banned by the apartheid regime for their political activities and sought refuge in Botswana. Mani and Cas, with whom we had stayed in Lobatse, were both from Dundee and had been in exile since the sixties. Cas became our very close friend as well. He had worked for one of the traders and lived in an old house on his own. Later he married, started his own business and lived a comfortable life. He nurtured friendships with leading Batswana politicians and later even joined the ruling Botswana Democratic Party. Politicians in Botswana at that time easily merged in with the local population and had little pretence about any elevated status. Lenyeletswe Seretse, the one-time vice president of Botswana, was Cas's close friend and spent many hours sitting on an old chair in Cas's shop conversing easily with villagers who passed by.

Bessie Head was a famous South African writer who also lived in Serowe. She was a well-known figure who lived in a little house that she had built for herself while she worked for the brigades. She was a volatile character who had the reputation of having posted on the wall of the post office an insulting letter to Seretse Khama for refusing to give her citizenship. We got to know her as a quiet, humble woman whom we often met at the mall riding her bicycle. She sometimes approached Roy for loans when money she was expecting did not come in time and she needed to buy food. Bessie was scrupulous about recording the money she borrowed and the day her money came in she would pay back every cent she had borrowed in the interim.

Life in Serowe was very exciting for us. We made lifelong friendships and became an independent little family. Our eldest son, Leon, was born at the local hospital on 15 November 1978.

Having left the employ of the brigades, Roy was working for a local South African trader as a bookkeeper. We left our brigade house even though I was still employed by them. We moved into an old abandoned Khama family house. It had been occupied by goats and snakes and we had quite a hard job making it liveable again. It had internal plumbing but the borehole was not working. We had to haul in drums of water every few days. An old Mosotho refugee, Re Moloi, who had married a South African, just arrived without any invitation because he had heard of our plight and set about fixing the borehole, using his tractor as a mechanical water pump. Such acts of unselfishness, solidarity and caring were part of the support system among refugees in Botswana. In a predicament everyone rallied, irrespective of political affiliations. We always felt that we belonged to a common South African refugee community.

While we enjoyed living in Serowe we started feeling isolated and much too removed from South Africa. Everything was far away and the dirt roads to Serowe really impeded easy travel. There are countless stories of driving on those roads after heavy rains. The car would assume a life of its own as it slithered and turned in all directions on what seemed to be a soft chocolate surface.

On a trip to Gaborone, Roy decided to visit the Botswana Housing Corporation where we had, in the first year when we were extremely desperate, made an application for a house. At that time we were told that getting a house was impossible, but Roy nevertheless filled in the forms and submitted them. We completely forgot about that application made in a moment of madness. On his second visit to the Botswana Housing Corporation, Roy was informed that they had been looking for him for several months as a house had been allocated to us. Roy immediately accepted the offer of a house and informed me that we were moving. We could not remain unemployed for long in Gaborone as there were bills to pay – rent, electricity, water and we had a little baby boy.

Kanye
Roy got an offer of a job as a bookkeeper at the Rural Industries Innovation Centre in Kanye, a large village to the southwest of Lobatse. Since the Centre was a little desperate, they offered to rent our house in Gaborone for the period Roy worked in Kanye.

In Kanye we lived in real luxury. We were not treated like refugees, but were given the same status as other expatriates. We had a beautifully furnished house with electricity and running water – all part of Roy's contract. Once it was known that I was a teacher, I was asked to teach local expatriate children. I started a little school and tutored children from Grades 1 to 6. It was a lovely experience. We spent three years in Kanye and once again made good friends, but felt our involvement in the South African struggle was not strong because of our distance from the centres of action.

Gaborone
We moved into our own house in Gaborone. We reconnected with our political allies and started study groups that strategised for the South African revolution. We recruited a number of people and organised for people to go illegally into the country and set up networks with the Unity Movement that had been reconstituted.

On 4 June 1983, my mother-in-law's birthday, our second son was born. We named him after our dear friend, Krish, who had been killed in Matola.

Our two sons were the centre of our lives and Lawrence Notha, Sefton Vutela and Pumi Giyose became regular visitors. We were able to easily balance our political lives and included our children in everything we did.

We were dealt a terrible blow when Lawrence died unexpectedly in January 1985. He had suffered for years with high blood pressure and on a visit to the United Kingdom was diagnosed with an enlarged heart. In spite of this he lived life to the full and was always larger than life, ever ready to jump in his car and set out on a new clandestine venture. He was buried in his home village in the Transkei. Attempts to get us included as family members allowed to travel through South Africa to the funeral were thwarted by the South African government who made it clear that we would be arrested. We said our goodbyes to our dear friend at a moving memorial at his home in Serowe. To the present day, I feel a deep sense of loss whenever I think of Lawrence. He was a mentor, father and comrade to us and his loss was catastrophic.

Our third son, Che, was born later that year on 25 October. Leon was already quite grown up and a great help with his two brothers.

SADF raid on Botswana

At about 1 a.m. on the night of 14 June 1985, the SADF raided Gaborone targeting and killing several South African refugees and Botswana citizens. Bombs were exploding all around us, for an eternal thirty minutes. Roy, who had been watching a late-night movie, *Of Mice and Men*, had just slipped into bed, only to spring up and hurriedly dress, putting on shoes, determined not to be found ill-prepared (or without his 'boots on') if the soldiers came for us. The SADF were all over Notwane Road, which separated our extension from their main target, the ANC house in Bontleng. That strong, stone-built house in the middle of the Bontleng low-cost housing area was repeatedly bombed to rubble. This was the house where in 1977 Roy had met Aubrey Mokoape, an ANC commander, to request permission for Vis and Krish to spend the weekend in Serowe.

Two-year-old Krish was woken by the noise but Leon slept through it. The noise was deafening as bombs dropped all over the city. When I left for work the next morning, the fear in Gaborone was plain. South African news broadcasts boasted about the successful cross-border raid into Botswana. The *Daily News*, the free-issue government newspaper, was filled with the gruesome photographs of the raid. The story that has stayed with me is of two young Batswana women, thought to be the girlfriends of ANC cadres, who were killed rather barbarically. Their home, servant quarters much like the place we had lived in Lobatse, had been blown up until not a single brick was left on top of another. One of the girls was beheaded by the blast and her head landed on the kitchen table of the main house.

That raid was the worst of the many raids the South Africans conducted into Botswana. Our lives were never the same again. Some time previously, around the time that Lawrence passed away, Vis had made contact with us again. Vis and Raymond Lalla, known then to us as 'Peter', used our home as their safe haven whenever they visited Botswana. They were both senior Umkonto we Sizwe (MK) operatives and functioned in very dangerous circumstances. Gaborone and Lobatse were heavily infiltrated by South African agents. As South Africans living in Botswana and clandestinely pursuing a political agenda, we expected to be in the sights of the South African regime.

Family reunions

Shortly after the first Gaborone raid, members of my family came to visit. In the years of our exile we had regular visits from my in-laws who provided us with sustenance and joy. In the early years my mother-in-law, who had never broken the law in her life, carried information to us in the inside of her sari. In later years, we advised them not to carry anything of that nature as they would become easy targets for the cops. They were regularly visited whenever they returned from visiting us. Fortunately, their passports were never taken away.

My family in Cape Town had not had such luck and were repeatedly refused passports to visit us. It was only in 1983, shortly before Krish was born, that my mother visited for the first time. My sister, Maria, had been more successful and had visited us some time before with her young son, Kevin. Maria arrived unannounced at the Gaborone airport and fortunately she bumped into Ismail Bhamjee whom we had met through association with Cas. He was kind enough to bring her to our home. As she emerged from the car, I did not recognise her at all. I remember thinking, 'Who is the white woman with the black kid?' We laughed about that afterwards. Our short time together was wonderful.

My mother's arrival was equally dramatic. I was in another part of the house when I heard my mother's unmistakable voice coming from the sitting room. We ran into each other's arms and cried like babies. I have photographs of that moment because Ferdinand, who brought her to Botswana, stood ready with his camera as I came into the sitting room. I had given up hope of seeing my parents and, although my mother and I corresponded regularly, we always spoke in code and had to be guarded in what we said as we knew our mail was monitored. For the first time in a long time, we could just talk and share all the stories we had missed in the past eight years. A few months later my father got his passport and he came to Botswana by train.

Born stateless

Leon only spent one year at school and then we had to take him out because we could no longer afford the fees. I home-schooled him until I got a job at Legae Primary School and he attended school again. But that job only lasted for a year. Once I was out of work, Leon was once again home-schooled with other children I took in to tutor.

Besides financial considerations, we also had security considerations for not employing anyone in our home. This meant that we did all our own work. Leon quickly learnt to do chores around the house.

His first visit to South Africa was a birthday present for his eighth birthday. It was also his first plane trip. He was the first person in our family to travel in a plane. A few months earlier, we had been forced by circumstances to send both Krish (two years old) and our baby, Che (ten months old), to stay for a while with our family in Durban.

Krish and Che were born stateless after the Botswana government passed a law that prevented children of foreign parents from getting citizenship. For a while they travelled on United Nations documents like ourselves, but we were concerned that our children would not have a country to call home. We applied for South African passports for them and were very pleased when they received South African citizenship and passports. This enabled them to visit the family home.

The next trip Leon made to South Africa was under sorrowful circumstances. My niece and her grandmother had been killed in a car accident on their way to visit us in December 1989. It was a dreadful year for our family. Earlier, on 12 September, Sonny, Roy's only brother and second father to our children, who had visited us regularly over the years and been our link with our motherland, died unexpectedly.

Sonny had been the rock of our family. Roy's mother and only sister, Mano, were totally devastated. We applied to the authorities to allow us into the country to attend the funeral but our request was denied. We listened to the wailing over the phone and sat alone in our Gaborone home as Sonny's body was carried out of our home in Merebank. Mani heard the news, closed his shop and rushed to be with us. Our friends came around to sympathise. For us it was like our world had been removed from under us. We lit a candle at Sonny's photograph and weeks later received photographs of the funeral ceremony. It was unbelievable to see our Sonny lying dead in a box, his face adorned with hundreds of flowers. Our grief was overwhelming.

Then in early December that year, when the news reached us that my sister, Jackie, and her family had been in an accident on their way to visit us, I became numb. My mother spoke calmly on the phone advising us of what had happened. Our dear Shelley, the same age as our son, Krish, and her grandmother had both been killed. The rest of the family had sustained injuries. Gonda phoned from Harare to tell us that she would join us so that we could comfort one another. We put Leon on a plane to represent us at the funeral in Cape Town. He was just eleven years old.

Going home
When F.W. de Klerk announced Mandela's release a few months later, we were ecstatic! We immediately applied for South African passports to travel home. Roy was constantly on the phone to Pretoria tracking the status of our application. He had had some experience with that office a short while previously when he applied for passports for Krish and Che.

I will never forget the day our passports arrived. We had been informed telephonically that our passports had been issued. Every day we visited the post office a few times to find out if they were there. When I opened the post box on that day, I immediately noticed the slip to pick up a registered article and knew that they had arrived. Tears welled up in my eyes as I nervously approached the desk. Yes, indeed they were there in their unmistakable government-issue, brown envelopes. I was shaking so much I could hardly open the envelope. The children were with me. Roy was at home, underneath the kombi, preparing it for the journey. Leon had already been taken out of school and had been waiting the past five months to go home to school in Merebank. I was overwhelmed with emotion. While the children understood the enormity of the moment, I don't think they had the same emotional experience. After all, Botswana was the only home they had ever known.

We were at the border gate (all packed, inclusive of a cargo of books) in our trusty old VW kombi long before it opened the following morning. The armed soldiers of the South African side seemed to know that we were returning and just waved us through. What immense pleasure it gave us to cross the border we had been looking at so longingly these past fifteen years. Driving to Zeerust was just beautiful. Even the busy streets of Johannesburg were not going to faze us. The children were squashed in the back of the kombi, all expectant and so full of cheer.

The thousand-kilometre journey home seemed long, though each kilometre travelled brought us closer to home. But we had to face a home in sorrow without Sonny. We arrived in Merebank shortly after midnight. My mother and Gonda had flown in from Cape Town to meet us. As we drove into Durban, Roy proudly edged his way through the new city road network. He drove us directly to our home with not a single incorrect turn. The family rushed out to the road to greet us. As we all gathered in the kitchen, my mother-in-law lit the God lamp and started her prayers of thanks. She walked into the road and lay prostrate in the middle of the road to thank God for our safe return – a day we had all only dreamed of. My mother, witnessing this great act of faith, joined the prayer declaring, 'It's the prayers of all the mothers all over South Africa that has made this day possible'.

For the love of my country

Mathabo Kunene

Rachel Mathabo Kunene was born in Rustenburg in the former Transvaal province and grew up in Cape Town. She received her primary education at a school started by her mother in the family home at Nyanga in Cape Town. She attended Adams College in southern KwaZulu-Natal for her secondary schooling and then applied to study law at the University of Cape Town, but was turned down by the university, which suggested that she apply instead to one of the newly established 'Bantu' universities. From 1966 she proceeded to train in nursing, obtaining diplomas in general nursing, specialist training in midwifery, obstetrics, gynaecology and ophthalmology.

In 1971 Mathabo left South Africa for London where she worked as a staff nurse in a children's hospital. It was here that she met and married eminent South African poet, Mazisi Kunene. Together, they re-located in 1975 to the United States where Mathabo obtained a B.A. degree in English and became increasing active as an anti-apartheid advocate and organiser. She founded the Los Angeles Youth Coalition, comprising fifty high schools in the greater Los Angeles school district, to help American youth to represent the voice of the oppressed children of South Africa. For her tireless and wide-ranging activism she was awarded the Winnie Mandela Women's Ministry Award for outstanding contributions to the fight against apartheid.

Mathabo returned to South Africa in 1993 and has since helped found and develop several economic and social enterprises to promote the professional empowerment of women. She currently serves as a company director in several corporate business groups and is the founder CEO of Nandi Heritage (Pty) Limited. She is also managing trustee of the Mazisi Kunene Foundation Trust, which seeks to preserve, publish and promote the literary works of South Africa's first Poet Laureate, Dr Mazisi Kunene.

I arrived in London in the late autumn of 1971, just as the leaves on the trees in Hyde Park were changing into their beautiful burnt orange and golden hues. Hyde Park brought back memories of Kirstenbosch Gardens in Cape Town. Only, in London 'Whites only' signs on benches were missing. I was soon joined by Mazisi on these walks in the park. His mood was often sombre and contemplative at times. This did not deter my fascination with the variety of trees and plants that filled this park. The early wintery wind on late autumn afternoons swept through the park making the bamboo trees from China sway gently over the large steady branches of a heavy-set tree from the Congo.

At times, I would read some of the little silver plates posted on each tree just to remind myself of my botany classes from Adams College. I noticed that there was a particular park bench situated beneath a large tree with beautiful purple berries. One day I ventured to read the identity plaque on the stem of this tree. The Latin name was *Syzygium Cordatum*. Reading it out loud made Mazisi laugh. He roared back: '*uMdoni lona isihlahla sangakithi*', the Zulu name for this tree whose natural habitat was the south coast of KwaZulu-Natal. I vowed to secretly return to the park alone and write down the name of this tree.

I realised that the trees in Hyde Park represented their own community of 'exiles' uprooted from far-away villages of their origin. The bamboo leaves muttering Mandarin sounds to the uMdoni branches were far from the sounds of the Zulu herd boys of Amahlongwa village in South Africa. Perhaps Mazisi felt a sense of kinship with this one tree that kept fond memories of a home far away. Only his poetic imagination could reach into the depths of nature to find solace from the pain of banishment from his native land.

By September 1971, I had been introduced to several senior women in their 'homesteads'. There seemed to be general approval of our relationship. Mazisi had arrived in London in the early sixties as one of the few members of the African National Congress (ANC). He had established his own home at 185A Gloucester Place. Because of its proximity to the centre of London, his place was known to many. And his reputation was that of a long-standing and available bachelor in London.

The battle to gain my passport was a well-orchestrated one that needed the help of Stanley Uys, then the editor of the *Cape Times*, and his old friend, Alistair Sparks, from the *Rand Daily Mail*. As a young intern with the *Cape Times*, Stanley had covered my mother's community projects in Nyanga Township in Cape Town. The very school I attended until Standard 4 was started by my own mother in our township house in Nyanga. It was a two-teacher school with my father ironically standing as the principal of the school (male chauvinism at its best). When two more teachers joined them and the enrolment grew to a staggering 400 pupils, the government stepped in to take over the school.

Soon my father started the concept of using the school for evening classes or 'night classes', as they were known. (Now it is known as Adult Basic Education.) White students from the University of Cape Town frequently volunteered their services at the school. Our little township house was always buzzing with activists from the suburbs.

One day, I arrived from school to find a number of kids ranging from three to five years of age, many crying for their mothers. My mother insisted on reading nursery rhymes above this din. The nightmarish scene formed a picture of the first

day-care centre or crèche in our community. Our lives ranged from rushing home
after school to be with our mother to taking the longest route home in order to delay
the hardships of nappy-changing. It was long before the advent of disposable nappies.

Women simply came in and dropped their babies at our doorstep and jumped on
the bus to work in the white suburbs to take care of other people's children. My
mother could not afford hired help, but some unemployed women volunteered a few
hours a day. This meant that we were the first line of caregivers. Stanley Uys's coverage
in the *Cape Times* of my mother's efforts drew the attention of foreign waves of
ambassadors and some women of the Black Sash who brought in food, toys and
other necessities. The crèche in Nyanga township, outside Cape Town, the first of its
kind there, was started in our home.

This piece of our family's history illustrates the broader role played by women in
various communities during the long years of apartheid. Their understanding of being
a woman in any African community, or village, for that matter, empowered them to
participate in nation-building. They were not in competition with their husbands; nor
did they qualify for the 'behind every successful man is a woman' theory. Women
were leaders in their own right, standing their own ground. Clearly, women arrived in
London fully equipped with this understanding of themselves and soon carved a
virtual 'South African village' all over the city.

Various 'homesteads' or *amakhaya* emerged all around London. One would often
hear people talk about we are going to kwa Tambo, kwa Bhuti Abe Ngcobo, kwa
Chonco, kwa Yengwa, kwa Bhuti 'Robbie' Resha, kwa Dlomo and the large family of
Joe Matthews and his brothers. Visiting these homes often assured one of a home-
cooked meal.

Life in exile was a mixture of the sad reality of being separated from your country
and family and the fantasy of the bright lights of a large metropolitan city like London.
Young men and women, brimming with youthful energy, found themselves in a virtual
enclosure where the males went on the hunt. But the balance was in our favour with
more males to choose from. That part will need to be told all on its own, as many
hearts were broken.

I must caution the reader against assuming that there were no checks and balances
here. No African village can ever survive without some form of order. In the early
days, men were often sent on far-away missions or to the various countries who
offered military training facilities for the political parties. Later, women were recruited
into active duty by their organisations. To their credit, nearly all South African women
living in London were professionals and provided a reliable source of income for the
families whose lives were constantly disrupted by these separations. Women took all
this responsibility in their stride and never saw it as a weakness on the part of the
men.

Stories of love and devotion have always formed part of the narrative of war. It would therefore be a fitting tribute to refer to some of the women whose stories of gallantry and devotion formed part of the 'gathering of women in London' in a particular way.

We constantly heard harrowing stories of young brides separated from their husbands. Perhaps the pain had become all too familiar as more and more men were sentenced to long terms of imprisonment after sham trials. Many of these women came to London. A new arrival would be 'presented' around the various 'homesteads', under the guise of 'paying respect' to the elders. I was no different.

I spent all my free days wandering in and out of London's fancy boutiques, pretending I could afford any designer clothes I wanted. After all, I had paid my dues all those years when my parents ran a 'two-teacher' school with us having to be the model pupils. I had migrated to a place far away and felt I deserved some time off for good service to the nation. I was therefore in no hurry to commit to any form of domination, be it marital or political. I had just escaped from the cancer that had been gnawing at my soul all of my life. For once, I was free to make choices that could heal my soul so that I could heal others. I certainly was not looking for a fight, not from any of my brothers and sisters. I needed spiritual restoration from the raw wounds inflicted by apartheid. We were all vulnerable and fragile.

My plan was to travel the world, experience other cultures, and even visit the big city lights in New York. I wanted to be free to negotiate my way through life without the mundane existence of wife and motherhood and the restricting limitations of choice. I could go to university to pursue my lifelong dream of getting a degree.

My plan seemed to move along quite nicely – until I met Mazisi Kunene. Our Hyde Park walks became more frequent.

Gloucester Place offered a very interesting meeting place. On any given day, one could meet the (now) Queen of the Royal Bafokeng and other Khama family members, guerrillas of the Shining Path in Peru, freedom fighters of Namibia's liberation movement, SWAPO, half a dozen ANC comrades arguing loudly with Pallo Jordan over the ideas of the Unity Movement, or Bhuti Abe Ngcobo espousing one Zulu theory or another. At the centre of it all, Mazisi would be busy cooking his famous *isitshulu*, otherwise known as stew.

There was one person whom Mazisi loved, feared and respected greatly: uSisi Sibongile. Edith Sibongile maDlamini Glenville-Grey, sister to Zanele Mbeki, first met Mazisi Kunene when he was a student at the University of Natal and she was a leader in the Young Women's Christian Association. Sibongile and Mazisi belonged to a group of long-time friends from that time. Her approval meant much to me and I looked forward to meeting her. I won her over with my cooking because she loved good food. I even have a favourite photograph of her towering over me doing the customary *ukuyala* (giving me a stern warning against ever abandoning Mazisi). '*Uzuke udlale ngomfowethu'* (Dare you play games with my brother!). She offered us her place as a venue for our wedding luncheon. This happened to have been a 600-year-old castle in Farnham. My wedding dress was pure fantasy. Everything else was pure Zulu tradition with Abe singing praise songs and the rest of the South Africans singing Zulu wedding songs. For a day, it was an African celebration. I will be forever grateful to Sis' Sibongile for her friendship with Mazisi. She kept his sanity intact during one of the most trying times of his life in London.

As I settled down as one of the citizens of this virtual African village, I began to sense that there was an underlying tension of a political kind. As I had stated before, I had no intention to participate in any way in such matters.

What I had seen and enjoyed at Gloucester Place was a cordial coming together of exiled South Africans whose political affiliations did not define their relationships. But there was another deeper personal power struggle waged against Mazisi and others within their party. I was prepared to 'continue running' away from such tensions until I reached a place of peace and calm. I believed that undue animosity could only distract Mazisi from focusing on his writing. We agreed to emigrate to the United States where he could take up a teaching post at Stanford University and later at the University of California in Los Angeles.

One cold, misty morning, we landed at San Francisco Airport to begin a new life together. Flying over the San Francisco Bay offered an uncanny feeling of landing in Cape Town with Alcatraz prison reminding us of Robben Island, the South African prison island in Cape Town.

Arriving in the United States, just at the peak of the civil rights movement, offered us an opportunity to inject the anti-apartheid movement. There my family became involved in a massive campaign. Lamakhosi, our first-born daughter, formed one of the most respected youth movements in Los Angeles – the Los Angeles Student Coalition. When this group called for a protest march around the South African Consulate in Beverly Hills, at least three to four thousand protesters showed up. Many of the middle-class, Beverly Hills students were children of the civil rights movement activists.

Finally, the disruption proved too much for the residents of Glitter City, Beverly Hills, and the consulate was asked to move to a location farther away towards downtown Los Angeles.

Lamakhosi had developed into a young firebrand. She spoke Zulu (growing up in the Kunene household offered few choices). As the apartheid police intensified their violence against the youth-led protests in South Africa, the American media showed 'restraint'. This was in line with President Reagan's Constructive Engagement policy. At the age of thirteen, Lamakhosi went around high schools in the area speaking on behalf of the South African state's atrocities committed against the youth. She was invited to testify before congressional committees on the plight of South African youth. She developed poetry writing skills and one of her poems, 'Mine eyes have seen America', was published by Amnesty International.

Our Los Angeles home, 3846 Chanson Drive, became the unofficial South Africa House, much like 185A Gloucester Place in London had been. I found myself creating my own *ikhaya* (home) surrounded by a group of ten women and their families. My role as an exiled woman, mother, nurturer and political activist on my own terms was realised. I even found time to achieve my lifelong dream of going to university. I enrolled at the University of California in Los Angeles and graduated with an English degree.

The anti-apartheid movement had picked up momentum, propelled by the sanctions against corporations trading with South Africa. Mazisi's teaching at the 32 000-student college offered a perfect place for the liberation movement. Students walked about with bright yellow T-shirts emblazoned with a huge map of Africa with the words: 'I am a Zulu' on their backs.

The student body built a makeshift shack city right at the centre of the huge campus for all to see. They threatened that they would not demolish it until the university had cancelled their loans with South Africa. We organised huge protest marches. As South Africa clamped down on all media coverage of the atrocities perpetrated by the regime, we collaborated with one of Mazisi's oldest friends in the media called Global Vision. Danny had been associated with anti-apartheid causes from his early student days when Mazisi first came to the United States in the sixties. He later left ABC Television to produce a show called *South Africa Now*. Television stations came to the house and broadcast live from our home. I had found a new 'gathering of women' and our home provided a safe haven for many South African refugees fleeing from the 1976 Soweto uprising.

Looking back on these days gives me cause to reflect on the importance of this collection of stories from women who were in exile. I have often wondered why women have taken so long to gather the courage to write about exile from their own perspective. It may well be that they were intimidated by the tales of self-proclaimed gallantry and, at times, exaggerated importance of our brothers-in-arms. Truth is, without the women's stories coming to the fore, only half the story would have been told.

And that's the story of exile. There's another truth that I would like to broach, and that is the truth that all forty-five million black South Africans who were born into and endured the years of apartheid experienced 'exile' in some degree or other. Some were exiled to townships and could only venture into cities under a limited 'permit', which came to be known as the *dompas* (Pass book). Severe penalties were imposed on anyone wandering about without the necessary *dompas*. When the South African government introduced the segregated homelands (or Bantustans), they designed a complex system of Pass laws under which the movements of blacks from the homelands to the cities were severely restricted. An identity document was specifically designed for blacks and it contained all addresses and other information on the individual. Police were authorised to demand to see this document, and failure to produce it could lead to immediate arrest. Africans viewed this as a foolish piece of legislation and nicknamed the document the *dompas* ('*dom*' is derived from an Afrikaans term meaning 'dumb'). The government deployed a large police force supported by the military whose only assignment was the monitoring and enforcement of the punitive laws of separating whites from blacks and blacks from blacks through the Bantustan system.

Indeed, Africans developed various coping mechanisms by depicting their own reality through the arts. Some of the most original artistic contributions in our country were made by pianist/composer Todd Matshikiza, singers Mirriam Makeba and Dolly Rathebe, whose original low base-sounding voice was like no other. There were also the Manhattan Brothers and many others. All of these great artists emerged during this era of oppression. The world-famous musical *King Kong* was the story of a talented athlete and boxer whose skills were suppressed by the limitations of growing up within the confines of a crime-ridden township like Sophiatown. Plays like *The Island* or *Master Harold and the Boys* ended on Broadway. Even our great actor, Zakes Mokae, won the coveted Tony Award. When Zakes passed away in the United States, his African American-born wife, Mandy, paid him the ultimate respect by bringing his remains back to his homeland for burial. In this, she was assisted by our own government. How great it is to be free!

As our country begins to assess its history of liberation, there has been a tendency to apportion varying degrees of praise to some above others. There are some who would venture that those who lived in exile may have made less of a contribution than those imprisoned on the island and in other South African jails. Others are of the opinion that those compatriots who remained in the country suffered less.

We will not forget those who endured the much-feared Saracens, speeding through their communities in the dark of night, instilling fear and domination and the attendant punishment meted at will by young police interns. And while rural communities seemed less exposed to the daily surveillance of the roaming *khwela-khwela* (police vans in the townships), their suffering was no less. Applying for a travel permit to the cities was tantamount to applying for a passport.

Who are we to bestow the highest 'Presidential Honour' upon any South African without due consultation with the forty-five million silent 'combatants' who lived through the horror of 'internal exile'? Perchance we should consider inscribing an honours roll of each of the names of the young students murdered in 1976, of all who went to the gallows singing freedom songs, of all those mothers who sat silently on the grass mat under the flickering light of a single candle, weeping silently for a child killed by a policeman's bullet.

In for the long haul
Baleka Mbete

Born on 24 September 1949, Baleka Mbete is a teacher by training and a mother of five children. She formally joined the African National Congress on her arrival in Swaziland where her fifteen years of exile began in May 1976. While in exile, she served as a presenter on ANC's Radio Freedom. She also served as the secretary in the regional and national ANC women's structures. Back in South Africa, she continued her activism and leadership in the women's sector, as secretary general of the ANC Women's League and, latterly, as national convenor of the Progressive Women's Movement.

Baleka became a member of the first three parliaments in the new democratic dispensation on the conclusion of negotiations of which she was a part. Aside from her role in the constitutional talks, she served as deputy speaker, speaker and deputy president of South Africa in her fifteen years of being in parliament. In December 2007, she was the first woman to be elected national chairperson of the ANC.

Given a chance, Baleka would mainly like to be involved in the arts and cultural sector. She loves singing and writing, especially poetry.

The abiding image which remains with me from a basket of jumbled memories of the day I left my matchbox home, E176 Mnyayiza, KwaMashu, Durban, in April 1976, is of my mother and me kneeling to pray that God should watch over my journey.

My journey was precipitated by a family friend and comrade. Sibongile had arrived from Johannesburg with a note that was to lead me to make one of the most difficult decisions in my life. It was from people, including my brother, Mphakama, who were all behind bars in John Vorster Square. These people had come to the conclusion that it was best for me to leave the country. After careful consideration of their motivation for this reasoning, I came to the painful acceptance of the sense in their proposal.

At the core of their argument was that my being a mother of small children could be used against me by the agents of apartheid. If I were out of the country, there was always the possibility that the children could join me at some point in the future. I would then be able to join African National Congress (ANC) structures in exile and continue to work for the country. That – in summary – was the argument.

I would have to leave two babies behind – a seventeen-month-old daughter and a son who was just over five months old. I was still silently reeling from the pain I experienced on a chilly early morning two months earlier, of having had to wean my son from the breast prematurely. His pink lips had held tightly onto my nipple as I pulled away. I needed to get ready to be picked up for a special task at 6 a.m.

Now, the day after her arrival, as Sibongile and I sat through the emotionally charged funeral of comrade Joseph Mdluli in Lamontville, my head was abuzz. Where was I going to go and how would I get there? What about my children? What if I met the same fate as Joseph Mdluli at the hands of the apartheid police? Frankly, I don't remember much of the proceedings of that funeral.

On Monday, after praying, I travelled by train to Johannesburg. Two days later, my mother followed with my babies. We all stayed at my uncle's place in Zone 3, Diepkloof. As soon as arrangements for my passage out of the country had been made, I couldn't continue to stay in my uncle's house during the day and was moved to a safe house. I could only visit my family at night.

At the shock of seeing my mother coming through the gate of the safe house one morning, I dashed into a bedroom to hide. I listened as she told my hostess, Zodwa, that she and the children were leaving that afternoon. She left the message 'just in case Zodwa had information as to where I was staying'. It turned out that my father who was working in the old Transkei had sent a telegram instructing my mother to 'go back home at once'. He, of course, did not know what was happening and he simply could not stomach the fact that his wife was at her brother's house. My father had apparently called my mother on the telephone at the Phoenix Clinic, in the Mahatma Gandhi settlement near Bhambayi where she worked, and had been terribly upset when he learnt that she'd left town without telling him. I suspect he actually expected her to ask him for permission to leave. I watched her back as she left, my heart sinking at the realisation that I would not be able to hug her and the kids for the last time and say goodbye properly. For her own protection, I couldn't have come out.

Swaziland

It was not long before the night of my departure. We used my uncle's VW kombi van; my cousin drove. Dressed like peasants, we left on 31 April 1976. By the time we had gone through the last of eight roadblocks, the rays of the May Day sun were emerging beyond what Comrade Inch told us was a border post. I'd never been anywhere near one before. We parked and stretched our legs as he explained that from there on we were going to jump over the barbed wire fence and walk through no man's land and into Swaziland.

Just then, a large South African Defence Force (SADF) vehicle approached from the direction of Piet Retief and parked right next to our van. Every stomach raged in silent turmoil. Having perfected our legend of being a grieving family going to a funeral outside Piet Retief, however, we managed to stay calm. The SADF soldiers looked – or rather stared – at us for a few minutes without saying a word, before proceeding to relieve their colleagues at the border post.

As soon as they disappeared from sight, Inch, one other comrade and I had dashed down the incline from the main road and jumped over the wire fence. From out of nowhere, dogs began to bark. We remained silent, following Inch. For what seemed like forever, the sound of our pounding hearts and the crackling of all sorts of dry vegetation underfoot were the only noises we made. At some point Inch said, 'We're in Swaziland'. Indescribable relief welled up inside us. We had survived the tight gap between freedom and the very real possibility of a bullet through our heads.

Later, in those first days of acute loneliness, deep pain and longing for my children, it was the knowledge that my mother was with them that was my only solace. Over the years, my brother and I had always marvelled at her amazing instincts. On one occasion, she decided to remove some banned books from the house and take them to Phoenix shortly before a police raid on our house. I salute motherhood!

In Swaziland, Mme Monare's story came out on the very first night I arrived in that large household. Sitting on her bed surrounded by faint candlelight, I was immediately made to feel like part of the family. She could not get over how she had left home suddenly to follow her husband. 'Leaving a fully furnished house just like that!' Nobody had ever explained to her why she should have to live a difficult life away from home. She pointed to her tattered nightclothes and recalled how, at home, she had been a well-dressed woman, with a job in a clothing factory.

For some years the Monare family had lived in rural Swaziland, far from services that are more easily accessible in urban Manzini or Mbabane. Mme Monare related how she had had to walk a long way to find help while in labour. Her waters broke and she delivered her child in the middle of a forest, in the dead of night. Luckily, she had a family member with her. She told these stories without anger or bitterness, just a vague puzzlement at the turn of events in the family's life.

We sat and talked until the early hours. The old man was out on a mission somewhere. Mme Monare loved and admired him totally, and she and her elder sister, Mme Meisie, looked after the whole household including whomever was brought to the house from across the border (people like Bab'uDuma and Bra Stan) with dedication. There was always chatter and laughter in that house.

Gradually, I explained to Mme Monare and Mme Meisie what work was being done outside South Africa. I explained about the need to tell the whole world, including the global labour movement, what exactly was happening in South Africa under apartheid. Trade unionists such as Ntate Monare, with a track record in the South African Congress of Trade Unions, played a critical role in this work.

They appreciated and understood what I was saying and even started making suggestions of safe routes between Swaziland and South Africa, usually used by petty traders from both countries. Much to Ntate Monare's shock, his wife offered to go to Durban and make certain contacts on our behalf. She brought back some young people to Swaziland. Regrettably, some were caught at Pongola because someone in Durban had tipped off the police. But mainly it was 'mission accomplished' for Antana (as she was referred to) in a difficult task she volunteered to undertake once she understood what was happening.

By the time I was brought to the Monare household in Ngwane Park, Bab'uDuma had already fully briefed me – a briefing I always remember with a smile. '*Vala la, uvale la!*' he declared, signalling with his hand at the mouth and at the private parts. 'Shut here and shut here!' Good advice from an honest man who had been a domestic worker, trade unionist and one of the most trusted cadres, one on whom a lot of work in exile had relied for many years.

Some years later, he went to collect the mail as usual from the post office. As he opened the post box, his arm was blown off. He continued to work for many years before he died, still in exile. May his soul rest in peace.

It was common knowledge that agents of the South African government operated in neighbouring countries such as Swaziland. There were even rumours that the Swazi police structures had been infiltrated by South African secret service agents. The same was suspected about Swazi government departments that had a role in processing South African asylum seeker applications. So, even in the relative peace and freedom of Swaziland, alertness and care had to prevail always.

For instance, I had approached a meeting with an elderly gentleman from the United Nations High Commissioner for Refugees with a great deal of hope and expectation. He must have sensed my vulnerability as he wasted no time in offering to arrange for me to be reunited with my children 'back in South Africa'. I was seething with disgust and anger as I politely declined his offer. It was obvious that he was part of the elaborate network of those who serviced the interests of the apartheid regime.

Within a fortnight of my arrival in Swaziland, as efforts were made to find me a teaching job, I was given my first task. I was part of a team that investigated the kidnapping, by apartheid agents, of one of our comrades.

Having arrived as a walking wardrobe of four pairs of panties, four bras, two petticoats and two layers of clothes, I was fortunate to be introduced to a South African who worked in Swaziland and regularly travelled legally to Durban. Within a week, I received a big suitcase full of clothes from home.

News reached me that my brother, Mphakama Mbete, Themba Kubheka and others had been released from the John Vorster Square Police Station in Johannesburg. I asked Inch to bring them over to Swaziland. On one occasion he told me he had received accurate information of their whereabouts in Johannesburg and that he intended to bring them with him during his next trip. Sadly, that never happened. Inch was caught and tortured almost to death.

Since I returned home in 1990, I have been promising myself that I would find Inch and thank him for his role in creating life-changing experiences for hundreds of South Africans. A little while ago, I saw a notice in the lift in Luthuli House, the headquarters of the ANC, announcing his funeral. I salute your courage, Inch. I hear you held out for a long time while they beat the living daylights out of you. I hear you were unrecognisable. I hear that while you suffered those blows, you gave your comrades enough time to get away. *Hamba Kahle, lamaQhawe!* (Go well, hero among heroes!)

Children

Children are gifts, angels who should be handled gently. They should remain with their parents while they are still young. They should neither be used as leverage by fighting parents nor as political pawns to achieve some or other desired effect from an unwilling source. One never feels the most appropriate words have availed themselves to express the value, beauty and divinity of children.

The 1970s was an era during which the children of our society were extremely vulnerable, taking on roles that should have been undertaken by adults. The country was in turmoil and many young people disappeared without explanation. The same happened to parents. One day children had parents; the next day parents had disappeared without saying goodbye.

I wondered what happened after I had 'disappeared'. There were very few people who knew I was going to 'skip' the country. That last Sunday evening I had discussed the matter with a friend. I drew her attention to a newspaper article about the National Youth Organisation trial in Johannesburg where there was reference to me being possibly required to be a state witness. That would happen, I said, over my dead body.

Six weeks after my arrival in Swaziland, the now well-known Soweto uprising exploded into world consciousness in June 1976. Living in Ngwane Park, we had first-hand experience of the waves of kids who came into Swaziland. I quickly got close to a young man who was on crutches. Unfortunately, as others' papers were processed and they proceeded to other countries, he remained behind. His condition made arrangements more complex and I noticed him steadily getting depressed.

I will never fathom the courage and determination of that teenager who, in spite of his physical challenge, refused to remain behind when his schoolmates and friends tried to discourage him from 'skipping'. A few years later, I met him in Tanzania on his way back from the Soviet Union. He refused to study. He wanted to go to military training. Sadly, he had become quite bitter.

It was a relief to find a job at Mater Dolorosa High School in Mbabane and to secure my own accommodation. It was while I was there that I was able to arrange for my children to be brought over from South Africa. Before a year was up, we (ANC structures) became aware that some youngsters who went to the school in which I had taught in Durban, Isibonelo High, had been sent to see if they could get close to me. This is something 'the system' did routinely, even if I did not feel I was playing a significant role. Our children were used to carry out the system's evil plans.

I was fortunate to have been placed with the Monares in Swaziland, who had already been in exile for twelve years. This was a big family with between ten and fifteen members, including children. One of them was Khethiwe, who was exactly the same age as my daughter. I got attached to her immediately, trying to fill the deep hole in my soul. No mother should ever be separated from her children if it can be helped.

So, I was elated when my brother arrived in Mbabane in December 1976, bringing my kids with him. He took advantage of the large numbers of fun-lovers for whom arrangements had been made to attend a music festival in Swaziland to bring them into the country.

It hit me hard when the decision was taken in June 1977 that I could no longer remain in Swaziland. Crossing to Mozambique was going to be as difficult as leaving South Africa, as we had no passports. This raised the matter of what to do with the children. After months of negotiating I finally came to terms with the reality that the kids had to be sent back home. That was the only sensible and responsible thing to do under the circumstances.

Mozambique

Crossing through the bush from Swaziland to Mozambique in the dead of that night in 1977, the image of my kids' innocent eyes burnt in my head. Their voices kept ringing in my ears. 'Bye bye, Mama!' they said, their little hands waving at me, little suspecting that we were going to be separated for many months and by momentous events.

We sacrificed a great deal as a society as our children were wrenched from the warmth of parental arms. Without realising it, our children contributed to the struggle by foregoing what was due to them so that their parents could participate in the struggle to ensure that they would enjoy a better future.

Once we were in Maputo, the nostalgia kept on eating at me. I spent long hours thinking of the life I had left behind. A husband and children; parents and siblings; the schoolchildren in the classes I had taught at Isibonelo High; the choirs I had been part of at my Methodist Church at G2 KwaMashu and the Durban Adult Choir. I longed for it all rather hopelessly. Something is so final about exile, like a door banged shut in your face. In Mozambique, people spoke Portuguese, just so you did not forget you were getting further away from home.

Tanzania

It was in Dar es Salaam, Tanzania, that I began to feel what it was like to be part of this large family in exile. Four women, all in our twenties, had been together in Swaziland

and spent a few weeks in Maputo. At twenty-eight, I was the oldest. The first time we were taken to the ANC office, we decided it needed a spring clean. Fortunately, we had been temporarily allocated a flat within walking distance in town. That Sunday we spent the day scrubbing the office from top to bottom. It was our office after all.

Mpule and I were soon deployed into the Department of Information and Publicity. We were part of a team headed by Tom Sebina that monitored developments at home and decided what to focus on and then allocated topics to individuals. We researched, wrote scripts and broadcast ANC messages through Radio Freedom into South Africa. We had to be up to date and talk about the most current matters inside the country. Regular news briefings came through our London office where South African newspapers were received daily. These were the pre-computer days, so there were no facsimiles or the Internet.

Radio Tanzania hosted Radio Freedom. We used their facilities. It is there that we met and worked with Tanzanians and made many friendships. One of them was a journalist with a deep voice by the name of Benjamin Mkapa, who subsequently became Tanzania's president. I also remember a kind lady called Halima and a sharp young man called Abdul Mtulya. The friendliness and warmth of all Tanzanians we came across mitigated the effects of being so far from home.

We were soon moved to a residence in Kinondoni just outside Dar es Salaam. It was good to be in a house in which we lived like a large family of about twenty people. There were separate bedrooms for females and males and everybody took turns to cook breakfast and dinner, guided by a roster, and to clean shared spaces. There were regular gatherings, political discussions led by a commissar who would arrange for various people to make presentations on specific topics. There was also a lot of singing, which kept our spirits high.

One morning, Jeff Radebe, who had also grown up in KwaMashu, came to me in stitches. Jeff related how it had been Mphakama's turn to prepare breakfast and he had set out to fry some eggs. Normally one would heat some oil before adding eggs. My brother had simply poured eggs into a totally dry pan. That is why Jeff was so amused.

It was in Kinondoni that certain features of our exile life emerged as strong pillars around which our individual and collective lives became anchored and regulated. Tasks enabling individuals to contribute towards servicing the exile community one way or another; participating in some strategic work; communicating with the people at home – these were some of the more gratifying activities.

Comrade Manto Tshabalala used to be part of the team that not only looked after the health needs of our community, but was also involved with the Organisation of African Unity (OAU) Liberation Committee, based in Morogoro, that trained ANC and Pan-Africanist Congress (PAC) cadres.

Different people who were elders in the movement, mainly from the generation of those who had left South Africa in the early 1960s and who were respectfully called '*mgwenya*', headed teams that looked after all our needs. Gradually, the younger comrades, referred to by *mgwenya* as '*o'Qiniselani*' (after one of the popular freedom songs), were brought on board and given different areas of responsibility.

There was the need to arrange education for new comrades flushed out by the ongoing turmoil at home and education also for children of families living in Tanzania. Travel arrangements had to be made for people going to all corners of the world, for military or political training or to represent the ANC at conferences.

I was elected as regional secretary of the first structure of the ANC Women's Section formed in 1978 in Tanzania. The first big task we handled as a Regional Women's Committee was the establishment of the Charlotte Maxeke Crèche in Morogoro. There were many kids born of young women who were either in the middle of studying or in military training in various countries when they got pregnant. These pregnant young ladies would end up being returned to Tanzania.

With the help of the United Nations Children's Fund, we sustained the project with the services of a team of older women headed by Mme Meisie Mntambo. She was a most caring, wise, humorous and hardworking woman. I had regarded her as my mother back in Swaziland.

Sometimes a young mother would wander off and spend a couple of hours at a bar with the baby. Mme Meisie put her foot down and insisted that the babies be fetched. If it was not for her farsightedness and deep love, many of those kids would not have survived. We buried her a few years ago, back in South Africa.

The ANC community in Tanzania, in Dar es Salaam, Morogoro, Dakawa and other outlying areas where we had a presence, all formed a region. There were many regions throughout Africa and abroad. As a regional structure of the ANC Women's Section, we reported to and were led by a national structure based in Lusaka, Zambia, which was where the ANC headquarters was situated.

As secretary, it fell on me to be the link with the Lusaka office. On one occasion, I met Mme Florence Mophosho, a member of the ANC National Executive Committee, when she visited our region from headquarters in Lusaka. By this time I was married to Willy Kgositsile and had moved to the University of Dar es Salaam where he was teaching. The first thing Mme Florence did after greeting me as she walked into our home was to scold me for being pregnant. 'When there is so much work, how can you be complicating things by making babies?' she said. She had a point. With the Department of Information and Publicity work and the Regional Women's Committee, ongoing political activities of the whole movement, writing articles for *Voice of Women* whose editor was Mavivi Manzini, one's hands were always full. There was never a dull moment.

The one big problem for me was malaria. A few years later, malaria would be the major factor in us moving from Tanzania, on the advice of some Soviet doctors. When my son, Duma, was born on 12 June 1978, I realised that I could now speak Swahili well enough to conduct a fair conversation. In 1977, I had left southern Africa for the eastern coast of the continent speaking only Zulu, a bit of Sepedi, some Afrikaans and English. Faced by the need to communicate with an old lady who spoke only Swahili, who looked after Duma, I surprised myself and spoke to her quite well.

As if I had not internalised Mme Florence's admonitions, I gave birth to Ipuseng in late 1979, exactly a week before Duma turned a year old. Ipuseng was born in the then Democratic People's Republic of Yemen in Khormaksar Clinic. The fact that she was born on 30 November, Yemen's independence day, led to a visit from a government official bringing gifts from the prime minister's office. We were guests of a well-known poet, Omar Algawy, who had befriended Willy at Afro-Asian Writers' Movement conferences over the years. At a small celebration to mark her arrival, Ipu was also named 'Arwa' by another elderly poet, after an ancient Yemeni queen.

For the first two weeks, my little queen got her baths in the sink of the Crater Hotel in Aden. Except for Duma's scepticism about the new addition to the family, things went off well until we left on her seventeenth day. The flight stopped in Saana on the way to Addis Ababa. A pretty Ethiopian young lady came over to play with the babies and chat. She asked about Ipu's age and when I told her, she began to scream, hands on her head, making lots of passengers rush over to see what the matter was.

She rattled off in Amharic (I learnt later) something like: 'Where have you ever heard of an African baby being taken out of the home at such a tender age!' Apparently she had been looked after by both her mother and mother-in-law for all of forty-five days after she had had a baby. I wish it had been possible for me to experience that sort of pampering throughout my childbearing years.

Nkuli and Zweli joined us in 1980 in Dar es Salaam, at five and four years old respectively. If it had not been for the communication challenges of exile life, this might have happened earlier. We were not allowed to post letters home or use the telephone, so that it took weeks or even months for us to communicate with loved ones.

In 1978, my mother had brought Nkuli and Zweli to Swaziland, with the understanding that either Mphakama or I would be able to pick them up from her. She had waited for three weeks before returning to South Africa when she ran out of money. A message from Mphakama eventually reached me through a convoluted hand-delivery route. It turned out that as I left Dar es Salaam for the south with one-month-old Duma, my mother was on her way back to South Africa with the other kids.

When we returned to Dar es Salaam in December 1979, there were some developments. A friend of ours, in the flat directly above ours, had started a relationship with a British gentleman. I do not remember us ever meeting this man directly although we were quite close to the girlfriend. After a month or so we no longer saw him around. Other friends told us that it had transpired that he was a South African agent who was quickly dumped by our friend as soon as she became suspicious.

Some of the poetry I wrote during this time was written at a house we moved into from the flat. Its address became the title of one of the poems. Other poems, 'Exile blues', 'I want to be an echo', 'Snake' come to mind, each reflecting the challenges and experiences faced at the time such as depression, cerebral malaria and asthma attacks which most people had never experienced back home.

Tanzania's invasion by Uganda's Idi Amin in 1980 brought about many shortages of items such as infant milk formula and baby napkins. There were long queues for bread. The ANC took responsibility for me and the children's monthly groceries, which sometimes helped, but not always.

We left Dar es Salaam at the end of 1981 for Nairobi, Kenya, where Willy had found a job at the University of Nairobi. I was sad to leave all my work in the Department of Information and Publicity and the Regional Women's Committee, the whole community and the great sense of belonging that we all shared. How were we going to replace those lively political discussions? The briefings by leaders from all over, especially Lusaka, had become our political lifeline. This process soaked you into an ever better understanding of why we could never give up on the struggle for the liberation of our country.

Being given tasks and finding your way through them, and being thrown in the deep end always helped one to learn to swim. Having to read ANC policy documents and prepare presentations for international seminars and conferences meant we learnt to explain ANC positions and defend them. We learnt to understand them enough to figure out answers to questions, but also – for our own internal purposes – to consider whether or when there would be a need to revisit or strengthen policies.

In the Women's Section, we had to take up the matter of student pregnancies, where the girls kept being sent back from abroad while the young men continued their studies and impregnated yet more girls. We took the view that the boys had to come back as well, in order to help them take responsibility and realise the seriousness of their conduct.

The other matter that caused us some grief was relating to the infliction of physical abuse of partners, mainly by men on wives or girlfriends. Situations would sometimes be so bad that a plan had to be devised to create facilities to lock our own people up for a few days in our residential area in the Solomon Mahlangu Freedom College (SOMAFCO) premises. This was better than handing them over to the host country's justice system, where we would lose control completely.

In some instances, women – having initiated the whole process to start with – would come back and want their spouse or partner released. We developed the position that the woman who had been beaten up was not the only complainant in the matter. ANC policy itself is violated when any of its members or anyone else is physically attacked. We then decided that insistence by a woman for the release of her abuser should be met with the possibility that she herself be locked up.

Kenya

Exile is a vast desert. It is a test that calls for you to dig deep and call on even unconscious inner resources for survival. I avoided allowing myself to miss home. I was afraid of the pain of thinking about it because I knew it was something over which I had no control. Exile meant statelessness, which required that the ANC continuously apply for travel documents from other countries such as Ghana for its members to move around the world.

In 1981, soon after settling into a university house in Nairobi, Kenya, Willy received instructions from ANC headquarters to attend a conference abroad. The next thing he was told to return via Mazimbu (SOMAFCO) and participate in discussions relating to the college the ANC had opened in Tanzania. He ended up being away for about six weeks, including Christmas.

With the few cents at my disposal, I prepared some sandwiches, boiled eggs and a chicken and took the children to picnic at a beautiful green sprawling park in town. Watching their joy as they ran around, rolling in the grass was the best present I could ever have asked for. I sat and watched them with a gratified mother's smile on my face until late afternoon.

We had taken the position that our children had to speak at least one South African language. They spoke fluent English and Zulu, which I insisted we stick to at home. My view was that if after school we did not let them speak one of our languages, nobody else would. One day I had to quickly stop Duma saying aloud, '*Mama kuyanuka!*' (Mama, it smells). The problem was that the Swahili word for smell is 'nuka' also.

Now and again, Duma asked questions I found rather difficult to answer. Washing dishes one day, I just found myself telling him that I was lonely, '*Nginesizungu*'. He responded by asking me to show him what it looked like, the '*isizungu*'. Another time I had suggested we 'take a walk'. He insisted I show him this 'walk' we were supposed to 'take'.

The South Africans we met in Nairobi were largely non-aligned. Some had drifted away from the confines of organisations such as the PAC and the ANC. But there were also ANC comrades who worked for United Nations agencies, people such as Stan Sangweni, Walter Msimang and their families. Bhut' Zola Ngcakane (a scientist) and Sis' Pulane Ngcakane's family were also there. I learnt a lot from Sis' Pulane about the realities of a political family. As a daughter of Professor Z.K. Matthews, she had grown up in one. We became a small ANC social collective.

At some point we were joined by the family of Thula Bopela who had recently been released from a Rhodesian jail. Night after night, listening to the stories of how the young Umkhonto we Sizwe (MK) and Zimbabwe People's Revolutionary Army guerrillas faced the militarily mightier forces of Rhodesia, often combined with those from Mozambique, left you in awe of the human spirit.

In Tanzania, we lived with a comrade called Elliot who had come out of fighting in Rhodesia with a distinct lack of fear – a rather positive attitude towards wild animals that the rest of us found unnerving. You never ventured into his room before making sure he was not harbouring a snake of one sort or another in it. One year, at a Women's Day (9 August) event, we included an item on events at Wankie/Sipolilo, where MK fighters had entered Rhodesia on 13 August 1967.

We used the opportunity for Elliot to talk, especially for the benefit of the younger generation, about that experience as well as about his relationship with animals. Images of the bush apparently were always with him. From time to time, he'd be seen diving into a shrub, pursuing something only he could see, or else hiding away from the enemy.

One Sunday morning in Mazimbu, the community heard a commotion which turned out to be a group of Masai men chasing a hippo. Apparently this hippo had wondered away from its herd and ended up in a donga, which had once been a flowing river. As soon as Elliot heard what was happening, he did what came naturally to him. He descended into the donga and slowly approached the frustrated hippo. I think he wanted to stroke it, to appease it; I don't know. This time he had underestimated its rage. It grabbed him in its enormous teeth and shook him three times like a rag doll. By the time he was rushed to the Morogoro hospital, it was over for him. He had lost a lot of blood. Elliot, a man of few words, was very well loved by our community.

Apart from the South Africans in Nairobi, we also met and became friends with people like Micere Mugo, Ngugi wa Thiongo, Shadrack Gutto and many other Kenyans who were not liked by the Moi government for their political views. Many of them ended up going into exile in other countries where – from time to time – we later came across them.

My first trip out of Africa was in 1981 to a seminar in Bommersvik, Sweden, where I met the then Swedish Prime Minister, Olof Palme. I remember being fascinated observing that the sun only just set at 10 p.m. My poem 'Solidarity' was composed along the lines of the freedom song, 'Beautiful Sweden . . . we shall never forget'. Sweden was one of the international friends that gave abundant support of different types to the struggle against apartheid. Being able to meet people like Vladimir Shubin in Moscow, who headed the Soviet Union's Solidarity Committee through which support for our struggle was channelled, further gave one a sense of the worldwide mobilisation against apartheid.

We ourselves did not last longer than two years in Kenya. In December 1983, after a scary attempted coup by some army officers, we left for Botswana. Moi's agents had turned their wrath on the university community, on both students and teaching staff. There were random killings and hundreds of arrests.

We left Kenya with no illusion that colour was the only or the main factor in countries' politics of oppression and exploitation of the majority of poor and working masses. The ruthless clampdown by a black government of any dissenting voices was as bad as in apartheid South Africa. In South Africa, race, class and sex were all rolled up into one massive knobkierie in the hands of a minority white regime against the majority of black people.

Botswana

We arrived in Botswana during the festive season. No sooner had we arrived in the Oasis Hotel than we were briefed about an 'alert'. We were not allowed to sleep at the hotel. We were whisked off, four kids and all, and for a couple of weeks huddled in some kind soul's four-roomed house. Two years later, in 1985, it was the Oasis Hotel that hosted South African agents who had massacred South Africans and Batswana all over Gaborone before disappearing without paying their bills, so we were told.

Being so close to South Africa was the best thing about relocating to Botswana. This was particularly so for Willy who was part of the early 1960s generation of exiles. We saw lots of people from home. As part of the underground structures based there, it was easier for us to arrange for people to come in and out of the country and for us to do our work.

I was soon in the regional women's structure and the music and writers' units of the Medu Arts Ensemble, something I enjoyed and found gratifying. I also tracked Willy's family down. As it turned out, they were just across the border in Mafikeng. This was important for our family, especially the children.

Bands with South African exiles such as Shakawe (led by Jonas Gwangwa) and Kalahari (led by Hugh Masekela) were key bands in Gaborone. I became the lead singer for Shakawe, while Tshepo Tshola was the lead singer for Kalahari. Yes, those were the days.

Without a doubt, Gaborone was swarming with enemy agents. But I hasten to say that, for me, it was the best part of exile. If I had been born in a different era, I would have spent my life involved in music and writing. Botswana gave me an opportunity to briefly focus on the abilities God gave me in these areas. Apart from a study group back in Dar es Salaam, the Medu Writers Unit was the next golden space that gave me the ability to share written pieces with a collective where we would help one another improve our writing skills.

The vibrant arts and music scene in Botswana led to us meeting Sis' Dorothy Masuku, Sis' Queeneth Ndaba, the Jazz Pioneers led by the late Bro Ntemi Piliso and pianist Bheki Mseleku. Among the many artists who came from home and who would perform at events we organised were Steve Dyer, Tony Cedras and Dennis Mpale, who were all members of Shakawe. Letta Mbulu and Caiphus Semenya would spend weeks at a time at a recording studio outside Gaborone.

SADF raid on Gaborone

On 14 May 1985, a young comrade was killed by an explosion as he turned the key in his car ignition. The presence of South African secret police in Gaborone was palpable. An Indian man, walking slowly past our house and slyly checking what was happening, became a regular feature. In June, an alert was put out. The children started spending nights at Dr Leloba Molema's house across the road. Mphakama, visiting from Lusaka, Willy and I took turns to keep watch at night. Later, we heard from a Tanzanian neighbour that the family in the house next door to us were frantically trying to move out. Their inability to relocate before D-day perhaps saved our family.

We did not sleep at our house on 12 June. We were at Kofi Mensah's house for a second night when the explosions and shootings started at exactly the same time, about 1 a.m., at different locations all over Gaborone. It went on for about forty to forty-five minutes; then you could hear vehicles speeding off. By 2 a.m., all was silent except for families and neighbours examining the damage left by the assassins and some wailing in the cold night.

The news on radio in the early hours of 14 June referred to a six-year-old boy and his uncle being casualties of the raids. A lot of our friends assumed it was Duma and Mphakama. Our friends, George and Lindi Phahle, were among those killed. A former guerrilla fighter and his handler phoned George a number of times before the raid recruiting him for the South African government. This man had once been accommodated by the Phahles on his way back from military training. Evidently he had become an askari (the term given to guerrillas who were captured by the South African army and 'turned' or converted into spies or soldiers for the apartheid regime) and had since defected.

Soon thereafter we were informed by comrade Thami Sindelo, then the ANC chief representative in Botswana, that our family was on a list of people whom the Botswana government had decided should leave the country because their security could not be guaranteed. Willy and I found a flat we occupied for some weeks while we tried to find alternative accommodation.

My mother had taken Nkuli and Zweli for a year, which somewhat reduced the complexity of life in a dramatic year. In the midst of days of driving around through the night, having run out of alternative places to sleep, we had discovered that I was expecting again. I had to have strict bedrest to avoid a miscarriage. My hospital room became a convenient indoor sleeping facility for more than just me.

The kids remained with Leloba. We dropped in every afternoon to see them. Once we let them stay with us – at the flat – over a weekend. This was most challenging. To start with we knew the owner of the flat whose door was directly opposite ours. This meant we had to ensure that he never saw us. We had to come in and out as stealthily as possible. Then, to keep kids of five and six years of age quiet for a whole weekend! Try that!

We then found a new place behind the Gaborone Sun Hotel. Living in that new block of flats was like a breath of fresh air for us. For some months there was relative normality after we brought all the kids back to live with us.

In the weeks after the SADF raid on Gaborone in 1985, I travelled to the Nairobi World Conference of Women. On my way back I stopped in Dar es Salaam and Lusaka. These kinds of visits enabled our communities to get first-hand accounts of developments. The important thing was to keep morale high and never give up hope. With each innocent person's life taken by an apartheid bullet, hundreds more recruits left South Africa to join the ranks of the liberation movements. I gave briefings and answered people's questions, reassuring them that we remained as determined as ever.

The day I was admitted to deliver Neo, Nkuli and Zweli had just arrived back from South Africa. Nkuli came with me to Bamalete Hospital. Neo was born healthy on 28 February 1986, a great joy that was sorely needed. We had started noticing some movements in the vicinity of our new home. Some of our neighbours had also tipped us off about strange cars driving or men walking up and down our street.

Once, the bedside cabinet door accidentally opened, revealing two pistols. Simultaneously Duma and Ipu went '*Ditlhobolo*!' 'Guns!' We had to explain as honestly but simply as possible to them that we had to be ready for a possibility of an attack. We took them through what they would have to do in case something happened to us, on the assumption that their lives would be spared. That they would go and report to the nearest family who were trusted friends across the road.

Zimbabwe

Soon we had to pack and move to Harare, Zimbabwe. Nkuli and Zweli stayed behind with Leloba so as not to disturb their school programme. In the year of our relocation to Harare, both Willy and I were immediately drawn into the regional political committee, the highest political structure in a region. In addition, I was elected onto the Regional Women's Committee.

Apartheid agents were all over Harare. There were rumours about some having infiltrated our ranks. We lived in a suburb called Avondale in an ANC residence. It was while we were there with Bro' Ike Maphoto that we got the devastating news of

President Samora Machel's death on 19 October 1986. We concluded that his death was part of a deliberate plan carried out by apartheid South Africa.

No one can ever prepare you for the loss of your mother. It is worse when you cannot mourn with other family members and benefit from the relative closure brought about by a funeral. I recall I heard about my mother's death on a hectic day in January 1987. We had planned a programme at a school in Harare to mark the ANC's birthday. As we entered the office of the school principal to finalise arrangements for that afternoon's event, I was told to meet Mphakama as soon as possible. I found him standing in the hotel lobby and saw he was quite dazed. After a brief greeting I asked, 'How long will this take?' He said directly, '*UMa akasekho!*' Then he asked for a lift. Without a word, I returned to the car. I also learnt Mama had suffered a stroke four months before. On the wise counsel of Sis' Thandi Lujabe-Rankoe, we arranged for Nkuli and Zweli to be driven to South Africa to attend the funeral and to enable us to at least get a first-hand account of proceedings.

In February 1987, ANC headquarters instructed me to relocate to Lusaka to head the preparations for the Women's Section national conference in September of that year. I went with Neo. I had met and developed a liking for Nosiviwe Maphisa at the Nairobi women's conference back in 1985. We reconnected and hit it off very well when I worked full time at the Women's Section offices. Part of the preparatory work took the two of us to the girls in the camps in Angola, where she represented the MK women.

In those years it was Nosiviwe's partner, Charles Nqakula, whom I had to rely on to look after Neo. He literally brought him up as he did a lot of his work from home. In the meantime, news came that Willy had been badly injured in a car accident in Harare. Our whole family subsequently relocated to Lusaka within that year. Then I was elected into the Women's Section National Executive Committee as administrative secretary.

In exile we each contributed to the collective according to our skills and where we were deployed. You gave all your energies according to your area of work, day and night. We forgot what it was like to earn a salary and allocate it to different aspects of life. This was the situation for full-time ANC functionaries such as myself. Others saw to our families' needs such as finding schools and uniforms, getting medical attention, groceries and clothing – '*mphando*' (piles of donated items). The second-hand clothing seen all over parts of Johannesburg today reminds me of the *mphando* from which for years we selected garments and filled up our wardrobes. We had, out of necessity, a strong sense of belonging.

You saw it on occasions when we were burying one of us. We came out in our hundreds, in an endless convoy carrying our sorrows and desires, our deep regrets that one of us would be buried so far from home. You heard it in our inspired singing when we gathered in Mulungushi Hall in Lusaka, in the camps in Angola, in Mazimbu, in any other part of the world. '*Savuma sangena kwamany'amazwe, lapho kungazi khon'ubaba nomama, silandel'inkululeko*' (Yes, we had gone to lands unknown to our fathers and mothers in pursuit of freedom).

One of a series of interactions between the exiled ANC and some white people from South Africa took place in Harare in 1989. This was a conference of ANC women in exile with women, mainly white and Afrikaner, from inside the country. We were asked – during preparations in Lusaka – whether we preferred to share rooms with counterparts from home. I thought, 'What a freaky idea, what if I end up with someone from the SADF?'

On the first day of the meeting, Zimbabwean women, black and white, talked about their experiences. Then presentations were made reflecting South African women's experiences. The white women related their stories of how they ironed their husbands' and sons' SADF uniforms with pride before they (the men) went to fight the 'terrorists' at the borders. The picture unravelled amidst tears of realisation about the pain inflicted by one another's children and loved ones on the other. Slowly, different realities emerged from sides never listened to, considered or appreciated before. One shift that was achieved at that conference was the revelation of a common experience evidenced by women's roles as wives, sisters and mothers.

At the end of the conference, the goodbye hugs were emotional. As they returned to South Africa, many of the white women were convinced that the ANC women were just ordinary human beings who did not deserve to be outlawed from the country of their birth. We knew as that year ended that the smell of home was in the air, though we could not fully anticipate how it would actually happen.

From 1987, I benefited a great deal from being based at the headquarters of the ANC in Lusaka. This enabled me to have a deeper understanding of challenges and to learn from interactions with many senior leaders and participate in many of its collectives.

Home-coming

I was part of the first group of ANC women leaders – led by Mme Gertrude Shope – who returned to South Africa early in June 1990, after the unbanning of political organisations. The drive to re-launch the structures of the ANC all over the country was our priority. We concentrated at launching ANC Women's League branches. I was deployed to the province of my birth where I worked with Comrade Willies Mchunu. We criss-crossed the region, visiting areas such as Sikhawini, Mpangeni, Nseleni and Port Shepstone.

I went to my mother's grave in Mqanduli within three days of my arrival. It gave me relief for me to finally be at her resting place. My first poem back in South Africa tackled the meaning and understanding of a word that I had found sacred throughout the exile period – home.

'Where is home?' (extract)
Is it the thorny path
to the family graveyard
could it be the shade
of the tall trees
whispering above
my mother's grave
or the sacred space
which permanently holds
her body away
from my hungry eye . . .

In our early days in Johannesburg, in June 1990, we were taken to Diepkloof, Soweto, where we slowly found our feet. For practical purposes, Thembi (the MK name for Nosiviwe) and I moved into a cheap flat in the city centre.

South Africa's physical beauty was striking after fifteen years of absence. The good condition of the national roads surprised four-year-old Neo. 'Where are the potholes, Mama?' he asked as we drove from Johannesburg to Durban once. When I explained that the road was in good condition, which is why there were no potholes, it still did not make sense to him.

South Africa is yet to fully appreciate the memories and records of life in exile. Perhaps the diaries of the family of a humble man, who went out on the instruction of his organisation to open up an external mission of the ANC, are a place to begin this appreciation. I know that the edifice Oliver Reginald (O.R.) Tambo created not only helped thousands of us to keep our sanity, but taught our people values and prepared the foundation for a free society.

His aura was omnipotent whether he was around or not. Mrs Mwanamwamba, wife of the current Zambian speaker of parliament, whose house was one of his safe houses, remembers how they had to keep out of the kitchen when it was *bhuti*'s turn to cook. Comrades from *mgwenya* told us how he would take his turn to do everything in an ANC residence. One of his last accomplishments before he became ill with a stroke was formulating a blueprint, adopted by the OAU and the United Nations, for a path to the new South Africa. What a leader.

'Thank you, Tata' (extract)
. . . We wish to dance
to your life
to say Thank You . . .

Under leaders such as Oliver Tambo and PAC leaders, Africa's understanding of the nature of apartheid was nurtured through the OAU. Our leaders' voices were also continuously heard at the United Nations where a special structure was created to pursue the goals of the worldwide anti-apartheid struggle. August 9 was officially marked by the United Nations as a day of solidarity with the women of South Africa and Namibia.

Not enough tribute has been paid to his wife and dedicated life partner, Ma Adelaide Tambo, whose sacrifices enabled O.R. to focus his energies on the struggle. Long after he had departed this earth, she carried on giving attention and love to us, 'Papa's children', as she would say. The two met when she was, independently of him, an activist in the ANC Youth League.

The significant contribution of women in the liberation process should not be underestimated. Thomas Nkobi, the late treasurer general of the ANC, used to publicly express appreciation for the work carried out by the Women's Section. According to him, the whole ANC external mission would sometimes be maintained, for some months, with resources raised by that section.

Reflections

Exile is not like deciding to move to another country from where you are free to call home or visit as often as you want. Exile takes you away from your natural environment, without you having the opportunity to prepare yourself or your family psychologically. You only have a choice at the level of principle, which leads you to decide to go. It is pursuance of an ideal and refusal to be prohibited in any way from that effort. Exile is not about enjoyment of life away from your country. Given that your country is at the core of what leads to your exile, you can never really enjoy being in another country. Your first and undying love is for your country.

The best conditions anywhere in the world can never be satisfactory to an exile because exiled souls always hanker after their home. A visit by someone from home was always a very special occasion. You shared your visitor with your other comrades as much as possible. Everyone had to get a piece of this person and, through them, get a glimpse, a whiff, a fleeting flavour of home that would have to last them a long time. So it was unfair for you to hoard a visitor unless it was about work.

With our children being born away from home, we had to figure out ways to mould into them a consciousness of being South African. The Young Pioneers of Walter Sisulu became a key programme through which we prepared our kids for a future envisaged back in South Africa.

At some point, I realised that my children resented the fact that ANC work kept me away from home a lot. They even vowed never to become members of the ANC when they grew up. Later, back home, they argued they were born into the ANC, questioning why there were now formalities to follow before they were able to join.

But, of course, they, like everyone else, have to decide for themselves whether or not to join the ANC.

From time to time, I observe the mood or listen with interest to accounts of get-togethers of kids from exile. There's something akin to nostalgia, but not quite like longing, to get back to a certain experience. The way a thirty-year old Ipu explains it is that, for her, this phenomenon is experienced in three different ways. There are people she has never lost touch with since her return, who have always been part of her life. There are those who are like brothers and sisters to her, by virtue of the shared exile-childhood experience, no matter how infrequently they might meet. Then there are some people she feels uneasy with. She senses that the latter are judgemental of her, perhaps because life has been harsher to them since the return home.

The 'exile kids' have a different perspective on life or sense of space and experience. It's not about being 'better'; it's just having been exposed to a different reality and set of values early on in their lives – such as non-racial human and social interactions in other countries and seeing or living in different parts of the world. Some years back, Nkuli told me about a young man in Soweto who said to her: '*Ngiyakuthanda*' (I love you). She asked me, 'But what does he mean, Mama? He doesn't know me. How can he love a total stranger?' Having grown up in a township myself, I understood where the young man was coming from. But I also understood Nkuli's confusion. To her it really did not make sense.

After coming home, we continued being referred to as 'exiles' and a new word – 'insiles' was coined. This is, in my view, an unfortunate phenomenon that has mischievously created artificial divisions between South Africans who all fought to liberate the country. I think it is crazy to evaluate people's contribution to the struggle or weigh their value depending on whether they were 'inside' or 'outside' the country. I think it was necessary for the struggle to be fought and won on each and every one of these fronts. If any one of these fronts had failed, the others could not have been successful, or would somehow have been slowed down or made deficient. To bring down apartheid, the support of the international community – including women, youth, workers, churches and cultural bodies – had to be mobilised and added to our people's capacity to fight the system.

Had I remained in South Africa, I would not have had the opportunity to '*rabula*' (drink) from the experiences I found beyond the boundaries of my beloved country. I would not like to return to exile even if I was paid to do it. But I do not regret living through, surviving and growing from it. For me two other experiences have since come my way for which I am as eternally grateful.

I got involved (through initial secondment by the ANC Women's League) in the World Trade Centre formulation of the interim constitution, which culminated in the finalisation of South Africa's Constitution, through the Constitutional Assembly in 1996.

Secondly, the opportunity not only to participate in the first three parliaments of a democratic South Africa, but also to be part of team that helped interpret the South African Constitution and led in the implementation of its provisions by creating institutions, has been more than a bonus.

The journey across that desert of exile has helped this society to become what it is now; has helped to formulate that space which can truly be called home. In the weeks of South Africa hosting the FIFA World Cup Soccer Tournament, I felt that we had entered that space.

'Thank you, Tata' (extract)
. . . Our tears have dried
into silver stripes
into lines of seasons
which point to our past
which in turn must point
to the future . . .

My life in exile

Nomsa Judith Mkhwanazi

Nomsa Judith Mkhwanazi was born on 20 July 1933 at Dukathole in Germiston, South Africa. She completed her secondary education at the Inanda Seminary and went on to obtain teaching qualifications at the Evangelical Teacher Training College and the University of Swaziland. In Birmingham in the United Kingdom, she undertook a range of tertiary and vocational study programmes. Early in her career, she held teaching positions in KwaZulu-Natal. While teaching at Mseleni Combined School, she pursued underground community work and was often threatened with arrest. Conditions prompted her escape into exile in Swaziland in 1963, to join her husband, PAC leader, Joe Mkhwanazi. When they were deported by the Swaziland authorities, they moved to the United Kingdom where Nomsa continued political work in the form of collecting material assistance for exiled South African refugees and cadres in Tanzania. On their return to South Africa after 30 years of exile she retired in Durban, where she currently resides with her husband.

It was in April 1963, after the birth of my second daughter, Zanele, that I had to make one of the most difficult decisions in my life. The security police were swooping on political activists, especially during the Rivonia trial which took place between 1963 and 1964. There was a lot of political unrest in the country. Robert Mangaliso Sobukwe, the leader of the Pan-Africanist Congress (PAC) was imprisoned. My husband, Joe Mkhwanazi, who was a member of the PAC, had already escaped the wrath of the South African security forces by fleeing to neighbouring Swaziland.

My baby was a month old. I was still breastfeeding and sore from the scars of childbirth. Unlike my earlier pregnancy, I had the support of my parents through the later stages of my pregnancy. Having had a stillborn earlier, in deep rural KwaZulu-Natal where I was a young bride with very limited access to healthcare, they suggested I come back home to Natalspruit, Germiston, in Johannesburg to give birth. Our opposite neighbour was a Dr Kunene. With such a support network around me, they were convinced that this time around nothing would go wrong.

Early one evening my parents asked to talk to me. 'We have decided that we should discuss with you the possibility of your joining *uMkhwenyana uMkhwanazi eSwazini. Asiyiboni into yokuthi uzohlala lapha nathi kanti ushadile,*' my father said. Loosely translated: 'We have decided that you should consider the possibility of joining Mkhwanazi, our son-in-law, in Swaziland. We don't see the point of you staying here when you are married.'

'What about my baby?' I responded. '*Umtwana akanalutho, uzosala nathi, simkhulise, kuzekufike isikhathi sokuthi simlethe kinina uma senizinzile,*' my father responded. Loosely translated: 'The child is no problem. She will remain with us. We'll bring her up until such time that we bring her to you, when you are settled.'

It was a thought that had not crossed my mind. While it was a difficult time of my life, I had taken one day at a time. Firstly, I was anxious that I get through my pregnancy. The political unrest raging through the country made me apprehensive about my husband, Joe. I prayed that he successfully reached his destination without being arrested. My prayers were answered and I was concentrating on healing and recuperating well. Mother and baby were fine.

That evening turned into a long night. The baby was restless, as if she knew that I was going through making a hard decision. She did not sleep all night. It was a decision that was mine alone, I could not consult with anybody. My parents were the only people that could have helped me through it, and their minds were already made up.

Knowing the way in which the South African security forces operated at the time, the loved ones of activists were a target for harassment, imprisonment and banning orders. I knew that I would not escape either.

These prevailing circumstances made my decision a simple one. As hard as it was to leave my baby, my parents, my homeland, and never to return, it was clear that I was not going to have the peace that I desired even if I stayed.

Three weeks after I had the conversation with my parents, I was psychologically prepared for the difficult journey I was to undertake. Packed and ready to leave for Swaziland, I held my baby tight with a hug I was never to forget. I felt a surge of the pain of separation from such a young life, one that I had brought to this world. I bade my parents farewell. I was to travel in a car that was commonly used to travel over the border. I was to undertake a journey that I myself did not know, with the hope that I would find Joe alive, that I would see my parents soon and that the baby was left in good hands. I thought my journey would not be that traumatic.

My breasts were a constant reminder that I had left a baby behind because they would fill up every time I remembered her. This also happened when I arrived at the Oshoek border post. The harsh realities of childbirth and the constant bleeding was a reminder of the difficulties that women go through in life to nurture life. It is so precious that it cannot be taken for granted.

The intelligence of the South African police forces at the time was very remarkable. My suspicion is that even though this had been kept under wraps, they already knew that I was travelling to Swaziland to meet my husband who they had been looking for to arrest for almost a month. As I stepped down to join the queue in immigration, they pulled me out for questioning. When that sort of thing happened, everyone who was travelling with you at the time knew that it could be the last time that they see you alive. I prayed hard that they would not kill me.

After a long period of questioning and interrogation, their suspicion was confirmed. Joe had indeed escaped into Swaziland and I was going to visit him. Having ascertained that, and just to inflict more pain, they were going to keep me in a prison cell overnight while they decided what to do with me. The decision seemingly was whether to allow me to go into Swaziland and return to South Africa, or whether to give me a choice of going into Swaziland and never be allowed to return to the country of my birth.

The horrendous experience of being in a prison cell overnight, constantly bleeding with no assistance or sanitary towels, was an experience that I will never forget in my life – a humiliation that is a constant reminder of what makes you a woman. The Oshoek border post can be very cold in the evenings whether it is winter or summer. I lay there all night, knowing that neither my husband nor parents knew where I was, even though they knew that I had undertaken the journey. The night was, once again, a long one.

In the early hours of the morning, a prison warder came to unlock the cell and inform me that they were going to release me. However, I should make the decision of whether they should send me back to South Africa or whether I would like to join my husband and never to return. Given that this was already a well thought-out decision, I had no doubt in my mind that I was going to leave the country of my birth, never to return.

Exile in Swaziland

Our exile in Swaziland did not resemble the realities of a harsh life being a refugee. Joe and I had settled very well. He had gone through a number of successive jobs, earning a living for the family. I had also been working as a teacher. We were in the process of building our own house after living in a railway carriage ('*eSitimeleni*') for almost a decade. My parents had been in and out of Swaziland.

They brought Zanele when she was four years old, no longer a baby, to visit us for the first time in 1967. They came again in 1969 when she came to start school in Swaziland. She clung on to my parents dearly as they were the only people she knew. Joe and I had also been blessed with twins, Themba and Thembi. In 1973, I was expecting my fifth and last-born child, Busisiwe, which means 'we are blessed'.

We experienced our fair share of tragedies in the family, first with the death of my brother, Lucas Dube, in 1971. It was painful being in Swaziland, a stone's throw away, and not being able to risk returning to South Africa to bury him. It was the same pain of not being there as an eldest child to support my parents as they were going through this loss. In the same year, we experienced the death of my father-in-law, Richard Moyeni Mkhwanazi, and once again we shared the pain of not being home for my husband to bury his father.

In 1972, I decided to send Thoko, my eldest child, and Zanele to visit my parents in South Africa. They travelled with a relative. Their passage to South Africa was very happy and a successful one – until they arrived at my home to find that my father, who had been ill for a long time, had died that morning. It was a sad moment indeed, even though my mother was grateful that the children had arrived and would fill our space.

The harsh realities of an oppressive state that sought to destroy its nation and humanity once again reared its head. The children came back and related stories about how they were visited by the South African security forces to interrogate them about our whereabouts, fundamentally not believing that we would not make the journey back to South Africa to bury our parents. The children would, from time to time, relate their disgust at the behaviour of the security police, how they would open the coffin of 'Mkhulu', my father, on the way to the graveside to check that he alone lay in there and no one else.

For me and Joe, the pain of being away from home was always felt when we received the notorious orange envelope with a telegram. This form of communication was always to convey bad news of the death of a loved one. The knowledge that we would not be able to go there and support the family was the greatest torture and reminder of the brutal nature of the apartheid machinery and its intent to inflict pain on a people struggling against the injustice of this system.

My parents, particularly my mother ('unaMabuza'), who was a remarkable woman in her own right, had always been a pillar of support to me. The closeness of both my parents allowed her to continue to play a significant role in our exiled lives. In fact, it was not until her death in 1973 that I realised that throughout my journey in exile I had her as my guiding light.

Often when the South African story is told, we reflect on the bravery of men, men like Robert Sobukwe. I always wonder who is telling the story of the brave woman, Mama Sobukwe, who endured the worst suffering in witnessing the incarceration of her husband at the hands of the apartheid regime and yet had to stand strong for her children, her in-laws and the rest of the family.

For me this was the most testing decade of my married life, as a mother, daughter and a wife. It was in 1973, when I was pregnant with my youngest, Busisiwe, that the volatility of this decade started. I was on holiday in January 1973, having visited some friends for Christmas at eMbabane, when Joe arrived to fetch me prematurely.

I knew there was something wrong as he would not divulge the reason why we were going home. As an obedient wife, I agreed to pack my bags with the children and follow him, as I had always followed him until this stage. When we arrived at home he broke the news of my mother's death. I always knew that my mom and dad were very close. However, I did not think that my father's death would affect my mother so badly. It was barely six months after my father's death that my mother died.

This was the bleakest time of my life – pregnant, having the twins with my mother at the time, knowing the role that she had always played in the rearing of my children. I could not imagine what life was going to be like without her. Once again, the greatest pain was one of not being there to bury her and see where she lay. She was gone, never to see my baby this time. As I was pregnant, I had to remember that I was carrying a life. I should not upset myself to a point where it could affect the baby. Life goes on. In May of that year, I gave birth to a bouncing, healthy baby, born after all our parents had gone.

Swaziland had become home. No one could say we were in exile. Our family life went on. Joe had continued his political activities, assuming the role of the external representative of the PAC in Swaziland. The political situation in South Africa had always been our concern. By this time it was fairly quiet. The apartheid regime had managed to crush the resistance movement, with the imprisonment of Nelson Mandela, Sobukwe, the banning of the African National Congress (ANC) and the PAC.

We kept in touch with events at home. Even though our parents had passed on, we often had visits from relatives and friends. We bought newspapers, listened to the radio and were well informed about what was going on in apartheid South Africa.

It was three years later, in 1976, when the tables turned. Early on the evening of the 16 June 1976, as we were listening to the radio, we heard about the Soweto students' march against a brutal system that aimed to enforce the Afrikaans language. So great was the resistance of these young people that they were prepared to die for their freedom. Like their fathers, they were not prepared to endure the brutality of the apartheid state and accept the oppressive nature of the system. This was the beginning of another chapter in the liberation struggle of our country. When listening to the news that evening, little did I know that the events of 1976 would affect me personally.

As mentioned earlier, Joe was the PAC representative in Swaziland. As the events unfolded inside South Africa, many children were arrested or simply went missing. A renewed exodus from South Africa took place. This time it was not adults or newly weds like myself. It was children as young as thirteen years old, fleeing for their lives. News of comrades and fellow activists being arrested and dying in prisons swept the country and the neighbouring countries. While in Swaziland the floodgates opened and we witnessed the arrival of scores of young people fleeing South Africa.

By this time my children, Zanele and Thoko, were at boarding school. As Joe was the representative of one of the liberation movements, they had to receive these children pouring into the country. A decade earlier, they had also had to facilitate the documentation of young refugees from South Africa. Very little activity had happened in the decade. The PAC headquarters was in Dar es Salaam, Tanzania. The military wing of the organisation was based there. There was little anticipation that there would be such an upheaval inside the country. A lot of these children were so angry, their aim was to join the military wing of any of the liberation movements and learn how to shoot and kill. They were not interested in anything else.

Swaziland was a passage rather than a place of refuge. The country itself was not prepared to harbour insurgents and was therefore keen that their passage be facilitated to leave the country. It was in these days that I experienced the absence of Joe from the home. It was as if the struggle had started all over again. I would go for days not knowing where he was, as he was involved in a number of meetings, with comrades being sent into Swaziland from South Africa.

Inside South Africa a year later, Steven Bantu Biko was brutally murdered by the South African security police. Mr Samuel Malinga, a prominent member of the PAC, and several other people had been thrown from the thirteenth floor of John Vorster Square, the notorious South African police service building in Johannesburg. Okgopotse Tiro, a prominent member of the Black Consciousness Movement, who had fled into exile, was killed in Botswana after receiving a letter bomb. Zephania Mothopeng, who was the PAC president then, was going through a trial for mobilising the young children in 1976. The country was on fire, the resistance movement was building up.

Personally, the feeling of being unsafe was creeping up, as the South African government retaliated by bombing neighbouring states like Swaziland and targeting specific activists in those countries. We had suffered the loss of a family friend, Victor Mayisela, who went missing. Until today his whereabouts are not known. Duma, a personal friend, had received a letter bomb and had lost his arm. Robert Sobukwe was ailing, having been imprisoned by the South African government. He died on 27 February 1978. That year would also go down in history as the beginning of another chapter in my exile life.

Deportation

As I was sitting at home with the children early one evening, I received news that Joe and a number of PAC colleagues had been arrested by the Swaziland police. Their arrest was followed by deportation. This, for a lot of people, meant the risk of being sent back to South Africa or to another country that was prepared to accept you on humanitarian grounds.

The first thing that came to my mind was that I needed to ensure that this was known by the organisations that could assist with ensuring that they were not sent back to South Africa. Luckily, I remembered that Joe was in constant touch with Bishop Mandlenkosi Zwane of the Catholic church who had assisted a lot of people in a similar position.

I immediately went to him to seek help to get in touch with organisations like Amnesty International to bring this to their attention. Fortunately, we were able to get through to Amnesty International in London, which sought a reprieve with the Swaziland government. It accepted the deportations and requested that Joe and his colleagues were not sent back to South Africa, but be allowed to leave prison to seek political asylum in one of the countries where this was possible.

In 1963, when Joe arrived in Swaziland, it was still a British Protectorate. By the grace of God, Joe had applied for and received a British passport. When Swaziland gained its independence in 1968 and recalled its passports, he did not hand it over as he was not a Swazi citizen. He had always used his British passport to travel in and out of Swaziland. He had recently used this passport when travelling on a trip overseas as a representative of the Coca-Cola Bottling Company, where he worked full-time while serving the PAC in exile on a part-time basis.

When he was arrested, I was advised that, as he held a British passport and was a British citizen, I should inform the British embassy and seek asylum. The British government, while not prepared to accept this as a valid passport, nevertheless offered us political asylum on humanitarian grounds. This meant that we could leave the country for the United Kingdom where we would be accommodated as refugees.

Exile in the United Kingdom

In August 1978, while Joe was in prison, I once again packed my bags, sold the house, and uprooted the family to the United Kingdom. This time round, I was not pregnant. However, the journey was as unknown as the one I had made into Swaziland a decade earlier. This time I was not leaving anyone behind. My parents had passed on. I was with Joe and he would be at my side. The United Kingdom, as far away as it was from home, provided a lot of hope for me. I was being given an opportunity for a fresh start. My family was going to have a stable life. As painful as it was being so far away from South Africa, it was, however, very attractive. In 1978 we left Swaziland as a family. Joe was released straight from prison onto the flight.

On 31 August 1978, I arrived in London to a very cold climate, ready to write another chapter in my exiled life. At that moment, I really wondered when it was going to stop. Would I be on the move for the rest of my exiled life? Would we ever get back home? Would things in South Africa ever change? Or were we a nation that was going to be oppressed for the rest of our lives? These were the thoughts that went through my mind as I was ready to start another decade in exile.

It had been almost twenty years since I had made that journey from South Africa into exile in Swaziland. The passage of time had passed. We were now settled in the United Kingdom. As cold as the country was, the warmth of the British people in welcoming us as a family was felt from all angles. The children had all settled well and were progressing with their studies. Joe had once again made a decision to continue with his political activities and join his fellow comrades in Dar es Salaam and pursue the struggle for liberation.

I was safe, I was happy, I was settled and there were no threats. My eldest daughter, Thoko, was preparing to leave us for the United States to pursue her studies at Temple University. Zanele, whose birth I started this story with, was preparing to go to university to do a Bachelor of Education Honours degree in 1984. The young ones were still at school pursuing their high school education.

I personally had undertaken a Bachelor of Education degree. As I was studying, the children were also studying. South Africa was a country that existed in our distant past. We seldom kept in touch with home. Joe had settled in Tanzania very well. At this stage in my life, I had taken the decision that while other wives joined their husbands in the struggle, my struggle would be to take responsibility for rearing the children and creating a home that Joe would always come back to when the harsh realities of political life turned against him, as they so often did in our exiled lives.

Our deportation and departure from Swaziland had been attributed to factional fighting within the PAC, where the leader at the time, Potlako Leballo, had advised the Swaziland government about the risks of allowing a PAC base in Swaziland. Who was to say that would not occur again?

My understanding of the dedication that Joe had to the liberation of our country made me realise that I could not stand in his way. When I took the decision to follow him, unlike other wives who remained in South Africa, it was clear to me that it was a decision that meant I would support him and also adopt the cause of the liberation of our own people.

It was equally a challenging period in my life. I was in a foreign country with no relatives, five children to support and bring up on my own. The children were in their adolescent years, a time that was difficult for any parent. I had to be their mother, father, aunt, cousin, everything. They had nobody else but me. I had to be there for them – their triumphs, their joys and their pain. It was a period when my health was also failing me. However, I knew I had to be strong for them. I took early retirement and decided to be a full-time, stay-at-home mom. The children were a joy to have around. They were very supportive of each other and of me.

Joe would occasionally drop by when he was on his way to meetings in Geneva, India and New York. Even though absent, he remained as head of the household. The children knew that he was a phone call away if they misbehaved. During this time I had always taught my children about the beauty of my country, the warmth of its people and their suffering. Freedom may not come in our lifetime, I said. However, with the knowledge that I imparted to them, I knew they would never get lost. It was a decade of achievements. Both Thoko and Zanele graduated with their bachelor's degrees, while the twins and Busisiwe were also admitted to universities to pursue their degrees. The younger ones settled well in England. It was the only country they knew. They had very little recollection of any other country we had been exiled in.

The political situation in South Africa continued to be volatile. The 1980s was the bloodiest decade – the height of the resistance movement and the international campaign to enforce sanctions against the apartheid regime. It was a decade when there were a lot of false promises from the South African government, first with P.W. Botha's 'crossing the rubicon' speech which he gave on 15 August 1985, and with the establishment of the tricameral parliament in the same year. It was also in this decade that a number of high-profile activists were attacked. Dulcie September, an ANC activist, was killed by a parcel bomb in Paris. Joe was also a recipient of a parcel bomb in Tanzania. Luckily, he did not open it.

For me, the time spent in exile in England was a time of reflection on my life. I had always, questioned: Why me? Why am I here? I had always wondered what I would say when I looked back on my life. I had always wondered what my life would have been if I did not leave South Africa. I was convinced that it was for the better. Emotionally, I was strong. I could not depend on anyone except myself. The kind of education that my children had access to could not be swapped for anything. The sense of independence, being far away from relatives, friends and familiar ground definitely made me a better person. I regretted not having a stable married life as so often the upheavals of life in exile separated Joe and I.

My hope was that one day South Africa would be free, we would return home and I would pick up my life with Joe from where we left off. I could not remember a time when I could say there was stability in our lives.

The journey home

On 2 February 1990, I heard on the news that the South African government, through the then President F.W. de Klerk, would make a speech that would change South Africa forever. As usual, announcements from the South African government offered only false promises and were given publicity that they did not deserve. This time around we expected the same. However, one of the things that exile taught us was never to give up. On that early afternoon we tuned into the TV to hear De Klerk announce that he would release Nelson Mandela and all political prisoners, and unban the ANC and the PAC. It was unbelievable.

Indeed, on 11 February 1990, we were all glued to the television to witness what was going to be history, the release of Nelson Mandela. When I saw him walk out of prison I then believed that indeed the journey home had begun. I was so full of hope. It was also in this period that I felt very much alone as Zanele, Thoko and Themba had already explored the path of discovering the country of their birth.

It was in 1992 that I took the opportunity to visit South Africa for the first time in twenty-nine years of exile. By this time, most of the political activists had returned.

The Convention for a Democratic South Africa talks had taken place and the country was full of hope. We were heading for our first democratic elections in 1994. I was eager and looking forward to being part of that history, a much brighter history than the history I had endured in the thirty years that I was in exile. It was a return journey that began three decades earlier when I left South Africa to join my husband in Swaziland. I had mixed feelings. I did not know what to expect. I wondered whether I would still find my parents' home standing. Who would be there? Would I recognise the people I had left thirty years ago? What of my future life with Joe as we were all returning home, full of hope and triumph? When we look back, would we indeed say it was worth all the pain and the suffering?

As I reflect on my life in exile, I would say it was a life well lived. If you asked me if I would do it again: yes, I would. My only regrets were not being able to bury my parents and my siblings. When I returned home, I found that only my younger sister remained. But I thank God that I came back alive with Joe, who was my main reason for leaving a country that I so loved, my parents and all. I also came back with all the children we had given birth to along our difficult journey of exile.

The prodigal daughter

Lauretta Ngcobo

Lauretta Ngcobo was born in 1931 in rural KwaZulu-Natal, at Cabazi, a village within the Ixopo district. From a very young age, Lauretta was encouraged to read and experiment with writing and, through the determination of her widowed mother, obtained a B.A. degree and a teaching qualification at the University of Fort Hare in the 1950s. In the 1960s, Lauretta was forced to flee South Africa and enter political exile with her husband, Pan-Africanist Congress leader, A.B. Ngcobo, and her three small children. For six years, they moved from country to country living in Swaziland, Zambia and eventually arriving in England, where Lauretta was to stay for a further twenty-five years.

In exile, she wrote *Cross of Gold* (1981), a novel chronicling the Sharpeville upheaval of 1960, as well as *And They Didn't Die* (1990), recounting the experiences of rural African women under the migratory labour system and the South African political climate in the 1950s. She edited an anthology of black women writing in Britain, *Let It Be Told* (1987), and has also written a children's book, *Fiki Learns To Like Other People* (1994). Lauretta was the winner of the literary lifetime achievement award from the South African Department of Arts and Culture in 2006 and the winner of the Order of Ikhamanga from The Presidency of South Africa for excellent achievement in the field of literature in 2008. Currently, she has a home in Ulundi but lives mostly in Durban where she remains as determined as ever to hear and read other stories of women in exile.

It was a still night on 21 May 1963. I lay curled up in my bed feeling very lonely and cursing softly under my breath. I had just arrived at Sydenham in Durban from a fleeting journey from Umzimkhulu, my home village 300 kilometres away, where I left my two-year-old daughter, Nomkhosi, with my mother. She now had both my daughters. My six-year-old son was with my aunt on a kind of long-term, loose, adoption arrangement. Without my children, I felt depressed. A tear slid down the side of my face to my ear. I felt a sense of shame and recklessness. I swore there was a conspiracy of circumstance against me and my family.

Just as I was wondering why fate had it in for me, I heard a knock on the window. I froze and in an instant I guessed it was the police. What now?

'Who is it?'

'It's Oliver, Oliver Munyaradzi,' came the reply from my new cousin-in-law from Rhodesia (now Zimbabwe), attending medical school in Durban at the time. I was flushed with another wave of shame at my brusque manner.

'Please go around,' I said.

There were two of them at the door; I did not know the other man. Without ceremony I asked if Bongiwe, my cousin, was fine. She was. 'And the children?' Slowly, he answered that all was well. Then I stopped prodding him. In his own time he told me that my friend, Doris Pamla, was up on the hill waiting for me to come to talk to her. I asked no further questions because I had known she was quite ill at the time. I surmised it was something quite serious that would bring her out so far at night.

When Doris saw us in the dim light, she got out of the car and came to meet us. In one wave of her hand she showed the two young men into the car.

'Lauretta, have you been writing letters?' Doris asked quite abruptly.

'To whom?'

'To different people . . . to Mdletshe . . . to Khanyi?' I drew a blank.

'All I've ever done is pass on information from Pretoria prison . . . I didn't write anything down,' I added limply. I was breathing hard and I was genuine in my denial.

'Then how come they (the police) say they saw two of your letters at different places in their searches?'

Doris told me that a common friend of ours had spoken to a Special Branch operative who had told him that they were about to take me into custody because they had finally linked my writing to seditious material.

Needless to say, I did not sleep that night. Neither could I resolve what my next move would be the following day. I was expecting my husband, A.B. Ngcobo, to come out of jail in the next few weeks after serving his three-year prison sentence in Pretoria. He had been in different prisons ever since the Sharpeville massacre of 1960. Then, what malicious fate would throw me into jail just as he was getting out? What spiteful plot would conspire to have me leave my children and my husband into timeless exile? It was unthinkable.

The following day the sun came out at about 6 a.m. I was teaching at Chesterville Secondary School and got myself ready for the day. At 7 a.m., a thought came like a thunder clap. It hit me so hard; I wanted to jump out of the bus. 'Of course I must. There is no other way. If I stay, I'll go to prison. Then my children won't ever see me again. God knows what will happen to me there. If I leave the country today, somewhere, somehow, I stand a chance of meeting them all in some far-away country. A.B. might manage to ferry them all across the seas to me in some distant future. Besides, I had myself helped some people to cross the borders, why not me?' Things began to fall into place.

There was no money to travel; there was no time to fit in every thought and action. There were exams coming for my classes at school. I had not finished setting the papers. I would have to burn all those political papers that I had hidden in my cupboard or the police would confiscate them and arrest all those contacts. I could not tell my aunt who lived with my son. I could not say one last goodbye to my little boy, let alone those daughters away at Umzimkhulu with my mother. Oh, my mother, my sister, my husband! Not to mention my brother, Phuthuma, who lived with me at the time! The world was crumbling in on me.

At the end of the day, my cupboards were cleared, my papers burnt. The keys were left on the table in the staff room. One last thing remained to be done and that was to tell Doris about my decision. I needed to tell her because I would need her that night when I had to go to the station without detection. She hollered and screamed, attracting everybody's attention. I had to pretend it was all a joke to be laughed at. Tears in her eyes belied it all. I did not wait to satisfy their curiosity. We soon disappeared around the bus stop and the bus mercifully appeared just in time.

We rushed to the bank to get the money that had recently arrived from an overseas organisation intended for A.B.'s studies while in jail. A.B. Ngcobo, my husband, officially known as Abednego Bhekabantu Ngcobo, had been away in jail for political reasons all those three years. He had actively participated as an executive committee member of the Pan-Africanist Congress (PAC) and organised what would eventually result in the Sharpeville massacre in 1960.

I closed the account and we headed straight off for the train station to buy the ticket. I was heading for Swaziland. My in-laws had another home there and some members of the family also lived there. The destination of my ticket was Golela in the middle of nowhere on the border of Natal and Swaziland. At the time, there were no border controls between South Africa and Swaziland. I did not need a passport.

From the station, I went straight back home to Sydenham, our main family home. In those far-off days, my father-in-law had managed to acquire for himself the property which was right inside Durban, in spite of the laws and regulations prohibiting mixed residential areas. There were a few other families who shared part of the property.

Things were hectic. I was packing, choosing what was absolutely necessary for me to take with me on the most definitive journey of my life – away from home and all that I had known – while trying to appear that 'all was well' with me. I talked and laughed loudly with all I met at the water tap and hurriedly went in and out through my kitchen door and back again through the front door. I had to pretend I was cooking supper as always. To be honest, I could not control my own voice.

My brother, Phuthuma Gwina, shared the space with me. I was only too happy to have him with me in the absence of my husband. When I arrived home that day it was hard for me to look him in the eye. I could hoodwink them all, but not my brother. He sensed that all was not well.

It was getting dark. The suitcase was ready packed. How to take it out through the back door was the problem. I darted out fast and whisked it right behind the flower bushes at the end of the garden. Quickly I ran back to see if I had left anything of importance behind. At the right moment, I slipped out and I could see the car lights flashing at the top of the hill where Doris's car had stood the night before. Heaving my suitcase with all the energy I could marshall, I swung it on to the top of my head and ran into the darkness.

In spite of her poor health condition, Doris had come in person to take me to the station in her car that night. She had planned everything to the last detail. But not before she took me to Dr Sikose Mji, another friend of mine who was a medical doctor. A medical certificate was essential, putting me on sick leave so as to give me time to cross the border before the police would know that I had left the country. My absence from school would have been an early give-away. So, Sikose's timely medical certificate would delay the alert. She scribbled the note. That meant two of my friends were aware what was happening to me. No matter, they were both political animals.

I hid behind the shadows and pillars at the Durban railway station, as Doris moved quickly to post the medical certificate to the school. In whispers and gestures she took the suitcase and loaded it in the second-class compartment of that puffing steam engine. By 11 p.m. my heart was thumping so hard I felt nausea pushing up my throat. It was seven minutes past the hour when I felt a chug – a chug, chug, chug, chug, chug – somewhere deep down in my being. The train was finally moving out of the Durban station. Something in me wanted to scream for her to let me off.

At dawn I was nowhere near the border. In fact, I had only travelled less than a hundred kilometres from Durban. It was a bright early morning with a promise of a beautiful day, but instead I was struck with a sudden sinking feeling as I turned away from the window.

My mind flooded with fear and a wish that all the happenings of the night before were just a dream. Well, they were not. Soon we approached Empangeni railway station. The babbling voices of the market sellers rose and mingled with the screeching railway wheels as they trundled fast into the station. Suddenly I woke up to another world: women selling all kinds of food and fruit that Zululand is famous for. All this stirred my appetite as I had not eaten anything for over two days. I ate greedily. For reasons I cannot understand or remember, I bought and ate layers and layers of honeycombs that the women peddled so generously. I even bought a plate from one of them for convenience.

I went on eating senselessly long after the train had passed through the station. A long day lay ahead of me, and the slow steam train went sluggishly round hill after hill. We stopped at every curve and the scene at Empangeni was repeated every time. To make things worse, I did not even know what time the train would finally arrive at Golela – that unknown place that lies on the border between Zululand and Swaziland. Those were the days before there was a border post dividing these two countries. However, crossing that imaginary line would put me beyond the reaches of the South

African police. The sky was pale and infinite and I feared asking anyone for such details, lest I aroused any curiosity.

It was about 3 p.m. when I suddenly saw a number of policemen going up and down the little station. They were white. I could not for the life of me understand or explain what white policemen would be doing in such a remote area. In those days carriages were divided into first, second and third classes. I reasoned that they must have come from the first-class carriage, which was reserved for white people only. I was in a second-class coupé; I withdrew into a corner and tried to make myself invisible under a coat. All that could be seen was the beating of my heart. When we finally passed that station, I was sweating and feeling faint. I feared they had sounded an alarm from home.

After many years, I gathered that my sixth sense might have been right because early that morning, before my train rolled into Empangeni station, the South African police had come in their usual manner, knocking and banging at every window and door, back at my father-in-law's house in Durban. They had roused everyone and swore at every passing bird and bee, speeding up the hill with their dogs behind them. They had sped off in their cars, about seven of them, and had gone to the other side of town into the township of Lamontville where my aunt and uncle and my six-year-old son, Luyanda, lived. They raised hell throughout the whole neighbourhood; they tried everywhere they thought I might be between the hours of 11 p.m. and 5 a.m., the last time I had been seen the previous night.

We were to reach Golela at about 6 p.m. and Swaziland was just across. The railway station formed part of the border. As soon as the train stopped, I got my luggage out, which was substantial, and put it on the platform. I could not wait to see what help I could get to move it. I sped right across and headed for my friend's house on the other side of the station. Dr Zamindlela Conco was not only a political fugitive himself, but he originally came from my home area of Ixopo/Umzimkhulu. We knew each other from childhood. He had been involved in the 1956–1957 treason trial, same as A.B.

Once he understood my plight, he dispatched a couple of young men to rescue my entire luggage. It was when I saw my luggage arrive that I realised I had taken a journey of no return – a strange moment when I accepted that I had cut myself loose, yet did not know where I was headed, and a stabbing realisation that I had just left all that I valued in my entire life including my children, my mother, my job – and instead I faced emptiness ahead of me. And for how long?

A few days later, after passing through my in-law's home in Swaziland, I landed in a place called Manzini. There, too, through referrals, I was fortunate enough to be received by an old friend who was working there, Nomusa Mildred Mali. Although she was happy to see me, she asked me many questions about my future which I could not answer for I had no future that I could see ahead of me. For her, I posed a problem. But for me, I just felt relief that I had a bed to lie awake on and think of my husband. It was a matter of weeks before his release from prison in Pretoria.

A.B. had spent part of the previous three years with Robert Sobukwe, and was later joined by Nelson Mandela. It had been a surprise to see the threesome together and to realise how intertwined their lives had become despite the different pathways that politics had led them. They had been together in the African National Congress (ANC) Youth League through the late forties; by the end of the fifties they had parted ways when Robert Sobukwe and A.B. formed the PAC. There, in prison, they were as fellow captives who had shared much in politics and together had seen the dark clouds gather in the future of their country. Old friends, now wary of one another, yet tied together in prison deprivations and so forced to carry the pains like oxen in a span under the same yoke. Under the circumstances, the old friendship prevailed and helped them give support to each other and to acclimatise to the ways of prison life whenever they could.

The last time I went to see them, they were happy together. But soon in early May, Sobukwe had been removed to serve an indefinite sentence on Robben Island. I was petrified, fearing the same prospect for my husband.

One evening, my friend, Nomusa Mildred Mali, came close to me and quietly sat down as if afraid to disturb me and told me that the famous school for girls, St Michael's Secondary School, had just lost a matron for girls. I listened silently. She went on to ask if I would consider taking that position for the time being. 'Of course I would,' I replied with disbelief.

The next morning I started a new job at St Michael's, looking after the girls at the hostel. The school was run by Anglicans and the boarders were girls mainly from South Africa on their own journey of escape from Bantu Education in South Africa. The school was staffed by mainly white nuns from England. The pastor was a white man by the name of Reverend Hooper. I had known him in political circles back in South Africa. Sadly, we did not belong to the same political organisation and he made me feel it. There were two other more fortunate black South African women teachers on the staff. They were on the right side of Reverend Hooper. As for the nuns, they were quite genial.

I settled comfortably in a place that afforded me a space to live, food to eat and even the good company of young girls to look after. I lacked for nothing personally, barring the haunting thoughts of home. But then nobody could set me free from the new path I had chosen. This was a time when South African refugees were pouring in. There were among them a lot of young men who I did not know, but I knew they were starving. They hung around the shops in Manzini. Some of them used to hover around the Manzini Hotel where they waited for scoops of food from the kitchen there. But my greatest concern was for the young wives of some of these men who had arrived with young children.

In an act of compassion a young nun, Sister Dlamini, based at another Catholic school, St Theresa's, took in about ten of those young mothers and children and accommodated them in a very large hut right in the middle of the school complex. Thank goodness the authorities at St Theresa's turned a blind eye and allowed her mission of mercy to continue. On the other hand, the girls at St Michael's School where I landed came mainly from comfortable homes in places like Johannesburg. I don't know if it explains why they ate so little, but a lot of the good food went into the bin, for many girls received food supplementation from home. After talking to them about the plight of our fellow South Africans, they were good enough to save neatly what they did not want to eat. I took those leftovers and darted a good distance to St Theresa's where the women lived. Needless to say, it was very much appreciated.

I was at St Michael's barely three months but, in that situation, time seemed long. Every hour held its own surprises and one tossed from event to event. One morning I woke up to the news that two South African white Jewish politicians had escaped from prison in South Africa and had found their way to Swaziland. It was even more alarming when in a few hours, I heard from the grapevine that they were actually somewhere within St Michael's School. The place was abuzz, in hushed tones, with the news. The pair was hiding in the same sanctuary that I was in, under the wing of Father Hooper! But, if the truth must be spoken, I never actually saw them myself. After a few days they were gone. Father Hooper had sheltered them successfully.

Then one day, in the midst of confusion, quite out of the blue, I saw a car come in and out of it came A.B., my husband. It was another moment of unspeakable excitement. I had guessed that he would have been out of prison by then. According to our calculations, it would be around 8 June. But that date had come and gone and I had heard nothing. I assumed the worst. By 16 June still nothing was stirring in the air. I feared he might have been sent to Robben Island, such as had happened to his friend, Sobukwe, in early May, a few weeks before. I also wondered whether the authorities had extended his sentence. I spent long, sleepless nights juggling with the possibilities. But then, in that great moment of joy, he was standing right before me, after three years of imprisonment. Stephen Mahlangu, an old friend, had risked everything to get him safely out of South Africa. News had reached them in Johannesburg that the police were spending days and nights around A.B.'s home in Durban watching out for his return. Mahlangu and other friends waited for him the day he came out of prison and they had whisked him away into hiding. That had been about ten days earlier. Needless to say, the day of his arrival was one of the happiest days of my life.

But there were immediate problems to be solved. There was nowhere for him to live, not even for that first night. I quickly approached Sister Prudence who was in charge of the establishment to show her the urgency of my family situation. I put my case to her, but when I saw her reluctance to let him use what seemed like an unused spare shack I knew there was no way. She was flushed with reluctance all over her face and said that the room was too close to the convent, even though it was well outside the perimeter of the convent. I tried twice to show her the urgency of our situation. As for my room, it was 'out of the question'; it was within the precincts of the girls' dormitory. She wouldn't hear of it. I then turned to the other male refugees who lived about five to seven miles away, on the other side of town, without transport. He would walk the distance and come to see me by day when I was at work. Now and again he would stealthily come over on some nights for us to get some private time. But even then the gossip did go round that he had been seen late at night, leaving me with an awful sense of shame, as though I had been caught tarnishing the good name of the institution.

In the old days in South Africa I had belonged to the worldwide Young Women's Christian Association (YWCA). Nomsa, who was already well settled in Swaziland, had been one of our leaders back then. So, one day she came to me and suggested that I write to the local chapter of the organisation and request assistance on behalf of all the refugee women in Swaziland. The local organisation would present our request and explain our destitution to the world body. Unfortunately, the idea was simply not acceptable to the local chapter, more so by the South African members who were already settled in Swaziland, working as teachers and nurses and other professionals. They had become active members of the Swaziland chapter of the YWCA and they swayed it against us.

A few days later, right at the bus stop where we stood to board the bus to Stegi on our way to the YWCA conference, I could feel the chilly wind of rejection. There were many South Africans in the crowd, but they were not prepared to support our request, nor even to talk to me. It was bitter to be among my fellow South Africans standing on foreign land and them displaying utter hostility. What for? I asked myself without answers. After all, they themselves had landed there begging for jobs because of the unbearable conditions at home. I could only conclude that they were reluctant to be identified with the riff-raff crowds that we had become. The experience was bitter and unforgettable. Needless to say, the appeal to the YWCA died a natural death because fellow South Africans had disowned us publicly.

Swept by the tide

Before I knew which way the tide of life was taking me, A.B. told me that an urgent message had reached them from Europe to say he and Jacob D. Nyaose – another executive committee member – and three other members from the Unity Movement were going to be picked up by chartered flight out of Swaziland through Mozambique to Dar es Salaam in Tanzania.

In the few weeks after my escape from South Africa, the border between South Africa and Swaziland was closed so there was no longer any possibility of escape from Swaziland to anywhere without trespassing over South African skies or land. But at the time, the Portuguese who ruled Mozambique were close allies of South Africa. For these reasons, I could not see how they could leave Swaziland by chartered plane. The PAC had always been a Cinderella organisation among South African exiles, but they were getting a lift from the Unity Movement who seemed better funded by their friends in the worldwide Trotskyite movement who could afford such flights.

So, on about 5 August, a very windy day, A.B. and the others left Swaziland at dawn via Mozambique. At the time, it felt like that was our final parting in our known world. In a very symbolic way, a very powerful, gusty wind broke the hostel doors wide open. I heard the noisy rush of the wind whooshing in and it felt like I was standing on the abyss, in a void. I didn't know whether to rush out to save A.B. from that wind storm. That was a futile thought. A.B. left.

I soon discovered that I was pregnant with Zikethiwe, our third daughter. Being pregnant with her was not easy. Everything added to a difficult pregnancy. By that time, I had moved to another school called St Joseph's Secondary School. It was headed by a young Catholic priest called Father Ciccone. He was always there deeply involved in the lives of everyone in the school, ready to help, right up to the night when my baby played games with me. It was a very wet night and I truly believed she was coming before dawn. Only it was a false alarm. By morning she postponed her arrival. After that day I decided to go to Manzini so that I would be nearer the hospital whenever she chose to come. I went and stayed with my friends, Judith and Joseph Mkhwanazi. I had been at school with Joseph when we were young.

They were now members of the PAC like us. When many of our members left, the responsibility of looking after their young wives and children was left with the remaining members. So they took the responsibility of looking after me as well. It was very generous of them, but they had just enough room for their one bed, leaving about one foot on each side of the wall. They insisted that I occupy the same bed as they did. It was Joseph on the right, Judith in the middle and me on the left. Talk about inconvenience on their part and embarrassment on my part! At first I thought it would last only for a couple of days.

As it turned out, it took about three weeks before Kethiwe would change that. I was very big. My belly literally used to hang off the side of the bed. There was no room even to turn round. As if to spite us, false alarms occurred night after night for all those three weeks. Kethi just would not come despite the doctor's predictions. It was pretty awful with me sliding out of bed during those frequent visits to the bathroom. Besides, I had never thought of a couple sharing their marriage bed with a third party for three weeks. But I was yet to learn the impositions of exile life. Years later, I heard that it had not been the last time that the Mkhwanazis had extended similar facilities to another friend in similar circumstances. If I have not had time over the years to sing praises to the whole world about this one couple for their generosity, then I have not shown my gratitude.

In the early hours of 6 April 1964, I could feel that it was like no other morning that had preceded it. In the silence of the morning, there I was tip-toeing to the bathroom. I heard Joseph asking 'How is it, my friend?' I faltered but could not hide my tearful voice. 'I do think this is the day, Joe.' At first I was not sure what he was up to. He jumped out of bed, put on his coat and, as he closed the door, he looked back and told us that he was going to pick up our other friend, Motsoko Pheko, who lived a short distance away. He was another member of the PAC who had been entrusted with the shared responsibility of 'looking after us', the young wives who were left behind when the men left for far-away countries. It was still dark outside and in a flick of the moment I woke up to the fact that I really was going to have my baby. They were faithful to their immense task for there were at least ten young women, some with very young babies scattered in every squatter camp all over Manzini and needing all kinds of attention.

We arrived at the hospital just after 5 a.m. I was rushed in immediately and I did not even get time to say goodbye to Joe and Pheko. But by 9 a.m. the pains were gone. I was afraid it was another false alarm. A while later the nurse came in with a bottle of castor oil. How I hated castor oil and all the fiddling that goes with labour. After that, Kethiwe lay peacefully in my belly for hours. Nothing moved. Right through the day, heavy, heaving women came in one by one and in an hour or so I would hear a baby cry. It was all over for them. I was beginning to feel tearful when the evening shift of nurses came in for night duty. My supper stayed untouched beside my bed.

Then, I turned once and I felt an overwhelming somersault in the pit of my body. Kethiwe's birth was the most difficult of all my children. That was the start of a long protracted labour. The nurses whizzed by fast, passing me by like I was part of the furniture. I was in agony. When things began to calm down in the ward the nurses came to my bedside and showed me a bell. 'If you think the baby is coming ring this bell and we'll come and attend to you.'

Hours ticked by and the crescendo of pain rose to unbearable heights. I had never suffered so much neglect in my childbearing experience. Then I let out a scream. I don't know where that came from for I was so faint I thought I was dying. It was exactly midnight. That brought a sudden flurry of activity as the nurses came rushing with confused instructions, some telling me off for not calling them earlier, others screaming for me to hold my breath. I was not listening to them anymore. Finally she came. She lay there, the smallest baby I had ever had and she did not even cry. Then the panic started. They were trying to help her to come to life, to catch her first breath. At that point I was beyond feeling. But in the end we both survived.

The next day, Joe and Pheko came to see me. It was strange for me to be visited at such a time by men friends and no other, not even any member of the family.

Grateful as I was, this experience drove it straight into my mind what exile really meant. I could not even recount to any other woman what a time I had had bringing Kethiwe into the world.

The next day, still in hospital, Father Ciccone came. I was happy to see him and he came straight to my bedside and, in his usual effusive way, he picked the baby up and swung her round once or twice, talking to her and, in the same breath, asking me, 'What's her name? What's her name?' For a brief moment I was quiet for suddenly I was not so sure he would like the name. Then I answered, 'She's called Badingile'. He stopped swinging about and asked furiously, 'What do you mean? This child is not exiled. She is loved and she belongs. She's open to the world. When I come back tomorrow I want you to have changed that name. Give her a name that opens the world to her.' And indeed I gave her the name Zikethiwe (the chosen one).

Soon after that, I was back at the school, the only place I could call home. It was not so comfortable being back at school in that poky little room with the other teachers in the adjoining rooms close by.

My mother had finally succeeded in coming over with the children at Christmas. She brought all three of them, my son, Luyanda, whom I had left with my mother's sister in Durban; my first daughter, Zabantu; and Nomkhosi, our second daughter. They came to find our new-born daughter, Zikethiwe. The family was overflowing with love and laughter. But towards the end of her month-long visit the house that had been so full of joy when she first came slowly changed. Mother grew quieter. She became more subdued. We could no longer hide our inner struggles, a time of pain and joy – truly indescribable when we first met after my escape from South Africa – but getting silently mixed with great foreboding. My mother dreaded the thought of me following A.B. beyond her reach. It was a time of very strong mental conflict for both of us, more on her part. She left with Luyanda who was virtually adopted by my aunt.

The baby would cry at night and I would be conscious of being of nuisance value. I will never know whether the other teachers complained or not but one day, Father Ciccone, out of the goodness of his heart, I'd like to believe, thought it good to build a separate shack from the other teachers to accommodate me and the children. The older school boys built the shack.

Then, a day after finishing the shack, one of the most terrifying electric storms in living memory struck. The children clung to me for dear life. Suddenly, in one big heave the whole structure fell down all around us. We sat down and watched the criss-cross dance of the lightening in the sky. For a moment the children held their breath, only to resume the loud chorus of their cries in that night of magic. I was left spellbound and could not explain to my five-year-old and my three-year-old exactly what had overtaken us. In the end, I left them alone with the baby in the dripping wet night sitting on the soggy beds. I had to go and find help from Father Ciccone and the rest of the community of nuns and students.

In the middle of the night a group of young hostel girls were woken up from their sleep and came along with me to pack up the children and the wet belongings against the unrelenting storm and take us back to their hostel. I will never forget the wonderful spirit of that small Catholic institution. It flowed straight from the head of the institution himself, Father Ciccone. Even though that night constitutes one of the most memorable days of my exiled life, it also remains a beacon of goodness shown to me in my long, dark years of exile.

Days went by and soon I was busy again running hither and thither. We had planned that I should soon find my way to Lusaka in Zambia or Dar es Salaam in Tanzania to unite our family at last. So we hoped. The possibility of travelling by car to Lourenzo Marques (Maputo) in Mozambique presented serious challenges. But we thought we should risk it anyhow. The date of our departure had been fixed for 17 January 1965.

What with the rush to get the yellow fever injections, suffice it to say I was very tired. I washed, I cooked, I ironed; I even went to the doctor at Mbabane, forty miles away with the baby on my back and the other two on the road. I must mention that the baby was teething. I was feeling even more ill. So in the middle of all those exertions I simply had to see the doctor.

At last, the trunk was fully packed. There remained one very important thing to do. All the calls that had been made to confirm the bookings at Lourenzo Marques remained unanswered. The line had been damaged by storms. On 16 January, I still had to go to town to make sure about my bookings from Lourenzo Marques (famously known at the time as LM) to Lusaka. Although I had feared a last-minute hitch, I had really never doubted that I would be booked through. But there I was at 12 noon on the day before my departure, with hardly a blanket in the house, without bookings for a flight from Maputo to Lusaka. From seasoned travellers, I got it that the planes from LM to Salisbury (in the former Rhodesia), through to Lusaka were seldom full. So I decided to risk it. After failing to contact LM, I rushed in that drizzle to see Joseph Mkhwanazi who was due to drive us to LM the following day. I did not find him in. I was desperate. But the Sililos came and drove us to the border. So on 17 January, we said our goodbyes to Father Ciccone and all the nuns and students and set out for the border gate at Kwanomahasha.

That drive brought a confluence of pain and joy. All along the way I was silent in the middle of all the chattering, happy voices of adults and children. I was looking back on my life, drifting back to my past and yet racing fast to a future I did not know. It was hard to believe that things had been so different only a month before, on 7 January, to be precise, when mother had left. I had been so full of life, hope and joy. I had obtained a passport – the document that meant all to me. I could still recall how I had literally scampered out of that Swaziland Home Affairs office. It was as if everything had been accomplished. Then, there was the day when again all my mother's fears were allayed for we got news that the air tickets had been successfully transferred from South African Airways in Johannesburg to Lourenzo Marques.

I suddenly woke up from my reverie when we finally got to the border post and passed from the Swazi side with some trumped-up excitement on my part. No problems there. That lasted a short kilometre. The story at the Portuguese border was very different. They looked at our papers once and brought our notice to the fact that there was no visa allowing us to go through Mozambique. In surprise, we took back our papers and raced back to the Swazi border.

The official on the Swazi side apologised profusely and immediately contacted the British High Commissioner, Mr Mike Fairley, who then authorised him to endorse the passport including the visa. At the time, Swaziland was a British Protectorate. Once more, in high spirits we ran back to the Portuguese post again hoping for a quick clearance. But instead we found a very remarkable change in the whole atmosphere. With that cold-cutting, immovable voice they waved us back, 'Come Swaziland, your husband fighting South Africa, come Swaziland'. At first I faked misunderstanding.

'Me not going to Swaziland, me going to Zambia,' I said showing him my plane ticket.

'Come, come Swaziland,' he repeated now full of anger and threatening gestures.

As we turned back, I wondered where we were going back to. I had said my goodbyes at St Joseph's that morning and that 'home' was gone. Yes, we indeed came back to Swaziland. We also had no place to sleep that night because I had been told that someone else was moving into our shack that very day. With my eyes full of tears, I looked into the eyes of Tom Sililo and he looked away into Marie's eyes. There was silence all the way as we drove back. I puzzled what they were thinking. As they turned towards their house I had the urge to scream and stop them for no family can be expected to inherit a family of four in an instant, with no foreseeable alternative plan. Without a word they took us in. Silently, they took our bags into their house. Their children quietly made room for us and piled into another room. I looked at my troop of many children. I looked again at my Zikethiwe and wondered how big that bundle of nine months had grown to be. We were a true army of invasion as we filled the house.

On the next day, 18 January, Joseph Mkhwanazi and I went to see the British High Commissioner to report the new developments. Mr Mike Fairley then advised us to take a charter flight and go through Johannesburg – and oh, how easily everything seemed fixed up. The right stamp in the right place. To follow on the suggestion of the High Commissioner to go through Johannesburg, we then chartered a plane for Wednesday, 20 January. On that day, we were waiting with Joseph Mkhwanazi at the little Matsapha airstrip. The little airplane soon landed and once more, full of excitement, we said our goodbyes. We boarded the plane. But just as it began to move, a hand appeared from the tower waving him to stop. Moments later, he opened our door and whispered to me that I should get down with the children. More than the shock and utter confusion, for me it was the ear-splitting screams from the children that have remained painfully lodged in my mind. None of us could believe it.

There was the explanation to be given to the children. Those who have not had to make empty but essential explanations to the young minds may not realise what a heavy side of the story this is. They knew no difficulty that could stand between them and their 'legendary' father. I had to make the impossible real to young people who didn't know the reality – how could a Portuguese stand between them and Baba for whom they had waited for so long to see?

Then I had to wait for several days for another try to get through to catch the next plane from LM to Lusaka. But we still needed to get to LM. The possibility of travelling by car back through Mozambique had already been discounted. Yet even at that point for me it still remained the only option left. We still had several days before we could make another attempt.

To make sure that there would be no more border incidents, we decided that we should charter a small plane, from Swazi Air to LM, even though it was expensive. On Friday, 22 January, we paid half the fare but had to go back in the afternoon of the same day to fix up an extra passenger (either Tom or Marie) to accompany us to LM.

It was on that afternoon visit to the office that I learnt for the first time that there was no way of escaping the border incidents for the plane would still touch down at Stegi for immigration clearances. The Portuguese immigration officers would be there. So that whole evening, we worried about a way out of the agreement between me and Swazi Air. We found a simple way out and on Saturday, determined as ever, we set out with Tom to the office on 23 January.

We need not have worried about finding them in the office on a Saturday. But we got more than we bargained for. We were told that we could not be airlifted by Swazi Air anyway for their headquarters in Johannesburg had refused permission. There were no questions to be asked or answered. The matter was crisp and finished just like that. They were to refund our money. We left that office feeling dazed. For the rest of that day, I felt and was told by my small circle of friends that there was no use attempting the trip. I saw this with my mind, but never with my heart. I could not tell my heart to give it all up.

That night I never did sleep a wink. At dawn, I was so tense, I was near breaking point. I knew I had to go and see for myself if they would refuse me permission to cross. I woke up early. How I wanted to cry and ease my soul, but not a tear came to moisten the dry sharp pain in the throbbing throat.

On Sunday, 24 January, at 8.10 a.m., hoping to catch the LM-to-Lusaka scheduled plane, I broke into Tom and Marie's bedroom and asked if they could arrest him as well if he took me to the border. I was ready for anything – even for an arrest. I

Brigalia Bam raised the plight of African people under apartheid in
South Africa for all the world to see and know (photo by Rogan Ward /
Independent Contributors / Africa Media Online).

Barbara Bell (right) at the Solomon Mahlangu Freedom College in 1982, with
husband Terry (left), O.R. Tambo (centre), secondary school principal Tim Maseko
(right) and some of the students on the steps of the primary school (photo by the
late Eli Weinberg).

Nomvo Booi in combat gear (photo supplied).

Nomvo Booi (far right) at a meeting with (from left) Mfanasekhaya Gqobose, Clarence Makwethu, Johnson Mlambo and Joe Mkhwanazi in a Pan-Africanist Congress executive meeting back in South Africa (photo supplied).

Busi Chaane touching a hollyhock plant
in autumn in Lauretta Ngcobo's front garden
in Hither Green, London (photo supplied).

Busi Chaane with her mother Thokozile in
Zambia (photo supplied).

Busi Chaane at her wedding back in South Africa
with her mother Thokozile and daughter Naledi
(photo supplied).

Thokozile Chaane (left), her husband George and her sister Bethukile (right) with Lauretta
Ngcobo back in South Africa in 2006 (photo supplied).

Ruth Carneson (photo supplied).

Artworks by Ruth Carneson (photos supplied).

Carmel Chetty reuniting with her mother on
2 January 1983 after leaving home in 1974
(photos supplied).

On the same day, Carmel Chetty relaxing with her husband Roy and her mother at their home in
Gaborone. Carmel is pregnant with her son Krish (photo supplied).

Mathabo Kunene (photo supplied).

Mathabo Kunene in her wedding gown (photo supplied).

Mathabo and Mazisi Kunene starting a new life together (photo supplied).

Baleka Mbete (photo by David Goldblatt /
South Photographs / Africa Media Online).

Baleka Mbete – ever committed to the struggle for liberation of her country and
people (photo supplied).

Judith Mkhwanazi on her wedding day
(photo supplied).

Judith Mkhwanazi – always happy and
accepting (photo supplied).

Judith and Joe Mkhwanazi and family in the United Kingdom, safe at last (photo supplied).

Lauretta Ngcobo at a writers' conference in Milan,
Italy, in 1987 (photo supplied).

Lauretta Ngcobo at home in Hither Green, London, in 1981. She never stopped yearning to
return to South Africa one day (photo supplied).

Lauretta Ngcobo with her class of seven-year-old children from many parts of the world at Larkhall, London, in 1985 (photo supplied).

AnnMarie Wolpe in Cape Town (photo by Sue Kramer).

Gonda Perez (photo supplied).

Gonda Perez with Thami Sindelo (left), chief representative of the ANC, and O.R. Tambo in Algeria in 1981 (photo supplied).

Rajes Pillay at her graduation from Durban
University of Technology on her return to
South Africa (photo supplied).

The Student Representative Council of 1966–67 at the University of Natal, Warwick
Avenue. Back, from left: Dr Soni, Paul David, Steve Bantu Biko, Sathia M. Naidoo,
P. Juggath, K.S. Govender. Front, from left: Steve Ramasuhva, Ben Ngubane, Rogeres
Ragavan, Rajes Pillay, Jonny Moseneke (photo supplied).

Ellen and Motsoko Pheko at the beginning of exile life,
wondering what the future holds for them (photo supplied).

Ellen Pheko back in South Africa with her granddaughter Mokhantso – happy
together in their new life (photo supplied).

Mohau, Mamello and Liepollo Lebohang Pheko – the three Pheko sisters (photo supplied).

Elizabeth Trew back in South Africa (photo supplied).

Elizabeth Trew with her husband Tony in Oxford in 1965 (photo supplied).

An anti-apartheid rally Elizabeth Trew took part in with 100 000 people. It was addressed by O.R. Tambo at Trafalgar Square in 1985 (photo supplied).

argued that seeing that there was no definite charge against me, I would get a quick release. I had planned it all at night. I was so desperate that my friends did not attempt to stand in my way for they felt it would have been useless anyway.

After finding Joseph Mkhwanazi, we all set out at 10.20 a.m. for the border at Mhlumeni this time, and not Nomahasha. Tom drove very, very fast, to get to the border before noon when they would close for lunch. We got to the border at 11.55 a.m. and we felt we did not want to exasperate them. We waited for 1 p.m.

At 12.50 p.m., we drifted to the border. But, even the dreaded moment of death does come. I walked into the immigration office on the Portuguese side literally shaking. Yet, strangely enough, the atmosphere around me remained calm, crisp and business-like. Without any effort they stamped my passport '*Entratta*' and I got through. Back in the car, I was praying, and not believing that everything had gone so smoothly. But Tom was still inside, fixing his own papers. Three minutes later, he came out, but I knew instantly that all my hopes had been dashed for he came to my side of the car and whispered in an unintentionally hoarse voice, 'We are going back, come and hear, for they wish to explain. Don't fear them, these are very polite.'

Back in the immigration offices, I was called into a private office where the chief officer started loading his revolver while he waited for the interpreter, so I presumed. Right through that interview, the revolver stayed in his hand being loaded and later pointing at me. It was explained briefly that because of my husband's 'crimes', whether committed in Durban or anywhere in the world, I could not be allowed to cross to Mozambique. Those were instructions from some office in LM.

Once we were outside on the veranda, they demanded my entire luggage and they proceeded to search for whatever. We began hoping for we felt at last they were taking us through. But at the end of it all they still told us 'Impossible', even though they had found no papers.

Back to Swaziland we came. I was no different from a sleepwalker. I felt the whole thing was grossly unfair on the Sililos – Tom and Marie and their children. Here were friends who had originally agreed to take me to LM for a nominal fee, who later found themselves bundled with a family of four (and believe me, children are a terrible class of people to invade any household). In that paralysed blankness, I knew I was not completely dead emotionally and mentally for I still felt this gross unfairness on the Sililos so keenly and with a deep sense of shame.

Now I had to write to the Secretary for External Affairs and Labour in Swaziland and retell my story officially – begging for his assistance in paving my way through the South African Republic – and thereafter it was waiting. I just had to learn to wait.

On Monday, 25 January, filled with a sense of defeat and weariness, I walked back into the Swazi Air office. Tom had forced me to go and find out if they would still refuse me chartering through South Africa instead of Mocambique. I was very reluctant, but my position left no place for likes and dislikes and pride. I had to do any and every possible thing if it promised even the remotest hope of success. Well, one thing I found out in my trouble is that the least expected is what almost always seems to happen. I was most surprised when, on that visit, the lady discussed the matter as though it was quite a possibility and promised to find out from her boss the next day.

Well, for the third time, I hired a plane. This time to take me over South African skies into Jan Smuts Airport in Johannesburg, and the air company allowed me. Remember, twice I had tried before and once, I had been jettisoned from a plane already taxiing on the runway.

Afterwards, the explanation was that the Swaziland administration, as a British protected territory, intervened with the South Africans and they had given their special permission to let me fly over South Africa with the children. Unbelievable! This issue had become an international issue for, just a little while before, the South African government had allowed the wives of two white political prisoners, who had escaped from prison and were in hiding in Swaziland, to fly out over South African skies in order for the wives to join their husbands in some other country. So Mr Mike Fairley as the British representative apparently managed to reach a compromise with the South African side. That is how I was finally allowed to fly over South Africa through Johannesburg on my way out to Lusaka. It was argued that Johannesburg airport was international space and not South African soil. While I remained within the precincts of that airport I would be guaranteed safety.

Our little chartered plane left Matsapha airstrip on Thursday, 28 January, and arrived at Jan Smuts Airport, Johannesburg, in good time and we checked in and waited for a few hours for our flight to Lusaka in Zambia.

However, also true to their nature, there was one last indignity that they had saved up for me before I left for Lusaka. Late in the afternoon the plane from Lusaka arrived and, like all the other passengers, I took my little troop and fell into line waiting to board the plane.

I was a few paces away from the door of the plane when suddenly I felt a grasp on my arm. It was a policeman. He pulled me over and the children followed us. I knew this was it. He took me behind a building that was under construction. When I turned round there was another man following behind us pushing my suitcase, the one I had checked in earlier. Fear and sweat was coming through every pore of my skin. Kethiwe, in my arms, tensed up and began to scream as always when she sensed my own change of emotions. They turned everything in the suitcase inside out, dumping it on the dusty construction rubble much like the Portuguese had done a few days before. I saw the children's clothes that I had washed and ironed so carefully just the day before. They were trashed and covered in dust. Then they stood up and looked at me straight. There were no words. Still rocking my baby I turned round and walked back to the plane with my other two following behind me. Back in the plane, I sat wondering if my case was still lying on the dusty floor or what they had decided to do with it.

The searing years of exile

After the relatively short flight and the relief it brought me, I stood on Zambian ground not believing what had been accomplished. If I had not been so preoccupied with the events of the moment, I would have raised a prayer, but that, too, was short-lived. As I moved forward I looked up and saw a pair of eyes that glared down at me in anticipation of something that I should have given him. I fidgeted and looked for my passport. He flicked through it once and looked back at me again. I looked back at him without comprehending. 'Your visa?' he asked with some anger.

Coming from South Africa and never having travelled anywhere outside that country before, I had no idea what a visa was. Nobody had ever mentioned that word to me before. Looking back, I winced with embarrassment, to think that at that age I could have been so ignorant. I saw his face turn red and he looked the other way. I believe he was angry with me or perhaps with a whole load of us. Zambia had just attained her freedom a month earlier, and the Sharpeville massacre in South Africa earlier had sent all of us helter-skelter in all directions of the globe. We all saw the newly independent African countries as our only refuge. I suspected that I was neither the first nor the only fool to stand before the exasperated Englishman.

He sat me down and was heard to murmur that had it not been for the children he would have sent me back to South Africa on the next flight. I sat patiently at the Lusaka airport while they went out to look for Mr Lesley Masimini. Masimini? Who was he? Well after midnight, he came to pick us up from the Lusaka airport. In Zambia at last! He was the PAC leader, one of the South African political party representatives. From that time on, we were left with him together with many others in his care. We were 'safe' at last.

Safe in our new life of exile – it was a four-roomed house which was home to many men, women and children. There was a constant flow of people going in and out. At night bodies lay sprawled on the floor of every corner of that house. At meal times, one saw voracious hunger at its worst. If one did not take good care that the children were provided for separately and in their own time, they would have starved. It was every man for himself and God for us all. I still cannot understand where Masimini and the other leaders got the food. The truth is that the food was inadequate, but we didn't starve. I now believe the food was supplied by the office of the United Nations. Needless to say, the people who bore the brunt of cooking, morning, noon and night, were the mothers of young children.

What irked me most of all was finding that while I dilly-dallied in Swaziland all those months earlier, A.B. had waited for us in Lusaka. Unfortunately, in the end he had had to be sent on some errand overseas. In those days, there was very little communication between South Africa and other African countries. It took weeks, even months, for letters to come, if they came at all. Political priorities always came first. I believe A.B. had gone to the United Nations. So it seemed to me, and no doubt to the children as well, that I was chasing an illusive shadow. Now that I was not so preoccupied with fear and anxiety I began to feel pain – pain that I had stifled over a very long period of time.

It stretched right back to the time when I carried Nomkhosi, our second-born, and A.B. was in jail just before she was born. In fact, a couple of days before she arrived, he came out of jail. In those two days a letter from the 'underground' had come directing him to report to the headquarters of the organisation in Johannesburg forthwith. Needless to say, he left and I faced Nomkhosi's birth alone. And by dawn of the next day, Nomkhosi was on her way at McCords Hospital in Durban. I had left my mother in the house to look after our older daughter, Zabantu.

By the time she came to see me in hospital that morning, she told me that she had not slept because the police had paced up and down and round and round the house beaming their lights through the windows. My mother threatened to leave my home for she was scared. Our friends, A.V. Shange and W.J. Ndlela, both offered to go and spend the night with my mother. So, two days later, with Khosi in my arms, I left the hospital in the company of Ndlela and Shange. We headed for the offices of Mr Swart, a sympathetic, progressive white lawyer who was persuaded to issue an interdict for free to stop the police from harassing us. Five days later, A.B. was arrested and tried in court for the second time. In those days I did not even care what for. This was 1960 still.

Five years later, we had raced round the continent and yet we had still not caught up with him. That's because from our meeting in court he had gone straight back to jail again. Now we were in Zambia and I had no answers left to explain the vain chase to the children.

Fortunately for me, in the middle of all this, we were lucky enough to be offered the opportunity to stay in one family house and to look after it while the owners went on holiday for a month. The house belonged to Dr Mogadime and his wife, Goody. I had known them in South Africa before.

On one or two occasions, Masimini came to see me and to tell me that he had made an appointment for me to see the education department so that I could apply for a job. The second time he came to tell me that he had been offered by various departments a few more houses to accommodate the many families that had recently arrived as refugees. He had chosen to give my family one of those houses. I need not explain what relief and joy this gave me. Soon after I moved into the bare house, A.B. arrived from his long absence. He was a stranger to our children. That meeting was marked by silence and coyness as though we were all playing hide and seek. As for him and me, we had these plastered smiles on our faces as we tried so hard to help the children to accept that we were friends, indeed more than friends. We hugged and kissed, all to no avail. When they saw him going into our bedroom after saying goodnight to them, they came scurrying to me whispering that he was lying on my bed. I was at my wit's end for it seemed clear to me that I had totally failed in explaining to them what being a dad means. We were reduced to gentle touches and smiles. What I could not understand was why they behaved like that when they had mixed with a lot of men, such as I have related throughout this story. They had never shown this display of coyness before. Zabantu was six. As for Nomkhosi, it was their first encounter in all her five years.

To be honest with you, A.B. himself behaved most awkwardly. He did his best, but it showed that he had no words for the children. He picked them up and tickled their cheeks and grunted a few meaningless sounds. As for Kethiwe, all he did was stare into her eyes wordlessly for many minutes at a time. Once or twice, he kissed her fondly and silently. And so began our first day as a family. Mind you, in the eleven years of our marriage we had never lived together as a couple for more than a few months at a time.

I got my teaching job at Prince Philip Secondary. Our little house next to the school was at number 7 Luangwa Road. Saying it was a little house is no reflection of the comfort and joy that it gave us. Indeed, it was better than most houses in the township of Kamwala occupied by the average black people of Lusaka. They compared favourably with the four-roomed houses that we had left behind in our own locations in South Africa. The children soon settled in their schools. On the whole, I shall never forget the wonderful treatment and respect that the people of Zambia gave us. Within a short time, we had friends among them and life was pleasant, even for the children. Soon they were speaking the local languages: Chinyanja, Chitonga and Chibemba. In that way, we the adults had very efficient interpreters. As for me, I can say honestly that my children made my adjustment so much easier within the community. I ascribe all this to the nature of the Zambian people as a whole. Needless to say, not all African countries were as welcoming as some of the Zambians.

Finally, we were in exile. Facing our reality, we began to think of the other women that we had left behind in South Africa with their children and their husbands who were in jail.

When we began to organise ourselves, we discovered that our own organisation was not ready to accept us as full members of the PAC because we were women. Over the formative years of the PAC inside South Africa, some of us had worked very closely with the men in the organisation. We had never been treated as 'women'. After all, we had shared ideas, discussions, debates and books by many pan-Africanists such as George Padmore of Trinidad, Marcus Garvey of Jamaica, W.E.B. du Bois of the United States, Kwame Nkrumah of Ghana, Jomo Kenyatta of Kenya and many others.

When we finally realised that our relationship had changed, we quietly backed off and formed ourselves into a typical women's group. We began writing letters to other women's groups all over the world putting the case of the women we had left behind and tried to collect funds for their needs. We did not get much in the line of money, but different groups sent us clothing parcels from Sweden, England and the United States, who solicited help from Robert Kennedy, brother to the late American president, J.F. Kennedy. We decided to sell the clothes to convert them into cash. We opened bank accounts and kept records and minutes of our meetings. When we had a tidy sum, we decided to send a delegation, which included Gertrude Mathutha, Madiapetsane Makhunga, Mengmeng Mokone and Vuyelwa Bolofo, to the women of China. We did not get much material support from them but a great deal of moral and political support.

Our fund-raising efforts did not yield much, but it was substantial under the circumstances and encouraging for a start. However, I shall not forget one Saturday morning when our team got summoned to the PAC office in Lusaka. There was Leballo and his new executive members. They told us that they wanted us to submit all the documents of the PAC women's organisation to him right there and then. He wanted the bank accounts in particular. Those men took all the books, went and withdrew all the money from the bank. They said they needed the money to feed their 'forces', meaning guerrillas (soldiers) of the movement. Yes, that ended the dream of supporting women on the home front. Needless to say, we had to close shop, too, in Zambia.

For a while, all seemed well for us in Zambia after that. But for those of us who were involved politically and who at that time lived in Tanzania and other countries in Africa, things were very different. Some may not understand what I mean. From the time we arrived in Zambia, the government of Zambia laid down regulations that only those who were involved in the actual war of liberation would be given refugee status. That had the immediate effect of separating the men from the women. Women had to take care of the children and only women were allowed to work and keep families going. This practice had the immediate effect of breaking families apart, with disastrous effects in some instances. Some of the couples were newly married and found they could not accept the cost of their beliefs and the reality of exile.

I shall not forget one young couple who were torn apart in this exercise. The young man was taken to the deserted, godforsaken borders of Tanzania, to a place called Mbeya. This was one of our camps where men were kept before they could be posted to some country for training. Under such conditions, rumours fly and imagination runs riot. The thought of leaving their young wives in some far-away country with virtual strangers was simply unbearable. So one young man took the easy way out: he hanged himself and died.

Solidarity among comrades demanded that his funeral should wait for the arrival of his wife and all the other comrades, especially women. This journey had to be covered over a distance of close to 800 miles through one of the hottest parts of Africa on the roughest roads. Without the benefit of any semblance of a mortuary, what we found there at the end of the long journey still haunts me to this day. But what made it stick in my mind was the decision by the menfolk that women had to sit there and guard the dead through the night, 'according to custom', and that they (the men) could go to sleep in the now cool air of the night. If I had not known until then what it means to be a woman in the eyes of men, I learnt that day. Not that we loved him less or sympathised less with his wife, but the stench of the little house-cum-morgue was so overpowering that it was utter cruelty that she should have been exposed to the mortifying remains of her once loving and living husband. What made it even more unbearable for me was the rumour that floated around to the effect that the real reason why he had killed himself was that one of the men who had so authorised this bitter separation had had something to do with this man's young wife. I often wished, as I do now, that it was never the truth. Otherwise, what painful bitter retribution that was.

We were settled in our jobs and the children in their schools and, on the whole, we began to accept our condition. It was all right for us who were far away from Tanzania, the political hotchpotch of those days for refugees from all corners of the continent. The continental Organisation of African Unity (OAU) had chosen Tanzania to be the central host country for all of us who came from the turbulent continent of the 1960s and 1970s when many countries fought for their independence from colonial rule. Often, there were several organisations vying for the same freedom from the same country and ironically quarrelling with each other instead of focusing on the enemy. It was double irony when the organisations would splinter and self-destruct. Such was the fate of the PAC, much as it is still mauling itself apart to this day.

I was a member of the PAC and my husband was the treasurer of the organisation. He had served his time in several South African prisons like Durban, Leeukop and Pretoria. On his release he landed in Swaziland as already referred to above. The first evidence of trouble for them and the whole organisation was when A.B. and J.D. Nyaose first arrived in Tanzania. They had barely landed when the very comrades, members of the same organisation, turned against them, ready to have them sent back on the next flight to South Africa. This was back in 1963. They had expected a happy reunion with their long-time friends prior to the prison days. Instead, they were quizzed like old enemies. They were saved from this fate worse than death by the long experience of Mualimu Nyerere, the president of Tanzania of the time, who intervened and stopped them mauling one another. So did real exile for them begin. The founder members of the organisation were targeted and expelled from the organisation. These included men like Nana Mahomo, Peter Molotsi, Jacob D. Nyaose, Peter Raboroko, A.B. Ngcobo and several other founder members.

At first, this was a blow and a great puzzle. This had been before they understood from the underground that while they (the leadership) were in jail, there had been a bid by another organisation to take over the PAC. In other words, the people who received them in Dar es Salaam were no longer members of the PAC, but thought to belong to the Unity Movement who were Trotskyites. This history is a subject of another research quest of the future; it does not belong here. The PAC had always been a Cinderella organisation for it had no relations with powerful countries like Russia, and no powerful connections like the Trotskyite movement. It seems plausible that this is why A.B. and J.D., financially poor PAC leaders, were given convenient airlifts to Dar es Salaam. For indeed, ever since they left South Africa and landed in Dar es Salaam, the PAC began to splinter. This is not to justify the failures of this organisation, but it is an aspect of a phenomenon that is difficult to explain. Up to today, the succession of takeover bids has continued, generation after generation.

It did not take long before the same vice crept into all PAC settlements on the continent. It spread into the camps; women fought among themselves and hate ruled. In spite of the dispersed forces, at some point around 1967, some senior members thought it best to summon a meeting to try to resolve the difficulties. This included all the members of the Sobukwe executive (founder of the PAC), except Potlako (P.K.) Leballo. He took leave and visited Nairobi instead. It was at this meeting that they tried to curtail Leballo's powers as the acting president of the PAC.

From that historic gathering, some of the members of the body had to go to the camps to inform the cadres of the new changes. That is how people like Tsepo Tiisetso (T.T.) Letlaka, A.B. Ngcobo and Jacob D. (J.D.) Nyaose ended up in the hands of a divided camp. They were divided generally along provincial and political lines. There were nationalists and socialists. Some were under the leadership of Templeton Mzukisi Ntantala, a Leballo man and the commander of the camp, and the others were what one could call the abandoned souls. So when the senior leaders came to report on the decisions of the meeting in Dar es Salaam, a conspiracy was formed to kill the delegation.

After three days, news reports reached us in Lusaka that these leaders were in danger of being killed. One of the cadres, Amos Mafukuzela Somdaka, was in Lusaka at the time. I feared for the lives of the leaders, one of them my own husband. I persuaded Somdaka to come along with me to the town of Livingstone close to where the camp was. We rushed to the office of the commissioner of police who immediately sent a squad of Zambian soldiers down to the camp and, at the same time, summoned Ntantala, the commander, to come to his office in Livingstone. In no time, Ntantala arrived. He was furious to see us there and he refused to speak in our presence. Meantime, the Zambian army squad managed to diffuse a very dangerous situation. The leaders back in the camp were very close to being killed. Their graves had already been dug days before. But some confusion among the cadres, whether to take them to the Zambezi River and have them killed there rather than killing them close to the camp, saved their lives. While they argued among themselves, the Zambian squad was upon them. Thank goodness there were no cell phones then.

All three men were immediately released to the safety of the Zambian army. Meanwhile Somdaka and I shot off to Lusaka (about 300 kilometres away). By the time we reached Lusaka, the matter had reached the political authorities there who had given orders that the would-be PAC victims should be driven off to some unknown destination. Pamela Letlaka, wife of T.T., and I were very anxious about our husbands and we sought to meet the highest political authorities to find out about their fate. We wanted to meet no less a figure than Vice President Kapwepwe himself. After some difficulty, we met him and he gave instructions that we were to be driven the next day to where our husbands were. We took our youngest children up to Kitwe where we left them with friends while we proceeded to a secret place which, we were later told, was a very high-security military camp. Even to this day, I am not ready to reveal the name of the camp just in case by so doing I might betray Zambian security.

We were allowed to spend two days there with our husbands. I mention this to show just how far the generosity of the Zambian state was extended to the people of South Africa in those days. But soon enough we came to know that the Leballo who had been suspended at the last executive committee of the PAC in Dar es Saalam a few weeks before, had convinced the Tanzanian authorities that it was dangerous to have two PAC factions fighting each other on the borders of South Africa. From then on, it was clear that the Tanzanians had reinstated him as the acting president of the PAC, regardless of the wishes of the leaders of the people of South Africa. At the time, the Tanzanians had political problems of their own and Leballo was somehow co-opted by Magombe (Tanzanian official in charge of refugee matters) on the Nyerere side, leaving Kambona the adversary on his own. But, seeing my story is not going that way, I shall skip that part. Suffice it to say, Nyerere chose to side with Leballo in this exchange of favours. So, Leballo not only convinced the Zambians to deal harshly with his opponents, but the Tanzanians as well.

Upon arrival in Tanzania, the Leballo faction was driven off in good government cars into hotels whereas the leadership, so-called opponents of Leballo, were driven off to prison. The Tanzanian government chose to take sides where South Africans could not agree among themselves. After another few days, rumours had it that the same unfortunate prisoners were going to be driven off to Dodoma many miles away, where at the time there was no kind of accommodation, no food, no shelter, just the bush.

Fortunately for them, there was a guardian angel in Dar es Salaam called Reverend Hayley who took it upon himself to collect food parcels and blankets and dishes to dispatch with them straight from prison to Dodoma. By the time the truck took them away, they had some provisions to last them for a few days.

They were in that godforsaken place for about six months. There was no transport to anywhere, no shops anywhere for miles and miles around. The local community taught them how to fish and lent them their tools. Father Hayley did not forget them for now and again he would send supplies whenever he came to know of anyone travelling in that direction. They were staring in the face a very unfortunate mistrial. Meanwhile, we, the wives back in Zambia, remained completely forgotten and ignorant of the fate of our husbands.

To cut a long story short, they finally stole out of Dodoma and ended in Kenya in 1968 where they were offered a kind of asylum on condition that if they ever left Kenya, they would automatically be declared 'prohibited immigrants'. But that is exactly what they proceeded to do, getting out of Kenya like thieves. This was with the hope that they could put their case before the college of OAU leaders in Ethiopia where there was a meeting at the time. They were so desperate that they thought the leaders of Africa could side with them against Nyerere's judgement. Needless to say, they lost their case before it even started.

In another twist of events, in the hands of the ever-changing African alliances, A.B. and T.T. were immediately dispatched to the then Zaire (Congo) as prisoners. Somehow, J.D. Nyaose managed to fly out to Sweden where he had made his home and had papers for travelling. A.B. and T.T. were in a far worse position now for they had neither diplomatic papers, nor could they speak any French. They landed in yet another prison in the Congo, (Lubumbashi, I believe).

But, for once, fate was smiling on them, for inside prison they met some minor criminal who was due for release. Across many barriers of language and lifestyle, they persuaded him to take their desperate situation to Holden Roberto who at the time had the favour and status of a legitimised government of Angola in exile. This gave significant powers to Roberto under the Congolese government, which he used sometimes in favour of those he went along with. So it was that A.B. and Letlaka were saved from another fate worse than death and which otherwise would have meant spending the rest of their lives in a Congolese prison, forgotten to all intents and purposes.

At the risk of breaking the trend of the story, I shall briefly take you back to explain why there was so much animosity among the members of the PAC. Back in 1963, when South Africa was seething in turmoil, Leballo had lost the confidence of many PAC members when he made his infamous announcement in South Africa of the date that the organisation had chosen as the start of the uprising in the country. In the eyes of many, he had sold out. Coupled with this was the blow that a certain political movement in Cape Town worked against the leadership of the PAC while they were in prison. It is alleged that they asserted that they were better able to lead the revolution than the PAC. And if the PAC is in tatters today it is because there were actually two organisations working under the same name. Ever since the imprisonment of the PAC leadership back in 1960, the PAC fragmented as a result of infiltration by one organisation in particular. When they left prison in dribs and drabs they found that there was no organisation to come back to.

Earlier in this story, I made reference to the arrival of A.B. and J.D. in Dar es Salaam and how certain factions agitated to have them sent straight back to South Africa. These were actually infiltrators posing as PAC members. About that time the split occurred. The leadership came back from prison to find that the organisation had been totally hijacked and from then on the PAC was altogether fragmented.

Back in Zambia, we, the women and the children, were left to our own devices. I will never forget our story as grass widows in Zambia. Pam Letlaka, for some reason, was soon declared a prohibited immigrant in Zambia. This was so inexplicable and to this day I still think it was unwarranted. But there we were. The mammoth task to get her out of Zambia would constitute another chapter in this saga. I still do not know how we finally did it. It could have been T.T. himself with the help of Roberto or it could have been ourselves. We, the women, had developed our own connections with diplomatic circles. She got out of Zambia to Kinshasa on a visitor's visa.

So it was that T.T. left A.B. to join Pam in Kinshasa. After more wangling, A.B. found his way to Holland where he joined his long-time friend, Dr Dan Ncayiyana. Together they linked up again with a member of the British parliament under Prime Minister Harold Wilson. There were two Martin brothers. They worked hard fraternally, opening the way for A.B. to get to Britain. Once in Britain, he worked with old friends like Colin and Margaret Legum to find a way for T.T. and his family to come to the United Kingdom. By this time, this faction of the PAC had come to accept that there was no home for them in Africa.

Unfortunately for T.T., as soon as he touched down in Britain, he was taken into Pentonville prison in England. However, that, too, in the fullness of time did come to an end. T.T. was allowed into the country and the family soon followed and started a new life in a new country.

One area of our exiled life that I have not touched on is the relationships between the various party organisations. The ANC and the PAC, from the start, were the only organisations recognised as liberation movements from South Africa by the OAU, perhaps the largest groups. Right from the time we left our borders, mainly the black majority were all exposed to the same hardships. We were homesick and disorientated and we faced all these challenges with a great sense of oneness. This spirit of comradeship pervaded all our social contacts, even across political lines. We shared our joys and our pains together. We attended each other's weddings, funerals and visited those who had received news of the death of their loved ones at home. We laughed and wept together as a community. This went on for many years. At these gatherings our common 'anthem' was '*Lizalis'idinga lakho tixo nkosi yenyaniso*' (Fulfil your promise, O God of truth).

But there came a time when we began to feel restless, especially the women, tired of waiting for the promised return home. I recall one year when the annual commemoration of the 1956 women's historic march to the Union Buildings approached, how a group of us sat talking about how we no longer celebrated even the women's day on 9 August. Among us was Zanele Dlamini (later Mbeki), who apparently had been talking to Hlophe Bam, who doubtlessly felt the same as many of us did. All of us in one voice decided we should celebrate the march in some way that year. Zanele and I were to co-ordinate the event. It was going to be nothing more serious than a meeting in memory of our motherland. At that time, there were no strong party alienations and the march was meant to be inclusive of all women regardless of party affiliations. I myself had been on the march back in 1956, as much as my own husband had been one of the treason trialists in the same period, indicating our common affiliations in the cause of our struggle. So we called together not only South Africans but those from fraternal organisations from other countries as well.

Later, it came as a real surprise to some of us when the ANC participants were called to order by their leaders for crossing some imaginary political line. To be honest, many of us took this rather lightly at first. Soon after that, there was another shockwave when we received a publication from the ANC about 'the expulsion of the eight'. Although this was an internal issue, we began to sense differences among exiles that were deeper than we had observed before. After that, there was a lull and we nearly forgot about internal differences. But, out of the blue, the Soweto uprising of 1976 exploded on the front pages of the world's media. It refocused all our minds. For some reason this suddenly deepened our political differences to the point of hostility. As if Hlophe and I and a few others had not learnt our lessons earlier, we proceeded to call another, even bigger, meeting of the women. Before we knew what was happening, Hlophe, who had remained politically neutral in her job and regarded all women exiles the same, got into serious trouble, this time with the ANC hierarchy.

On the night before our conference of women in London, Hlophe and I were called by the senior women of the ANC for a gruelling meeting which took up most of that night. The meeting on the next day was a fiasco for the ANC had recalled many of their women members from all corners of the diaspora. They had come to destroy all our efforts to work together as women through their votes. It was one singular signal of things that were to come. At that meeting we quarrelled as we had never done before. For me, the fragile relationship among our political rivals today dates from that time. Some analysts suggest that the political strategies were copied from Vietnam and its 'people's war strategy', 'throwing dust in people's eyes, and subverting the truth and turning it on its head'.

However, to go back to my own party, the PAC, the paradox of it all is that those who had hounded out the whole executive of Sobukwe and got them flung out to all corners of the world in all the years of exile ended up being hounded too. Internal insurrections surfaced. Maybe, in the end, at another time, that story, too, will be told. Even Leballo himself, the bane of many in the PAC, ended up in exile. From the security and protection of the various African states, he became a refugee and died in

England in his second exile home, ironically in the arms of A.B. Ngcobo. His apparent friendship with the leaders of Africa had ended up in alienation.

I have tried to avoid the personal experiences of our lives. Perhaps turning a total blind eye to our lives as communities might give my story a kind of falsehood. Yet, living under our desperate conditions, there were bound to be very human stories. Earlier, I did mention how responsible male refugees respected and protected the very vulnerable women refugees. But, of course, as time went by many women did not need that much protection. I recall one man who had remained to run the party office in Lusaka and how he began having one or two liaisons with lonely women. He had one such relationship with a woman whose husband was around. We all came to know of this. Then, his appetite carried him further so that he began yet another relationship with another young woman. Being one of the leaders, he had the privilege of sharing one of the smaller rooms. His mistake was sneaking them into this confined space which he shared with another deprived man. Out of frustration, the other man woke up in the middle of the night to report this inconsiderate behaviour to the husband of the other concubine. Needless to say, the matter was morally very challenging to the small community, and instead of the matter being dealt with officially, the other woman went berserk and ran straight to the nest stripping them naked as though she wanted to see for herself if the infidelity could be true. In a community with little to occupy their interests, the hoo-hah lasted for a long time. We thought it a joke and could not stop laughing.

Then there was another case, far less amusing. One husband died. In a situation where the death of a husband meant serious sexual deprivation of the remaining partner, one 'friend' saw the need of the remaining wife as a humanitarian challenge. So he confided to his wife, persuading her to 'understand' her friend's needs. He felt called upon to 'help' her sexually starved friend. The trouble came when, at the height of her enjoyment, the friend would scream at the top of her voice, awakening those around them. The matter became unbearable. On one occasion, when they all visited a common friend, the wife could not contain her jealousy. Again, painful, but none could stop the cackle for months. Enough of the flippancy of our exiled days.

And so, many years later, I had also ended up in England on our third leg of exile. After the children were settled in schools, it was time for me to find a job. A.B. had no job, never having worked in all our married life except as a student here and there.

Arriving in England brought new perspectives to the meaning of exile. There were children to be acclimatised, the weather, the language, the confined spaces, the playground, the why, the where, the how, the lot. As for me, I found both the English playground and classroom an altogether unique experience, especially in the first two years of teaching. I was so stressed that on Monday morning I would count the hours from then until Thursday afternoon when my week would end. In those first two years or so, I worked four days a week only and it was enough. At first I feared the

British children had an antipathy for a black teacher seeing there were very few black teachers in England at the time.

However, one episode in the staffroom changed my mind altogether. We had a new teacher who was originally English but had moved years earlier to teach in Italy. She was happy there with the Italian children until some circumstance brought her back to London. For a few weeks, I assumed all was well with her and the children 'she knew so well'. But one day, she came in on a tea break and broke into hysterics, much to the surprise of everyone. It was the children. They were breaking her down. From that day, I knew what I had to do. I observed every move that the other 'successful' teachers did to get the right response and soon my classroom was humming and full of order. I shall not tell a lie here and say that I never experienced problems after that. Sometimes it varied with the change of school. One had to keep on one's toes all the way. But, on the whole, after many years one can claim to have enjoyed those years in English schools, at half of which I was deputy head. During the last two years, I was actually the acting head teacher at Larkhall Infants School. Altogether I taught for twenty-five years in a few schools. Today, I hold on to a mixture of good and bad memories of my teaching experience there. I will say it was an enriching experience and I learnt a lot in matters of education. In very many ways, I benefited a lot in spite of all the undeniable difficulties. My personal experiences in this area are recalled in my short story: 'Some Londoners'.

I cannot say the same for many of our children. To this day, I nurse deep pains for what our choice of exile subjected our own young children to. If things were hard for the teachers in the classroom it was sometimes hell for our children. In the end, it was for this reason that the whole English teaching system of education was forced to adopt what was called Multi-Ethnic Education in our schools. It was designed to assist teachers to understand the needs of our children on both sides of the colour line. I know it because many of our exiled children suffered deep emotional breakdowns at times. Few people in South Africa know that on our return we left some people in mental homes in various countries. Some died in such institutions. Their stories remain untold. Many people died in exile. We left them there.

On a personal note, I shall refer to my own daughter's agony. I had known for some time that my second daughter, Nomkhosi, was good at art in school. From her first year at secondary school, she had shown a deep interest in the subject. But I got no feedback from the subject teacher even on those one-to-one visits to the school. This had been the case until the very last end-of-year school meeting. The school hall was full of parents and pupils when the headmistress, Mrs Zakerwich, stood up to give us a review of the work covered in the school, the good and the bad, the successes and the failures. With reference to the arts department, she suddenly raised her voice and said she was very proud of the art display on the wall of the hall – adding that we may not believe that the whole display was the work of one child – pause – Nomkhosi

Ngcobo. I was stunned and overjoyed, but as we all stood up to leave the hall, I felt it was not the time to seek out the subject teacher. I put it off and thought, I will return later. Two days later, I returned to the school to collect my daughter's outstanding work and to express my joy and gratitude. I stared into the eyes of Mrs Zakerwich who looked at me blankly and told me that all of my child's art work had been taken by teachers. It did not make sense then. It still does not make sense now, more so in Nomkhosi's life. My child was devastated and, to this day, she has never attempted another piece of art work. The only thing she did for me thirty years later was a pencil portrait of my head and shoulders; otherwise she does not attempt work of art in any medium. I often sit and wonder what sort of teacher could do this to a child, any child.

Yet, it was the children in their first years in school who assisted me to understand the adults that I interacted with on a daily basis. This was so in spite of the so-called 'horrid English school child'.

One great gift that England brought out in me was giving me the opportunity to develop my skills as a writer. The lifestyle is calm and people leave you well alone to do what you want to do. It has endless resources in the form of libraries and television is used most profitably for those who want to learn and better themselves. In the beginning it was cathartic after my unspeakable earlier experiences in South Africa and on the long journey through the thirty years or so through other people's countries.

When I was not in the classroom, I was busy pouring out my pain on paper in anger. At first it poured out like froth with no order. It took a persistent friend like Margaret Legum to draw my story out slowly. She came to know that I was actually writing secretly, taking my 'froth' out of me. She saw me through those early stages and I shall be eternally grateful to her for the final publication of my first book, *Cross of Gold*.

Through my writing I saw the world differently. I read more than I had ever done before and grew in my thinking and in the portrayal of my inner world. Besides, I travelled a lot, being invited to most countries in Europe, Scandinavia and the United States. I visited Italy most frequently for I had a friend, Christine Panks, who often gave me room to sit and write in her house in Bagni di Lucca on Monti di Villa, not far from Florence. Here I was privileged to be exposed to the best I could have wished for and I learnt as much. I owe a great deal to her and her partner, Matthew.

The best cultural experiences that only the rich take for granted were mine for the taking. You should have seen me walk so proudly through those select corridors of the ancient University of Bologna! My greatest joy was actually being in the Verona of 'Romeo and Juliet' fame. It was wonderful! What of the Tower of Pisa!

Through all these experiences, I came to understand just how much South Africa as a country, through its apartheid policies, had deprived me and all of us, as blacks, the most valuable right that defines humans wherever they may be. And that was food for thought.

Few of our many dreams come to fruition or fulfilment in our real life. Yet on 2 February 1990, a frosty English morning, I actually heard F.W. de Klerk, the president of South Africa at the time, talking on the radio for all the world to hear, that political organisations would be unbanned, that Nelson Mandela, the South African prisoner of twenty-seven years, would be released together with many other people whose dream of freedom we had foregone completely, even though we knew it could never die.

In the height of my disbelief and exuberance, a thought came through me like a sword. It was the picture of Mangaliso Robert Sobukwe, better known among his friends as Prof, who died in his nameless exile. Sobukwe, the leader of the PAC, had been sentenced to three years' imprisonment back in 1960 after the Sharpeville massacre. He was held responsible for these atrocious events. On 3 May 1963, his sentence was over, but instead of going home he was whisked away to the prison of Robben Island without any further charge or sentence. He was the first of our latter-day prisoners to be sent to that infamous island prison and the first to go there without any charge or prison sentence. Parliament simply sat and formed the General Law Amendment Act, No. 37 of 1963, allowing them to detain somebody without reason, even if that person had already served his sentence. It became known as the 'Sobukwe clause'. All this was the extension of the government's displeasure of the political influence Sobukwe had exerted on the black people against their oppression, which had resulted in the Sharpeville massacre.

In the end, Sobukwe had spent a total of nine years in complete isolation from other political prisoners. For company, he had a pack of dogs baying day and night in their kennels that surrounded his shack. Finally, he fell ill and was discharged from his exile to die a short while later in 28 February 1978 in Kimberley where he had set up his final home. He lies buried in Graaff-Reinet, his original home.

From the Cape Flats to exile and back

Gonda Perez

Gonda Perez grew up in Cape Town in a family that strongly promoted social awareness and a commitment to fighting for justice. While at school, she joined the South African Black Scholars' Association and the Young Christian Students. Later, she joined the South African Students' Organisation and the Black Consciousness Movement. In 1974, she married Jaya Josie who, through his political activities, was banned, house-arrested and frequently visited by the police. In 1975, together with Jaya, her sister, Carmel, and Carmel's husband, Roy Chetty, Gonda fled to exile in Botswana. Carmel Chetty's story is recorded elsewhere in this collection.

Gonda was in exile in Botswana, Algeria, Zambia and Zimbabwe for fifteen years, during which she trained and worked as a dentist. Her Umkhonto we Sizwe training took place in Cuba. On her return to South Africa, Gonda continued building her professional skills and experience in teaching, research and service in dental health. She has since worked as the director of Health Promotion and Communication in the Department of Health, as head of Ministerial Services, Welfare and Population Development in the Department of Health, and as chief director in Communication and Ministerial Services in Public Service and Administration. Currently, she holds the position of deputy dean at the Health Sciences Faculty at the University of Cape Town with a focus in the area of undergraduate education.

I was born in Bridgetown on the Cape Flats on 4 September 1956. I am told that my mother was making curtains when labour started and Nurse Barlow was called to deliver me. My family was much better off than the others in the neighbourhood as my father had a regular job, a car and our house had a telephone – a huge luxury in those days. My mother did not go out to work, but growing up I remember her being engaged in different projects to try to increase the household income. She decorated and sold hats, sold dressed chickens (we children had to dip the chickens in hot water and pull out the feathers!) and worked as a casual in a catering company making and selling hotdogs and hamburgers.

With only one regular income, it was not easy for my parents to raise six children. I was the third after Anthony and Carmel. Maria, Jacinta and John followed later. Each of us had one pair of shoes to be worn to school and church; the rest of the time we had bare feet. Later, when things improved, we got Christmas shoes that we could also wear to church on Sundays. I wore my sister's hand-me-downs that were in turn passed on to my younger sisters. My mother sewed our clothes herself with some amusing results, like having the pins left in when wearing the garment for the first time – not so amusing when I was a teenager and wore a dress my mother had made and the boy I was dancing with got pricked by one of the pins she left in.

I and all my siblings went to St Theresa's Primary School in Welcome Estate, the closest Catholic school where we also went to church. We had to walk through a bush where cows grazed. I remember my brother, Anthony, leaving me alone to guard his books while he went off to ride the cows, a source of great fun for him and his friends. Often we would come across young men who were going through initiation rites in the bush.

My parents ensured that their children knew what was happening in the world around them. At the supper table we talked of the repressive laws that were being introduced; we heard of friends who were being evicted from District Six, a sprawling, cosmopolitan area in Cape Town, first settled by emancipated slaves in the 1800s and later inhabited by people of all races. It was declared a 'white' area in 1966 under the apartheid government's Group Areas Act and people were forcibly removed to the Cape Flats. People with whom we went to school and church, who were classified 'Bantu' by the apartheid government, were being moved out of the area (declared a 'coloured' area under the Group Areas Act) to Langa and Gugulethu, which were set aside for African people. We heard of my mother's school friend who was deported because of his protests against oppressive laws.

My father refused to allow us to speak Afrikaans at home as this was considered the language of the oppressors. It was bad enough that we were obliged to learn it at school. It was a natural progression to be involved in activist structures as teenagers. My first defiance was not standing to sing 'Die Stem' (white South Africa's national anthem) at school and getting into trouble with the teachers. In 1971, we refused to participate in the 'Republic' celebrations, which marked the tenth anniversary of the declaration of South Africa as a republic and independent of British rule. We refused to celebrate what we considered the further entrenchment of our oppression. In Standard 9, I went to Livingstone High School where teachers like R.O. Dudley, G.L. Abrahams and Stella Petersen from the Unity Movement further developed my sense of justice.

In 1973, when the students from the University of the Western Cape went on strike and were expelled from the campus, my father invited them to set up their base at our home. We were then exposed to the Black Consciousness Movement (BCM). In Standard 9, I was part of a grouping called the South African Black Scholars' Association, which was set up to mobilise scholars against the apartheid regime. We participated in various protests and community projects around Cape Town.

We woke up at three or four in the morning to hand out pamphlets to workers at stations and bus terminuses to mobilise their support for the various projects we were involved in. We made the pamphlets ourselves with old typewriters and Roneo machines. The repercussions were that the police soon noticed us. Our telephone was tapped. Our friends were picked up for questioning. One of them was brutally tortured. The bravado of youth prevented us from being intimidated. Sometimes we had to run from the police and their dogs at protests. My sisters, Carmel and Maria, my brother, Anthony, and I were fortunate to participate in a residential youth leadership programme run by Jane Abrahams at the Christian Leadership Centre. This helped us to focus our efforts more and to develop skills that stood us in good stead throughout our lives.

Through my involvement in the BCM, we met with students from other parts of the country, including Jaya Josie, whom I married in 1974. He was banned and house-arrested between the hours of 6 p.m. and 6 a.m. at the time. There were of course restrictions placed on his movements so we could only invite a limited number of people to the wedding. Despite that, many South African Students' Organisation (SASO) students came to the reception.

In 1975, the liberation movement was buoyed by the news of the coup in Portugal and the liberation of Angola and Mozambique. The Mozambican resistance movement, FRELIMO, became a household name. SASO organised pro-FRELIMO rallies around the country. At the same time Jaya's sister was very ill, dying of breast cancer, and we were taken by one of the more friendly Security Branch people to visit her in Pietermaritzburg. On the journey the Security Branch man revealed that they were about to arrest a number of people and that Jaya was on his list.

We then started making arrangements to leave South Africa. Abraham Ongopotse Tiro, a SASO friend, was in Botswana and had invited Jaya to join him there. Unfortunately, Tiro was killed in 1974 by a parcel bomb before Jaya could respond to his invitation. We still thought that Botswana would be the best option. There were stories of exiles being kidnapped and sent back to South Africa from Swaziland.

One Monday morning in May 1975, Jaya and I went to sign at the police station in Wentworth, a township near Durban, as per the terms of his banning order. A comrade picked us up on the highway and in the car were my sister, Carmel, and her husband, Roy, who were going into exile with us. As we drove out of Durban we were conscious that both Jaya and Roy were in contravention of their banning orders. The comrade drove us to Johannesburg where we were picked up by another comrade who drove us to the border area near Zeerust.

As we approached the border, we were followed by a person on a motorbike who put his (I assume it was a man) headlights on our front and back number plates and followed us for some distance, sometimes turning his headlights off. He passed us, made a U-turn, came towards us with headlights on bright, then passed, turned and followed us again. He did this until the wet gravel roads became a problem for the bike.

We continued to the point where we were to be dropped off. The rains this time worked against us. The map showed a small stream – it had changed into a raging torrent and it was impossible to cross in the small car. We decided that we should walk the rest of the way. As the driver was about to leave us, the car got stuck in the mud. You can imagine the noise it made with the engine running and the wheels digging deeper into the mud. Finally, we managed with grass and stones to move the car out of the mud. I still remember the absolute darkness and silence once the car left the area. We had to cross the river waist-deep in water in absolute darkness. The area around the river was a marshy bog and we walked into and out of the mud, getting scratched and poked by the thorn bushes. I can still feel the fear. It was terrifying for a young, city-raised girl.

At some stage we came to a relatively dry area. We stopped to relieve ourselves. Carmel put down the bag containing our money, maps and documents. When urged to hurry, Carmel assumed Roy had picked up the bag, only to find after we had walked some distance that he had not. Roy tried to go back to look for the bag. We kept track of him by whistling softly. Roy returned not having found the bag. We had to go on.

The crossing of the border was supposed to be easy. Across the river (that was supposed to be a stream), up the hill, across the two fences of the border and a short walk to Lobatse. The reality was very different. We waded across the river and climbed the hill. As we reached the top of the hill we heard the sound of a car. We thought it prudent to hide behind rocks. Just as well. The car stopped and spotlights were shone onto the hill. We speculated that the motorbike driver had gone for reinforcements and they were looking for us. It seemed like hours before we were able to climb the rest of the hill. As we reached the crest of the hill, a huge light rose and flooded the hill. As one, the four of us ducked behind a rock until one of us tentatively looked out and found out that it was the full moon that had bathed us in its light.

We cautiously reached the top of the hill and were completely disoriented. We had lost the maps and our money when we had stopped and then had to hide from the people who were chasing us. We had no idea which way to proceed. We decided to find a sheltered spot to sleep and proceed first thing in the morning when there was better light and we could see the direction from which the sun would rise. We slept – woken up in the night by my brother-in-law's loud snores and rain from the trees dripping down on us. As dawn broke, we started our descent from the hill and towards the border. Just as we started out, a huge thunderstorm broke and the area was plunged into darkness again. We could not see the person in front of us. Jaya took off his belt and used it as a link between the two of us. I held on for dear life and stumbled after him.

It proved too difficult to proceed and we stopped again in a bushy area. The exhaustion of walking for so long, the interrupted, uncomfortable sleep on the hillside and the events of the day before took their toll and we were soon all fast asleep. When we woke up, the sun was up and we could hear herders in the area where we were supposed to cross the border. We had been warned that we should not be seen during the day time. We decided to try to rest until the evening and cross the border when it was dark. That evening, we came across the border after walking for ages.

We crossed the two fences. By then we were thirsty and hungry. We squeezed water out of our wet socks and sipped it. Jaya and Roy found berries that the birds were eating. Carmel and I were more reluctant to eat them. Jaya picked cactus, peeled off the skin and got us to suck the moisture. We walked until about ten when we came across a farm. The workers gave us water and told us to hide from the farmer. They showed us the way to Lobatse.

As we entered Lobatse, we headed towards the Coca-Cola sign in the distance (we actually passed by other shops but all we could see was the Coke advert). We had something like R1.13 on us, which Jaya had in his pocket. We bought a tin of pilchards and a loaf of bread and ate, not noticing anything else around us until our hunger had been satisfied. We asked the shopkeeper for directions to the Lobatse pharmacy where a pharmacist friend of Harry Nengwekhulu worked.

Harry was a SASO member who was also in exile and he was supposed to look after us once we arrived. We were taken to a house where several BCM exiles were. They discussed our situation and it was agreed that we should report to the Botswana authorities in Gaborone as in Lobatse they had the tendency to imprison South Africans who presented themselves as refugees at the police station. The next morning we were taken to Gaborone. There we reported to the police who took down our details and asked us to report to the Botswana Christian Council (BCC) and the United Nations High Commissioner for Refugees (UNHCR).

We soon discovered that there were tensions among the various BCM groups in Botswana and each of the groups wanted our allegiance. We decided to be independent, much to the disgust of these groups. Immediately we told them of our decision, we were without accommodation. We went to the Catholic church, but they refused to assist. The Anglican church put us up for a while in a church guest house. We had no money and no food. We stole vegetables from a shop in the African shopping area to survive. A Zimbabwean exile who worked at the University of Botswana, Lesotho and Swaziland loaned us his house while he was away for a week.

When he returned, we asked the chairperson of the BCC for help and he put us up in his home for a few days, after which the BCC gave us blankets and placed us at a camp where they 'housed' refugees from Zimbabwe. The camp was a run-down, old farmhouse where ant heaps occupied most of the space in the rooms. Someone at the BCC remembered another exile, Iyavar Chetty, who maybe could assist us.

Iyavar was most helpful and gave us his daughter's room and we stayed there until we found jobs and a place to stay in Lobatse with some German volunteers, Klaus Hummel and his partner, Solveig. Jaya and Carmel taught at a community school, the Itereleng Secondary School in Lobatse. We stayed in Botswana for eighteen months. During that time we were helped by many people including Sisa Mvambo, principal of the school where Carmel and Jaya worked, Mani Pillay (an exile and shopkeeper who gave us a place to stay), German volunteers and other expatriates from Europe. The solidarity was phenomenal.

Jaya and I pursued our wish to study further and applied to a number of universities. We wanted to study and to pursue the fight for freedom in our country. We decided to join the African National Congress (ANC) after being recruited by Dan Tloome. Keith Mokoape came to see us after that and made arrangements for us to leave Botswana. The ANC sent us to Algeria to study. We travelled from Gaborone to Rome and on to Algiers on refugee passports issued by the Botswana government on behalf of the UNHCR.

We knew very little about Algeria before our arrival there. We had heard and read of the struggle for independence from France. We had visions of the romance of the battle of Algiers. Our arrival there brought us back to earth. It was a Muslim country with many traditional customs – very difficult for a young woman from South Africa. There were many places where I was not welcome because I was a woman. This was difficult for me to adapt to. I could not walk alone in the streets without being followed by men. After dark I had to be accompanied by a man.

Our comrades in the ANC were wonderful about looking after me and protecting me. On one occasion, Comrade Ngesi chased an Algerian man down the stairs with a broom after he had followed me right up to the door of the ANC offices! The Benmosley family, our neighbours, adopted us as part of their family and ensured that we were invited to all their parties – weddings, birthdays and Muslim festivals.

They ensured that we were never hungry and were integrated into the community where we lived. We met up with Cameroonian exiles, Marthe and Reuben, who invited us to be part of their African solidarity group. There we met Gaby Cottenceau who took us under her wing. Munir and his sister, Nacera, Algerians from the south of the country (dark like us and also taunted in the streets) often invited us to their home. We also formed lasting friendships with many people. Christine Abdelkrim, a journalist with *Afrique Asie*, is still my friend today.

At first, we had to study French before entering our respective programmes. I studied dentistry and Jaya economics. Besides our studies we had to help out in the ANC offices, doing all the chores assigned to us, including making posters that were taken to various meetings to tell people of our struggle. We attended meetings of the women's and youth groups and told them of the struggle for freedom in South Africa.

Everywhere we went we were assured of the support of the people of Algeria. While we had high-level support, the reality in the streets was very different.

Black people were given the name of '*kalusha*', meaning black. Children in the streets would run after us shouting '*kalusha*' while their parents looked on and laughed. After a few months we became a familiar sight and were welcomed in the souks (markets) of Bab-el-Oued and the Casbah. Few people knew where South Africa was. We had to struggle with the local people for scarce resources. Sometimes during droughts the water would be switched off for many days. When there was water available we had to fill every available container with water and use it sparingly as we were not sure when it would be available again.

We competed for places on the bus. There was no tradition of queuing for the bus. Everyone crowded around and when the bus arrived there was a great surge. Often we did not board the bus and had to take the long slog up the hill to Notre Dame d'Afrique on foot.

Every year Algiers had a trade fair and we were expected to assist with preparing the ANC's exhibition. We made posters, mounted pictures and helped the comrades from the South West Africa People's Organisation (SWAPO) and the Zimbabwe African People's Union with their exhibitions. We then helped to explain our struggle to people who visited the stand – initially in halting French, but we grew more confident as our knowledge of the language grew. There were student groups that were supportive of our struggle.

In 1979, the year Solomon Mahlangu was executed, they mounted posters in protest. Some of the Muslim brotherhood did not like their involvement in this foreign struggle and assaulted the students putting up the posters. They hit one person with an iron bar and broke his hands. Some of our friends were the secretariat of the Pan-African Youth Organisation (Jenerali Ulimwengu, Patrick Etoka-Beka and others). They ensured that we had a good social life and interacted with the rest of the African community in Algiers.

Studying in Algeria was not easy. Algerians had a much higher level of education than ours in South Africa and the first year was very difficult. I had to practically relearn all the maths I knew and learn things like calculus that I had never been exposed to, even at matriculation level. The hours were long. I had to depend on Jaya and other comrades to see that I travelled to the place where I studied. It was most frustrating. We spent seven years in Algeria and finally completed our studies and returned to southern Africa, specifically to Lusaka for deployment by the ANC. I was told to seek work at the University Teaching Hospital and Jaya worked in the economics unit analysing information that came from South Africa. Jaya was recruited to Umkhonto we Sizwe (MK) and sent to Moscow for his military training.

Life in Lusaka was very different from life in Algeria. The ANC community was much bigger and we felt much more at home there. Zambians are among the friendliest and most welcoming people in Africa. We lived in Lusaka with Ilva Mackay and Mandla Langa, first in Chilenge and then in Kabwata. Before starting to work at the University Teaching Hospital, I helped in the South African Congress of Trade Unions offices and assisted Kay Moonsamy with some of his office work, corresponding with progressive trade unions around the world.

In those days, the ANC gave us each K14 (fourteen kwacha, about $1.40) a month to survive on. We were also given whatever vegetables were available – usually cabbage and potatoes (I still try to avoid cabbage today). Sometimes we were lucky and were given big tins of meat from the Soviet Union. We called this meat 'skop' or 'Mugabe' (I'm not sure why). We tried all kinds of ways of cooking the meat to make it more palatable. I once even tried to make meatloaf but, without essential ingredients, this was not very successful.

Occasionally, the word would go round that second-hand clothing had arrived and we would go to Awolo, the comrade responsible for distribution, to queue for our turn to rummage through the *mphando* (clothes pile) for clothes that could possibly fit us. Later we were told the secret – grab whatever looks reasonable and sell it in the market to Zambians and then buy whatever else you need with the proceeds. When I was employed at the University Teaching Hospital as a dentist, life became slightly easier. I earned a basic salary and I was able to apply for accommodation, and when I was assigned a flat comrades could come and live with me. One of them was Ronnie Kasrils (a leader in the South African Communist Party (SACP) and MK, responsible for military intelligence at the time). Ronnie, with other comrades, had to leave Mozambique with the signing of the Nkomati Accord, a non-aggression treaty between the Mozambican and the apartheid governments in 1984 under which the Mozambican government would withdraw its support for the ANC.

While we suffered hardship in Lusaka, we were part of a community and we shared whatever we had. We had a common aim: to work to go back home. We snatched at little bits of information that came from home, read the news briefings prepared by Gill Marcus with great eagerness to find any bit of information to confirm our belief that the apartheid regime was crumbling. Joe Slovo (head of the SACP) had a stock answer – we would be home in five years.

We had occasions when we cooked meals and invited one another around. At every possible opportunity we reminisced about home and planned where we would live on our return. We talked about our families and how we longed for them. There were some of us who had not had contact with their families for decades. We argued with one another about the most beautiful part of our country and our favourite foods. I remember longing for Sunday morning koeksisters.

We looked out for one another and were really a big family. If we had differences, they were kept in the family. We defended one another to any outsiders. Diek, Ardie and their two children, from the Netherlands, whom we had first befriended in Algiers, came to work in Lusaka. We and all our friends had access to their home and swimming pool.

Often in Lusaka we would be told that the South African Defence Force (SADF) was planning a raid and that we should not sleep in our homes. Everyone would be ordered out of the known ANC houses and we had to sleep wherever we could. We were lucky that Hugh and Louise Africa (and later Diek and Ardie) invited us on those occasions to share their home.

On one occasion, the SADF bombed the wrong camp – a camp of SWAPO dissidents. I was on duty on that day and was there when wounded people spilled out from the ambulances with blood gushing everywhere. On another occasion, Ronnie and I were in the flat when we heard gunfire outside. I fell to the floor and crawled to Ronnie's room to see if he was okay, only to find Ronnie leaning out of the window trying to see what was happening – against all the rules that he had taught me. On that occasion, it was a battle between the Zambian police and local criminals rather than an SADF raid.

Despite these interruptions in our lives we tried to live as normally as possible. I worked at the University Teaching Hospital on those occasions when we had water. Sometimes, for many days no water was available at the hospital. We waited around to do our work. Sometimes we had to extract teeth that could have been saved if we had water to drive the machines we needed to do fillings. On Saturdays we attended ANC meetings in preparation for the Kabwe Conference in 1985 and participated in the heated debates about 'open membership'.

Some Saturdays I worked on comrades who were going back into the country, ensuring that they would not have toothache while on sensitive missions. I also made them false teeth that would assist with disguise. I was asked on a few occasions to take money and materials to comrades in Swaziland, Zimbabwe and Botswana. My innocent-looking face, an Indian passport and professional status were all that prevented border guards and immigration officials from searching me.

Eventually, the decision was made that I needed to be trained militarily and in the art of disguise so that I could be more effective in the work I was doing after hours and during holidays for the ANC. Joe Modise and Jackie Molefe ensured that I had weapons training on the farm outside Lusaka. I was sent to Cuba in 1986 for training in clandestine work and disguise. To get to Cuba, I travelled with other comrades to Luanda and spent a few days there, waiting for transport to Havana. The water situation in Luanda was dire. We stayed on the eighth floor with no lift and the only water available was on the ground floor. We had to carry huge containers of water upstairs to ensure we had enough for cooking and cleaning. We used to walk down to the beach with our toiletries and bathe there – even wash our hair with shampoo in the sea.

The beach was also a source of money. We used to walk along the beach in the evenings at the weekends when most people had left and pick up coins that had been dropped. Most times the coins would enable us to buy bread and, when we had enough, to buy fish that we cooked – it was delicious!

We travelled to Cuba with soldiers returning home after a stint fighting South Africa. We marvelled at their wonderful spirit of solidarity. What struck me about Cuba was that everyone read – on the buses, in the markets, in the parks, you would see people reading. Young and old would be found with books or newspapers. I also marvelled at their work ethic. They had what was called 'Red Sunday' and everyone would pitch up at their workplace and do a day's work for their country.

Back in Lusaka later that year, it was decided that Jaya and I would try to find work in Zimbabwe or Botswana and work in military intelligence under Ronnie Kasrils. Jaya soon found a job and I went to join him. I worked at the Parienyatwa Hospital in Harare. Here we were a bit lonely as we were prevented from meeting up with our South African comrades. But the advantage was that we regularly had visitors from home, including our families. Some of our contacts provided intelligence information about the SADF's plans for Cuito Cuanavale that we were able to feed into the ANC machinery. This information confirmed intelligence that the ANC had from other sources.

In Zimbabwe, from 1987, we had to be more conscious of security and often took a very long route home to ensure we were not followed. Once I was asked to go into the notorious Chikurubi Prison (a high-security prison in Harare) to see a prisoner. It was scary walking down the long corridors and being shouted at by all these male prisoners. I was taken through numerous gates until we came to the medical centre and a dental chair in the centre of the prison. I waited there and the prisoner was brought in.

I was horrified to find that the prisoner was one of the South African men who had killed a Zimbabwean security guard when they (South Africa) had bombed a house where they thought ANC comrades were living. I had to remind myself of all the ethics and professionalism I had been taught and to treat the patient like I would anyone else. I was tempted to hurt him, but had to put my personal feelings aside. He tried to engage me in a discussion and find out where I was from. He kept asking about my accent. I just kept asking him about his dental complaint and gave the necessary treatment. I was very relieved to leave the prison and be back at the hospital.

Tragedy struck our family when my sister, Jacinta (called Jacky), and her family were involved in an accident while travelling to Botswana and Zimbabwe to visit Carmel and me in December 1989. My niece, Shelley, and her grandmother were killed in the accident. My family has still not recovered from that accident.

On 2 February 1990, I was at home ill in bed listening, as usual, to the BBC for any information from home. The announcement came – F.W. de Klerk said that all political parties would be unbanned and negotiations would start to take the country to democracy. Conscious of the Zimbabwean worker in the house who did not know we were South Africans, I went into the bathroom and wept and danced for joy. At last we would be able to go home! Jaya phoned and asked if I heard the news. We were overwhelmed. It seemed like the whole of the South African community came to Phyllis Naidoo's (she was mother to us all) house to celebrate. This bonanza was so unexpected yet so welcome.

Our high spirits were dashed later in the year (I think it was March) when we were at an economics conference organised by the ANC with comrades from home. We heard a loud explosion. One of our comrades immediately asked what the time was – you have to check the time when there is an explosion. Then the phone call came – the explosion was at Michael Lapsley's house. Michael Lapsley was an Anglican priest from New Zealand who worked in the ANC structures. He was alive and being taken to Avenues Clinic for treatment. I immediately thought of Aunt Phyll (Phyllis Naidoo) who had been at a farewell party for Mike earlier in the day. I found her at Derek and Trish Hanekom's house, just leaving for home.

She got into my car and we drove to Avenues Clinic. Aunt Phyll was allowed to see him. He asked her to pray for him and she couldn't remember the words of 'Our Father'. We heard that Avenues Clinic was not happy to have Mike there and wanted to transfer him to Parierenytwa Hospital. I rushed off to make the arrangements at the hospital. Mike arrived in great distress and pain. Both his hands and his eyes had been severely injured. His hands had to be amputated, he lost an eye and he was deaf from the explosion. This was a huge setback. We wondered if the olive branch offered by De Klerk was genuine.

It was decided that I would go back to South Africa. I left Zimbabwe on 15 June 1990, still with my Indian passport containing a visa to enter South Africa. My passport was checked and stamped – I thought the immigration man took a long time looking at it. He then said go through there – I was terrified that behind the door would be the dreaded security police.

I found, instead, the baggage hall. I grabbed my bags and went through customs at some speed and through the automatic doors where a huge crowd of friends, including my dad who had travelled up from Cape Town, had gathered to meet me. Reshie, Ingrid (a childhood friends of Jaya's and mine) and all their children had come from Durban to be there when I arrived. Imagine the tears and laughter all at once in the middle of Johannesburg airport. We had a party that evening at Bobby and Shamim's (childhood friends of Jaya's) and the next day my dad and I left for Cape Town.

I could not stop the tears when I saw Table Mountain as we came in to land, my father holding on tightly to my hand. I could not believe that I was back home. Again, a huge crowd was there to meet me. My family had a bunch of balloons as if they were meeting a film star. We drove home in convoy. The neighbours came to greet the car as it pulled up at my family home. There was more family there to greet the prodigal daughter and to party and feast. What a welcome!

Disconnected from family and home

Ellen Pheko

Ellen Pheko was born in Qhoboshaneng, Eastern Cape, in 1937. She joined the Pan-Africanist Congress soon after getting married and actively served in the struggle by hosting and supporting comrades and by acting as an information courier. She left South Africa in 1963 to join her husband in exile in Swaziland. Two of her three daughters were born in exile. The family went on to settle in the United Kingdom where Ellen remained until she could come home for the first time in 1990. In 2007, she returned to live permanently in South Africa. Today, she is retired and spends her time in South Africa, England and Japan where her eldest daughter is serving as South African ambassador.

From the moment I finished my primary school education, I was given choices. My father wanted to know what I wished to do with my life, whether I wanted to pursue my education or stay at home and get married.

I learnt later that there were several parents in the community who wished to have me as a daughter-in-law, but, without any hesitation, I told my father that I wanted to study medicine. The schools in South Africa – Mariazell, to be specific – were full. My father was referred by my former primary school teachers to Qacha's Nek in Lesotho. He rode his bicycle to Qacha's Nek, and fortunately, there were a few spaces left. So, I managed to get into college in Lesotho. I was very excited to be in high school and worked very hard to obtain good marks so as to be able to study to become a medical doctor.

My father died towards the end of the year, before I completed Form 1, my first year in a secondary school. I felt as though my whole world had collapsed. I thought I was definitely going to have to stay at home and get married, but my cousin offered to pay for my studies. Of course, he could not afford to pay for me to study to become a medical doctor at the Durban medical school. He was a family man with two children of his own. I was advised to take a shorter course that would enable me to get a job and look after my widowed mother and seven siblings.

I completed my course and started working. Then I was made an offer of marriage by someone I had known for a while. He was still studying for a teaching degree, but the plan was that we would get married eventually, and then his parents would send me back to college to study medicine. However, another offer of marriage was made, which I accepted, and which was totally different from the first. In this arrangement, my two siblings were sent to school. I never became a medical doctor. My husband-to-be was a journalist with an adventurous streak and a strong sense of purpose. The young man I chose came from a village called Mangoalaneng, not very far from my own. Growing up, I had heard of his family. They were known to be educated, firebrands, progressive and of good stock. He was Motsoko Pheko, who was later to become president of the Pan-Africanist Congress (PAC).

All the while, there were political upheavals going on around me which I did not even fully understand in the beginning. The man I chose to marry was detained; fortunately, I was working and able to support the family. My husband had to leave the country at some point as the case against him was very strong. I had to choose, once again, either to stay at home and work, or follow him into exile. There were two good jobs to choose from. Three friends offered to take me to Mbabane, Swaziland. At the time, I was then about four months' pregnant with my second daughter, Mamello.

My friends tried to tell me what life in exile would be like. They suggested that I stay in South Africa and face whatever problems might arise with the South African security forces, and said that, in the end, everything would settle down. However, I chose exile because I was married and believed that the right thing to do was to follow my husband and retain our family unit.

I was a very young bride when my husband and I arrived in Swaziland in 1963. Some Christian friends managed to find us a beautiful house that belonged to American missionaries in a place called Bethany, which is between Mbabane and Manzini. The house had a thatched roof. It had three bedrooms, a cosy sitting room, dining room and a small kitchen. There was also a sizeable bathroom. There was running water in the house that was drawn from a small spring over the hill, though the plumbing was very simple. The toilet was not the type you could flush, even though it was very well built. The orchard there was beautiful: there were guavas, oranges, lemons, pears, avocados, pineapples, peaches and bananas. This was complemented by the front lawn.

There was only one major drawback – there were snakes everywhere. Green mambas took up residence in the roof of the toilet and in the orchard. I used to scream most of the time because of those mambas. Then there was another snake that liked to slither across the sitting room window, a very cheeky snake that would strike the window, almost breaking it. One day, my second daughter, Mamello, was resting on the settee. Suddenly, I heard her crying. I could not understand what had made her wake up because she was usually a good sleeper. The next thing I heard was a thumping sound on the window. There was this huge snake, trying to break the window. I picked the baby up and ran down the village to uMkhulu, the snake killer. He was a very calm man who walked around the village with a stick. I explained what had happened. He told me that he had been tracking the snake for days. It was a green mamba. He killed it that afternoon with a stick.

At first, the Swazi people were not warm at all. I perceived them to be tribalist, steeped in their own ways and disliking of foreigners. The fact that in South Africa my husband had been a managing editor for a Christian Magazine called *Our Africa*, that he had been arrested for political activities and jumped bail in South Africa, alienated them from us even more.

It certainly did not feel accidental that each Sunday, the reverend felt the need to remind the congregation, which included us, that people should not have one foot in the church and the other in the secular world. We were seen as a bad influence on the community and were only tolerated because we looked after the church mission while the American missionaries went home on leave. The fact that we were outsiders who had been given permission to live in the big white man's house created such tension that, on the Sundays when my husband was scheduled to preach in church, only a handful of those who lived in the village would attend the service.

The environment was so inhospitable, we dared not even think of asking anybody in the community for help. Things were bad financially; there was no electricity and we could not afford to buy a generator. We used a paraffin stove to cook – it was a good stove with four plates and an oven. However, we only used one plate as we could not afford to cook different ingredients separately. I had to cook the meat first, then the mealie rice (the cheapest we could afford), and then the vegetables – all in one pot. If I had tried to cook everything separately, the primer stove would have run out of paraffin before the meal was cooked. Mealie rice, potatoes and cabbage, all in one pot, to save paraffin! Often, I cooked enough food in large pots to last several meals.

Over time, relations began to change slowly with the Swazi community. I found I got used to the place. It actually felt like a home, but the concerns of not having money spoiled things for me. Even the beautiful house had no curtains. We had stuck newspaper on those windows so as to have a shred of privacy. I used to sew and sell beautiful children's clothes, which used to bring a bit of cash for paraffin, tinned fish or beef, potatoes, cabbage and mealie rice.

There was a primary school in Bethany and almost all the teachers there were from South Africa. They were not really aware of my financial need, but they were aware of our other needs, such as for curtains in the house. The school decided to change the navy blue uniform with pink collars to something which I was to suggest. I was given the contract to sew uniforms for about three hundred girls. We calculated the cost and half of that amount was given to me as a deposit. I ordered rolls of materials from a wholesaler in South Africa and started sewing. My first daughter, Mohau, was in the same school.

I used to sew with my second daughter, Mamello, strapped on my back. With the money I got from the contract, I ordered material from South Africa and made curtains for the whole house. We were even able to buy some meat. I made many Swazi friends in the community. I found them very helpful. They validated me a lot and complimented me in telling me I was a resourceful woman, sewed beautiful clothes, kept a clean house, did plumbing, did the typing, made sour milk (*amasi*) and cultivated my own vegetables.

Each time there was a wedding in the community I was consulted. Then I would be asked to arrange everything from sewing clothes for the bridesmaids to preparing the menu. I was sometimes asked to do things at the last minute and this alone made me well-liked. It was a great comfort to me to feel accepted. The prices I charged for these events were quite low because I had no idea how much things were supposed to be.

By now, I had made a lot of friends and they used to bring me eggs, beans, chickens, goat meat or pork from the village. I had a manual Remington typewriter that had been brought for me by some missionaries when they visited from South Africa. I started teaching typing and had five students.

My husband had already gone to Rhodesia (Zimbabwe) to work there. He had left me in Swaziland with the children – Mohau and Mamello – and we were to follow. My mother-in-law came to visit around the time we were preparing to join my husband. She found me organising weddings, teaching typing, sewing clothes for kids and selling fruit and tinned meat. She was warmly welcomed by friends in the community and they brought her gifts. In her eyes, I was this clever, gifted, young woman who was on top of things. She asked me not to move to Rhodesia, but to stay in Swaziland. She even offered to stay with me and the children in Swaziland. But, again, although I wanted to stay in Swaziland and settle there, I believed the right thing to do was to follow my husband. That is what married people do – stand together.

I travelled to Rhodesia by road, via Mozambique. Mamello, my second-born, still a baby, became very ill during the journey. I travelled by bus from Manzini to the border post of Mozambique and Swaziland, a place known as Nomahasha. It was a day's journey. It might have been a bit shorter, but the bus driver went into the village to drink some local beer.

When we finally reached the border at Nomahasha, a Shangaan man, part of a group I had travelled with from Manzini, asked me to carry some secret documents for them. They feared they would be searched and get into a lot of trouble for having the documents. I was furious that they did not seem to be concerned about my own security. They suggested that a young woman like me would not be searched. As soon as we entered immigration, every white Portuguese officer wanted to serve me. The Shangaan man's theory proved true. They, on the other hand, were interrogated and searched for about an hour. The bus finally got into Nomahasha at 7 p.m. that evening.

We had left at about 8 a.m. in the morning. The trip would continue to Lourenzo Marques (now Maputo) the following morning.

My new friends tried to find a place for me to stay in town, but we had no luck. We decided to sit in a cafe and eat and hopefully come up with a plan. They asked the manager for a place for me and the baby to sleep. The cafe owner said he would not help me as I was a married woman with a baby. My friends were very angry to hear the manager's reply.

I did not understand the language. I only saw them picking up my belongings and taking the baby from me. I asked where we were going. They said we were going to sleep in the bus. I was given the long seat at the very back and they said they would sleep in the other seats and I should not be afraid, they would protect me and the baby. The baby slept soundly. I, on the other hand, could not sleep at all. I was flooded with regrets for not taking my mother-in-law's suggestion to settle in Swaziland and make a life there. I had left my first-born with some family friends and that was contributing to my worries.

When morning came, my companions woke up, got water from a nearby tap with a jug. I was asked to wash my face and freshen up the baby. The driver came and set off for Maputo. The music in the bus comforted me. My companions, too, asked me to cheer up as I would soon be in Rhodesia to meet my spouse. When we reached Lourenzo Marques, there was no train to Rhodesia on that day. My companions and I started looking for a bed and breakfast for me and the baby all over again. Again we had no luck. They said they had to catch their bus to their final destination. I asked them where they thought I could spend the night. Even as I posed the question, I wept.

There was silence. All of a sudden my companions started discussing something among themselves in Shangaan. They asked me to stop weeping while they suggested a solution. One man remembered that he had a cousin in the township, but had not seen her for ten years. Fortunately, the cousin was still there, running a shebeen (an unlicensed drinking establishment). She owned about three bamboo huts, surrounded by trees and white sand. She was more than happy to accommodate all seven of us. The arrangement was that the baby and I would share her hut with her and the five men would sleep in another hut. I was relieved to have a place to sleep. The men went to the shops and came back with rice and fish because the host had no food to offer us. The baby was fed clear soup and jelly. She had not eaten for two days.

The baby's temperature came down and she began to sing and clap her hands – another relief and an indication that the environment was safe. I was sitting under one of the trees with the baby on my lap. The noise of the drinkers eventually lulled me to sleep. At some point I was woken up and told by one of the companions that the room was ready for me to sleep. They said I had nothing to fear. In the room there was a single bed with bits of dirty cloth to make a mattress. I had never experienced such poverty. I was moved by the shebeen queen's generosity. This was the best she had to offer and she treated the baby and me as her special guests. She slept on the floor and gave me the bed. All my reservations about how dirty the place was faded. There was a small, blue paraffin light the size of a sparrow on the floor. That was all I noticed before I fell asleep, too tired to observe anything else in my surroundings.

I slept until morning. I offered to pay the host for the bed; she refused and took only a token amount from her cousin. I was then taken to the train station by my travel companions, before they embarked on their journey. At the train station there was a Shangaan police officer who spoke Zulu fluently. They left me in his care and departed. I felt very emotional. It was as though I had known them all my life. I learnt to treat a Shangaan person with respect from that day until now.

The officer took the responsibility of looking after me. He helped me to buy my ticket, offered me some food from his office and finally put my luggage on the train and waved me off.

Once the train had crossed the border into Rhodesia, a well-dressed man came into my compartment and asked me many personal questions. I was quite relaxed and conversed with him. It was daytime and I did not feel the need to be cautious. He left the compartment only to come back a few minutes later with a cake. It looked appetising. He put it on my table and left. At the next stop, I was joined by a female passenger who noticed the cake and asked me about it. She advised me not to touch the cake. I was still too naive to understand that secret police where everywhere, tracking the movements of political activists such as my husband and me. She actually put the cake on the floor next to her and beyond the baby's reach. She was Rhodesian and seemed to have a lot of knowledge about politics, and she talked about the history of cultures plundering other cultures. She told me not to take food from anyone under any circumstances and not to befriend anyone. Before she left the train, she opened the window and threw the cake out.

It turned out that the well-dressed man was a secret policeman and had been tipped off that I was on the train. I learnt later that the cake was poisoned. When I related the story, those in the know confirmed that it was common for secret police to move around trains looking out for dissidents or people who were on their target list.

I fell in love with Rhodesia and the people as soon as I landed there. But I also missed the people in Swaziland. While we were beginning to settle down, we even tried to buy a house. However, it was time to move again. Then my husband was detained for what turned out to be about six months. The support I received was overwhelming. I was immediately offered a job where my husband worked. They arranged for a girl who was a teacher to stay with me. I worked part-time, from 8 a.m. to noon. The teacher started work at 1 p.m. so she looked after the baby until I came home. These arrangements were all made without my input. It worked out really well and the teacher and I became like family.

Each Saturday, when we visited my husband in detention, there was a long procession of cars from his workplace, from church members and the community. I was asked to carry only a change of clothes for him. Things like food and fruit were prepared by friends. To this day, I cannot forget the kind of support I got in the former Rhodesia.

The South African intelligence machinery caught up with us and we were deported to Zambia. In Zambia we stayed for about a year with Sis' Lauretta, A.B. Ngcobo's wife, and their three daughters along with our first daughter whom I had since collected from Swaziland. We had great times there and Lauretta was a good friend to me. There were many wonderful women in exile such as Priscilla Gumane (whose husband was part of the Mozambique cause), Violet Chikoore (who was a Zimbabwean freedom fighter) and Victoria Mahlomahkulu (a midwife who was present when my youngest daughter, Lebohang, was born). It made me feel that families could be created. We were not connected by blood, but by the common thread that existed from home. Not knowing if we were ever going back home created a strong bond between us.

In Zambia, I came to know a lot of political exiles. Mrs Nokwe and the other women from the African National Congress (ANC) often met for tea at each other's houses. They lived two streets away and our struggles to adjust away from home and continue living 'normal' and productive lives bonded us. We never discussed party political matters. Everybody had their political cause, but what I recall was the strong sense of support and community among the exiles who lived in Zambia. It transcended factionalism. We were not enemies. We had a common cause of liberation – bigger than political parties. Our children played together, we went to each other's weddings and funerals and, on occasion, gave each other vegetables, sugar and tea. Many of the young ANC cadres would come and solicit advice and assistance from my husband, seeing a father figure in him. We never turned them away.

When I reflect on exile and the choices I made, it seemed even to me that I chose to go into exile. But, on deeper inspection in my thoughts, my true belief was that the injustices of my country did not require me to leave. I could have fought the system right here. What I chose was to support my husband who did not seem to have the same choices. He *had* to leave and my commitment to him was to go with him.

Family life in exile can be a very difficult affair. Far away from home, in a strange country, it is difficult to resolve some of the problems that young couples face without a familial place to complain. If my mother or mother-in-law had been nearby, it would have been easier to have somebody mediate and arbitrate some of the challenges of a young marriage. I had to mature long before my time. It also took time to make friends you could trust with some of the problems you had.

All the same, life in Zambia was good and they were far more welcoming than the Swazis initially had been. Salaries were better than in Rhodesia and we bought a lovely home and a car. My children and I learnt the local language, my husband had a good job and we got on with life. We were respected members of the community; we attended church; my husband grew lovely vegetables; I sang in a local choir and nurtured a pretty flower garden; the children were growing well.

Many times our home was the site of meetings and organising and several people, who are now forgotten heroes, would come and stay with us. My children called them 'uncle' and, in some way, that was the comrades' only connection with normal family life. One of them – a great PAC ideologue – would often leave our house with a suitcase full of clothes for his children. This went on for years. Every time he came back from a mission, he would have some clothes for them. Once he was gone for so long that the clothes had been outgrown by his children. We often wondered if they knew how often he thought of them, even as he went on missions, and how deeply he loved them.

The exile community was so small. Everyone knew everyone's business. That was not a comfort to me because I was, and remain, very private. When my daughters grew older they became my sounding board. This is the downside of exile. As parents, we tend to load our children with problems that are at times beyond their comprehension. Of course, the apartheid machine was always hovering over our shoulders. Many times, my children and I got phone calls saying my husband was dead or had been in an accident, or had left us never to return. As time went on, I developed nerves of steel, but to this day I resent the alarm that the system tried to inflict on my children and me.

Life in the United Kingdom proved to be different. It was cold and harsh and again we were starting over. While in Zambia we lived a 'good life', London was tougher and the people were hard to handle. I arrived there in the 1970s and skinheads were on the rise, punk was still alive and it was all so strange. We bought gas and electricity through installed coin slots. My older girls were at boarding school in Kenya and later both went to the United States to study and work. My little one – Lebohang – was the one who had to deal with bullying and the nastiness of children who were raised to think Africans were monkeys. Every day she went to school, I felt knots in my stomach. She proved to be resilient and quickly learnt to fight her battles. She was also very brainy and this caught the attention of her teachers who were more willing to pay attention to her adjustment.

Life in London was humdrum, but we gathered a community around us. Lauretta was also in the United Kingdom then, as well as many friends from Zambia and Swaziland. Unlike Zambia, though, political lines were drawn sharply and, as the 1980s drew on, the politics of funding and media propaganda had divided the ANC and PAC even socially. It was a great pity, especially at a time when we needed each other more than ever. An atmosphere of distrust developed between us. Life in Margaret Thatcher's United Kingdom was designed to be difficult for immigrants and refugees.

We found some solace in the vibrant and diverse community around us and again I rediscovered that family is not only blood and, of course, not only South African. Family was extended to include Nigerian, Ghanaian, Turkish, Pakistani, Grenadian, Jamaican, Barbadian, Trinidadian, Cameroonian, St Lucian, Dominican, Irish, Italian, Greek, Somali, Sudanese, Chinese and Vietnamese. Friends like Greta Paterson and Teresa Straunn remain sisters to me. The church also offered some support and sense of community. My children's friends in the United Kingdom and the United States were a 'United Nations'.

As time drew on in the 1990s, two of my children made the choice to come home. As age set in and the cold winters continued, I decided it was time to hit the road again – after thirty years in the United Kingdom and almost forty-five years in exile. I was barely more than a girl when I left South Africa. I came home a pensioner. It is a lifetime spent away.

Now that I am home, there is also a perception held by many people that I am some sort of 'exile queen'. You see it in reactions to our lifestyle, my children's education and the fact that we have flown in an aeroplane as many times as they have taken the minibus taxi from Durban to Johannesburg. To many people, my life is one of privilege. After all, my daughters are doing well, and are respected and successful adults. According to belief commonly held by South Africans, money is the one thing everybody in exile has. Yet, nothing could be further from the truth.

Sometimes, when I count the cost, I think of my relatives with whom I did not spend time and those I could not bury. Both my mother and my mother-in-law died before I came home. One of my brothers died a year before we were able to come home safely to visit in 1990. My children grew up without their grandparents, aunts, uncles, cousins and this pains me.

Communication was tough because letters had been intercepted over the years. Often letters from loved ones came in strange handwriting using a tone that just did not seem like them. Some letters denounced us and told us never to write to them again. Then some months later the same person would write asking why we were so quiet. They, too, received the same disinformation from people pretending to be us. Relatives at home were also harassed by the secret police. This affected both my mother and my mother-in-law. They never complained, but often begged us to be careful or just come home.

Some of my friends who are still alive are lost to me – too many events passed in those many years of separation. I am left now, forced to accept that I have to redefine what home and family is. The real legacy is the marriage I chose, the traditional vows that I held to and the children that we raised.

On our return from exile, my husband became the president of the PAC and served as a member of parliament in the National Assembly for two terms.

Exile was a key that opened many doors and windows. When I watch my daughters getting on with their lives in South Africa, it is with some amazement because a part of me did not really think there was a train or anything that would physically bring us all home again. Exile is about finding the resilience to survive anything. My children seem to be able to adapt to anything in any setting and live their lives on their own terms. Now that I have come back, I ask myself if I might have left anyway, if I might have become a medical doctor after all, if I would also have made more choices on my own terms. I may never know and I am at peace with that.

I have, however, found a new sense of purpose and enjoyment in watching my grandchildren grow up. I have travelled to Canada and, at the time of writing, I am in Japan. My children have grown up. There is nothing to keep me from living out my life fully. It is interesting that the sense of adventure that drew me to my husband is the one that is taking me on new travels. I may never be a doctor now, but I am able to look at my life and what it has been with a sense of achievement and pride. It has been a winding road to take, but it was (and remains) one that I was supposed to walk.

Destination Azania . . .

Liepollo Pheko

Liepollo Lebohang Pheko was born to exiled parents in the 1970s in Lusaka, Zambia. She continued to live in exile with her family, moving to the United Kingdom in 1981. She remained in the United Kingdom until 1993 when, at the age of twenty-two, she came 'home' to South Africa for the first time. In 1997, she returned to live in Johannesburg where she writes, teaches, researches and trains people in the areas of socio-economics, development policy, political theory and feminist theory. She is also a development consultant. She has published several articles, essays and poems in journals and contributed to three books.

'Chuh the bo' . . . 'chuh it!' Half a dozen voices screamed impatiently at me, their tolerance for this new African girl stretched by my apparent inability to follow a basic children's game. I stood holding the ball as children of various hues all looked at me as though I had a spare head growing out of my left shoulder. As months progressed, I realised that all that was required of me was to 'chuck the ball'. Throw the ball to the next child. And so began, at the age of ten, what has seemed to be a lifetime of feeling half a step behind, of feeling that I had just missed the punchline or appeared just after the moment of shared laughter to school friends' or family members' anecdotes.

Adjusting to a working-class, slightly rough-around-the-edges, South London neighbourhood in the United Kingdom, was nothing that my middle-class, private-school upbringing had prepared me for. I was accused of being posh – and in the middle of Peckham that was the kiss of death. I had been exposed to French lessons, horse riding and karate classes. I could have done tennis, but did not since it clashed with choir and drama rehearsals. I was what we call in *Mzansi*-speak (South African slang) a 'cheese girl'. I knew I was different and so did everyone around me. We just lacked the shared vocabulary and EQ to define what made me so different. No one could understand why the soggy cabbage, flavourless beef and lumpy, mashed potatoes served in the school canteen did not excite me. They concluded that it was because I thought I was too 'nice', as in too special and too posh to eat the school fare. With hindsight, I think they were right. After a month of this food, I began to run home for my mum's lunch and dash back to school glowing with appropriate specialness.

None of this made it less clear to me that we were going home 'soon'. We were in a place called exile and I grew up with the assumption that I was on my way to Azania via settler South Africa. We were always on our way to somewhere despite having to create 'home' where we were. I was ten years old, with no understanding of the political machinations of the apartheid government or the social conditions that my age-mates in South Africa/Azania were enduring. The notion of home to me was where I stood.

More puzzling for my new acquaintances in Peckham was that I did not fit any of their stereotypical ideas about Africans. I had heard of Tarzan and was amazed that anybody took that myth seriously. More difficult than the assumptions about Africa being full of huts and malaria, with wild animals roaming the streets – which, alas, many Europeans have yet to grow out of – was the notion of what being an African means. This was hostile territory in 1981. Google had not yet been invented, the information highway was not as advanced as it is now and there were numerous weak excuses for the ignorance, racist presumptions and prejudices that abounded. The terrain was hostile in its assumptions about me and others like me – hostile because it sheltered us conditionally. It was not just the food that was admittedly awful; it was not just the sub-zero temperatures that lost their lustre over the years; it was not just having only my family to speak seSotho with; it was not just the fragments of memories that were all we had to keep 'home' alive; it was not only that photographs were the only sense of extended family I had; it was not just the stupid questions about riding to England on a crocodile – it was all of these things and so much more.

There was a price to be paid for being me, with my strange unambiguously African name, extensive vocabulary and good manners, high marks and short uncombed hair – aka 'nappy head'. I was roundly bullied by various characters, perhaps themselves grappling with their own sense of disconnectedness, since they were all children of colour from immigrant communities. One might have expected solidarity but, knowing what I now do about the politics of vulnerability that dictates that you pick on anyone who seems weaker, more confused or less adjusted than yourself, their reactions were not surprising. I spoke to my mother about it after daily bouts of anxiety-related diarrhoea for the first term became almost too much for my young ten-year-old being to deal with.

Things subsided soon afterwards, but this had less to do with my mother's strongly worded letters to the school than with my well-directed fists. One bull's-eye punch landed successfully on one of the chief bullies, in full view of my classmates, sealed my 'aggro-free' school career and solved my gastric issues thereafter. If anything good came out of this, it is probably that I began to discover a strength that has kept me on solid ground ever since. I did not confess my very physical intervention to my concerned mother for twenty years after the fact.

Another good thing that happened was that two girls – one Turkish, the other Pakistani – planted kindness and acceptance in my life by inviting me into their circle of friendship. This made the new-African-girl-in-Peckham experience much better, gentler and kinder. I paid it forward many times when others who seemed lost, vulnerable or ill-adjusted crossed my path during our school career. And, in one of the girls who extended that lifeline of kindness, Zambia has been a lifelong friend.

My parents had enough on their plate, trying to navigate the complexities of exile. Their story had begun nearly twenty years earlier than my English playground adventures, when they 'skipped' South Africa and fled to Swaziland, Mozambique, then Southern Rhodesia, Zambia, the United Kingdom and the United States. It was all much more intricate than getting on trains, packing up home, putting children in new schools, finding work and setting up new homes.

I recall like yesterday my father's anguish because he was unable to travel to my uncle's funeral in South Africa in 1977. I also recall that was the very year my late grandmother joined us in Swaziland for what is still for me a profound time of fellowship. It was the closest my sisters and I got to being grannied and, as I watch my own small daughters twirling around and singing for their grandparents today, I vicariously enjoy the belated glow of family.

Prior to living in the United Kingdom, our longest stopover was in Zambia where I was born. Perhaps because I was born 'into it' and understood how to say 'chuh the bo' in Nyanja, Tonga and Bemba, I did not feel half a step behind there; I was not too nice or too clever. I was, however, too light and even in relatively friendly Zambia, being light-complexioned brought with it accusations from our Zambian playmates of being 'coloured' or even worse, a '*muzungu*' (whitey). Clearly, belonging was something my sisters and I had to fight for.

Zambia was nicer and simpler to relate to than the diaspora later proved to be. It was calm and, although the welcome was not entirely unconditional, it was easier and less emotionally violent. My sisters and I were comfortable in our 'otherness'. Well, at least I was, probably because I did not know I was an 'other' or because it was a 'familiar other'. My mother tells me that when I was born theories abounded about how come I could be so light although I had been born in Lusaka. Wrapped in a yellow bonnet at church, my complexion was a source of fascination. Later on, in the United Kingdom, it evoked confusion and envy, since all Africans are supposed to have complexions as dark as midnight.

In Zambia, I didn't know that I was in exile. Perhaps it would have clicked if I stayed on longer and if I had not been forced to confront and contest my identity in the United Kingdom. The streets surrounding our home in Lilanda (a township in Lusaka), formed a snapshot of the southern African liberation movement. We were Africanists, the ANC house was a walk away, the Zimbabwean struggle families remain our family to this day, the Namibian and Angolan comrades were often in our home exchanging strategy with my parents. Uncle Duma and Auntie Tiny Nokwe were firm fixtures in our lives, as were the Ngcobos, the Konosos, the Ntloedibes and many others. In addition, there was a plethora of Congolese and later Senegalese neighbours. It all seemed absolutely normal. Probably because it is absolutely normal. We are all from somewhere and many people in our neighbourhood had their own interesting, complicated, tragic or exciting reasons for living outside of their country of birth. That period in our lives remains the picture of authentic diversity for me, as opposed to the microwaved construct of the rainbow nation that was forced upon our gaping wounds in the name of reconciliation in South Africa.

Fast forward a few years to the United Kingdom, still in a place called 'exile en route to Azania'. We were in the midst of constant news and images about the Ethiopian famine and, because I was African, I had to answer questions about why everyone in Africa was so hungry and whether South Africa was close to Ethiopia. I was even asked if perhaps hunger was why my family had come to the United Kingdom in the first place. Apart from being a devastating indictment of the British state-school geography curriculum, that experience continued to speak to the many complexities of what home was. As much as I did not want to be directly associated with the despair and victimhood that the Ethiopian famine represented, or with Bob Geldof's hollow ranting or the media's perverse lack of geo-political analysis, I realised I could not choose which bits of Africa to be from or to love. Loving Africa was like a marriage to a great guy with bad breath. I had to kiss him anyway.

In all the years I lived in the United Kingdom, I had the strong sense that I would eventually come home. My only dilemma was where home was and what it meant to me. South London had become slightly friendlier to me as the years progressed. Food from home that I could relate to, like *pap* (soft cornmeal), tripe and okra, became available. There were African music festivals and people like Lucky Dube, Mahlathini and the Mahotella Queens, Dorothy Masuka and Hugh Masekela came and embraced us with rhythms from home. I survived secondary school and was even elected class president for three years running. I was still posh, knew way too much about Marxism, Malcolm X and Maya Angelou and still went home to eat lunch. As a schoolmate said to me years afterwards, 'We just didn't get you and you sort of scared us.'

My local library had books by the poet Don Mattera, who articulated the complexities of his own identity politics in *Gone with the Twilight*. Mark Mathabane's *Kaffir Boy* and writers Bloke Modisane and Sindiwe Magona all contributed to my knowledge of 'home' and its challenges. The South African community in exile was close-knit and we went to each other's weddings and funerals. We were the closest thing to family that any of us had.

And then, somewhere during the 1980s, South Africa became fashionable. Nelson Mandela was successfully, albeit undeservedly, branded as the symbol of the South African struggle. In the midst of this, the colonial question was forgotten. Some of my friends even refused to eat Cape apples and invited me to picket against the South African cricket team. Later, there was black history and the Nelson Mandela concert to help construct and reconstruct popular ideas of what Africa and South Africa were. I found the Mandela hype infuriating and, when a college friend asked me if I was going home in the wake of his release, my life flashed before my eyes and I wondered if decades of struggle, bloodshed, sacrifice and the kind of trauma that many people of my parent's generation had undergone could possibly be reduced to one human being.

In July 1990, my mother and I finally came home. For me, it was a debut. For her, it was the first time in twenty-seven years. It was longer than I had been alive. At the time I was unsure about my ability to translate cultural codes, to speak seSotho as quickly, melodically or effusively as I imagined was required.

It is difficult to express in full the extent of this pilgrimage on me and my psyche. From landing at what was then Jan Smuts Airport to leaving nearly two months later, I experienced a rollercoaster of emotions – tears, expectations, discoveries and at last a face to what 'home' is. Photos and stories about aunts, uncles, cousins, grandparents, nieces and nephews came to life. People who looked like me, sounded like me and walked like me became real. After years of acquiring family across the world, my blood family in Johannesburg, Mangoalaneng and Qoboshaneng, living their lives, some of them thinking about us, some wanting from us, some longing for us, finally emerged in real life. Meeting both my grandmothers remain seminal moments in my life.

My maternal grandmother – Maria Pakkies – shared my anxiety about my communication skills. We were both delighted that my linguistic competency not only met requirements for a conversation, but they exceeded expectations – not least my own. Spending a week in her rural home was like visiting an oasis of love and restoration. I felt as though I were being birthed again and that all these people who looked and sounded like me were the catalyst for this birth.

The birth of my sense of home was truly profound. I cannot to this day express what I felt. I spent much of the trip in tears that went beyond joy at meeting and sadness at parting. It was partly the understanding that 'home' is a choice. Home is acceptance of the warts that one does not like to deal with about one's country. And home was my grandmothers who, over the years, had sent gestures of love, letters, ponchos and blankets. As it happens, I never met either of them again after 1990. They passed on before I came back in 1997. As if she knew, my paternal grandmother – Mohau Moerane – bought me one more blanket, one final gesture of love, of welcome and of parting.

Might I add that in the midst of this halcyon pilgrimage, we stopped at my other 'home', Zambia, and spent moments with adoptive family there. The tears began flowing upon touchdown and watered the parts of me that I thought had been lost while 'chucking the ball' in the United Kingdom. For those couple of months, I got some of the punchlines and even helped to create some new ones.

Upon return to Babylon, things in my head were clearer, firmer and more finite. I was no longer coming home 'someday'; I was coming back before I was thirty. I watched the elections in 1994 from a surreal distance. I felt as though the struggle had in fact been betrayed by the negotiation process. During this time, the South London neighbourhood I grew up in evolved. My neighbours and friends were now Nigerian, Trinidadian, Somalian, Liberian, Ghanaian, Jamaican, Guyanese, Pakistani, Vietnamese, Greek and Ethiopian, among many others. I did African dance classes at Brixton Recreation Centre, hung out at Africa Centre in central London and felt as though I was in whatever I imagined a shebeen to be. I worshipped at a multiracial church in Kensington and visited many Nigerian and Ghanaian churches en route. I gave my tithes to the work of the Kingdom not only as part of my spiritual discourse, but perhaps to ensure that my heavenly home would be surer than the earthly one I had so far experienced.

Life progressed; I got through university, worked for some noble organisations, doing stoically virtuous work. In December 1996, my father who had repatriated back in 1995 sent me a ticket to 'come and see'. In January 1997, I boarded a plane and waved the grey clouds goodbye. My friends knew that I would be back in six weeks, in time for some occasion or other in March. And a part of me believed it when I said it.

So I boarded a plane from the familiar to the terrain I had sampled seven years prior and decided to call home. It is an odd thing this 'home' stuff. Initially, I was ambivalent and there were moments where the violence of change was as acute as if I was ten years old once more. Again I struggled to 'chuh the bo' and again I seemed to be missing a beat. The first year in particular was a combination of heaven and hell and my vocabulary does not extend to the spaces I traversed emotionally and spiritually. An intensely visceral experience, it improved once I got a job and made a new circle of friends to chill with in Newtown, Yeoville and Rosebank, all suburbs of Johannesburg.

But still, there were codes and mores that I struggled to understand. What I realised a long time ago is confirmed daily – that, in many respects, I may always be half a step or half a beat behind, out of synch or ahead of people around me. Even at home, I am still 'other' because of my accent, my reference points and sometimes obtuse sense of humour. But it's fine because it is an 'other' that more of us understand. It is an 'other' that many of us share, of being of this land and from this land, even if we did not grow up here. We 'exiles' daily carve out our own sense of belonging and define what home means to us, and we keep creating our own punchlines that feature our own experiences. And, more and more, it feels as though the reference points and conversations of the ones who left are melding with the ones who remained and are increasingly and necessarily mutually enforcing. We keep on learning to 'chu the bo' at each other.

After thirteen years in what I have chosen as 'home', it's easier and smoother and I am able to construct a reality that works and functions and feeds me. I may be off again to other shores at some point and reconstruct 'home' as the place where I land, but I understand where my 'North' is and will use it to centre me wherever my feet take me. I am uneasy with the idea of 'South Africa' as my final destination, but remain in transit here on my way to Azania.

My shades of light skin, 'othering' and exile

Mohau Pheko

Mohau Pheko was born in Roodepoort, South Africa, in 1959. She grew up in Zambia and Kenya where her parents were in exile. She was educated in the United States under a United Nations Expanded Program of Technical Assistance scholarship. When she returned to South Africa in 1995, she worked for several organisations including the Women's National Coalition, promoting the rights of women. She founded her own consulting firm working on international trade and economic literacy. She is a member of several international networks concerned with economic rights. Recognised for her leadership and strategic vision, Mohau has served as South African High Commissioner in Canada and has recently been appointed as South Africa's ambassador to Japan.

There were throngs of them behind us. Their ages varied from six to fourteen years old. There were boys, there were girls and their chant was not new. Whenever my sister, Mamello, and I dared to venture out of Lilanda, the township where we lived in Lusaka, Zambia, hostile, childish, threatening and menacing crowds of children besieged us. What was peculiar to me was the fact that parents and adults always stood in the doorways of their shacks, not scolding or discouraging the children's chant as we passed by.

I am not certain if we were a novelty because, after all, how many light-skinned girls walked through the George and Matero compound townships? Was it because they really thought we were coloured or white, or that we were so different from them? What incited them to chant the same song and slogans each time we passed through the neighbourhood? Why did I not feel different from these kids? Was I so oblivious to my own skin colour that the shades of toffee, caramel and butterscotch playing on my body did not define me as different enough? As far as I was concerned, I was an African child. Or, was I too indoctrinated by my pan-Africanist parents and indifferent to things such as skin colour?

We were all living on the same continent. We met often at Happy Grocery, the local shopping centre. I had even spied them from time to time in front of the shop dancing to the music of bands from Zaire. Those days, the grocery store transformed itself into a tavern after 7 p.m. The adults often chased us away from there or questioned why we were buying bread at an hour that was for adults only. It was those same kids whom we met on a one-to-one basis that would place their bread and milk on the stoep of the grocery store and gyrate to the music. I would always follow suit. Why would the same kids who danced with me on the edge of the grocery shop 'other' me and treat me so badly when they were in a crowd with their friends?

A taunting chant like that never leaves you. It undresses you in front of everybody. You feel like you are walking naked down the street and everybody is laughing at you. '*Chimpalala gumugumu letha nyama ni wose*' (Bald head, bald head, you look like a lizard. Your head is shining like a hotplate. Let me roast some meat on your head). This followed by '*Muzungu!*' (whitey) and '*Mu-coloured*' (coloured), They would jeer this painfully behind my sister and me.

What could my mother have been thinking when she asked my father to take us to his barber under a tree near the taxi rank, beside Matero township market in Lusaka? The fact that the barber himself was perplexed but too polite and respectful of my father to explain that the idea of cutting two young girls' hair was not only out of his area of expertise but was also unheard of. Worse for us, there was a group of old men who always seemed to have nothing better to do than hang around the barber shop all day, unashamedly making comments about women who wore short skirts, the affair a pastor was having, you name it. If my mother had known our ears were being filled with all the community gossip, I am sure she would have found another place for us to cut our hair.

As usual, the barber never gave us the cut and style that we wanted even after a long explanation and description. Not that it was any of their business, but the old men also thought it was their duty to join the discussion and recommend what they thought would be a good haircut. Of course, this was all discussed as if we were invisible, without voice. The issue of the colour of our skin was always the centrepiece of the discussion. We spoke Nyanja fluently and understood Bemba well enough to get the drift of a conversation. We conversed in these languages with the barber, but it seemed to matter little.

'Why are you so light?' one old man asked for the hundredth time. The conversation was so predictable. 'Is someone in your family white?' 'No.' I would give the usual terse response, but not so terse as to be rude. We were well brought-up children, with manners, who had been taught to respect adults even when they talked rubbish.

'So why are you coloured?'

'I am not coloured, I am an African like you,' was always my response.

That a conversation about what haircut style I should have, and not-so-kind mutterings about my skin colour should become a refrain, as it were, was an indictment on my father, who always unceremoniously dumped us at the barber's tree, making noises through the driver's window to the barber about settling the bill on his way back from town. The fact that the styling occurred in his absence meant that we would have to live with whatever haircut the barber decided upon – and it was usually the French cut that was only for boys. A French cut is the worst kind of haircut you can give a girl child. The barber would shave our hair as low as possible, and then leave this ridiculous-looking 'V' shape on the top of our heads, while completely shaving off the rest of the hair. Even more humiliating was the fact that after these haircuts, we would have to traverse all the way from Matero market through three hostile neighbourhoods to get home, with kids chanting their usual song and slogans of *Muzungu! Mu-coloured!*

The taunting from our darker-skinned Zambian peers said a lot about our place in terms of class, race and gender in the township and shanty towns near where we lived. Walking through at least three working-class communities on a Saturday afternoon was bound to elicit a wild reaction. Strangely, they had only ever seen us drive by in what they considered a posh mode of transport, the family's blue station wagon. Any time we went out of the boundary of Lilanda, children came out in droves to chant at us. Even mangy dogs would take the opportunity to bark at us, in solidarity with our jeerers.

There was always, though, the privilege of sweet revenge. The taunting, jeering children learnt very quickly that when they came into our neighbourhood, especially Iboza Avenue, they were walking into our territory. The lines were drawn and the boundaries set. Unlike them, we did not have the power of numbers behind us. However, we had an even better weapon to fight them with. They must have wondered how we were able to identify them. Inevitably, the protagonists would come into our neighbourhood selling vegetables. Then and only then would we prepare our secret weapon to fight this war in which we were constantly being made the 'other'. 'Tomato, onion', they would shout at the top of the streets. Various people in our street would stop them and buy vegetables from the big dishes they carried on their heads.

Our house was situated more towards the middle of the street. This lulled the sellers into a sense of comfort about their excursion. Little did they know that my sister and I were about to strike terror in their hearts. Patti, my mother's dog, was a mix of fox terrier and Pekinese. She was black, obedient, compulsively co-operative and knew the drill. We had trained her to be on the lookout for the vegetable-selling kids. When she heard them, she would run from the back of the house to the front gate and lie down quietly. As the children approached our house, we would push the gate slightly ajar to let Patti out to settle our score. She was not a kind dog to strangers. Even worse, she had sensed our antagonism towards the children and all her protective instincts came out. Small as she was, her aim was strategic. She would give small nips at the ankles and snarl and bark so viciously, even the meter reader was scared of her. It only took us three attempts to stop the jeering. I would say 'Sssaaahhh!' and Patti would take off, running after the unsuspecting kids, their produce spilling onto the street. Tomatoes and onions would chase after each other down the road, while the kids took off in a different direction. It was a mean thing to do. I had neither concept of class nor an understanding of the economic damage I might have done to a family that was not as fortunate as I was.

I was about ten years old when this was happening. That other children, students and even teachers, perceived us as different was difficult. All my life I had been socialised under an African identity. I may have gone to white schools outside the township, but I could speak seSotho (my mother tongue), Nyanja (spoken in Lusaka), as well as Swahili (spoken in East Africa), fluently. I could even throw serious insults in Bemba, a language spoken predominantly in the Copperbelt province of Zambia that could easily undermine your mother's or father's sexuality.

I don't know what it is about light skin that made so many Zambian women bleach their skin with creams that were corrosive enough to turn their dark skins red. This prompted my mother and her friends to whisper 'Fanta – Coca-Cola' each time one of these women walked past them. Fanta depicted the bleached lighter skin on the face, while Coca-Cola was the obvious demarcation of the darker complexion untouched by the bleached from the neck down. What was hilarious was to hear the same women ask my mother what she used on her face to be so light – a strange question to ask a woman born light-skinned. What was it about light skin that would follow me into adulthood? Was it just the experience of living in exile or was it something more?

Immigration issues, border-crossing and nationalist tendencies have been a part of my life ever since I can remember. Living in Swaziland, Rhodesia (now Zimbabwe), Zambia, Kenya and the United States bestowed on me multiple identities. I belonged somewhere and everywhere. In reality, I did not belong at all. I was and am an African child of the continent – a Mosotho, born in Dobsonville in Johannesburg. However, my sense of belonging or 'home' was never on the basis of being a South African because I did not and still do not know what that means. I left South Africa at a young age and therefore had no real attachment to it except through photographs of me when I was younger. I did not remember my grandparents or my other relatives enough to have formed roots or a sense of place that says: 'You belong here.'

If belonging and identity are based on culture, language, heritage and statehood, exile has given me multiple cultures to which I had to adapt in order to belong. I am fluent in a suitcase-full of languages that I had to integrate into my life to fit in. My heritage is not just from one source, it carries so many universes, nuances from different places and people. In the white schools where I was the only African girl in my class for six years, I had to accept that I was 'white enough' to become a great interpreter. I was bombarded with questions such as, 'Why do African people straighten their hair? Why does your skin tan and other black people don't tan?'

I was Azanian because that's what my parents told me. I had to understand the liberation struggle because my country South Africa was dominated by white people; so said the comrades from the Azanian People's Liberation Army who stayed at our house for months at a time. They said I had to develop a political consciousness, yet it was this very political consciousness that alienated me from my white classmates who could not deconstruct the liberation struggle in South Africa.

In the African communities where I lived in various countries I did not really belong. This was never more evident than when I had to cross the border into different African countries. Who are you? Why are you going to a white school? Why are you travelling on this passport? Which country are you a resident of? I had no state of my own and my acceptance in different groups was conditional, sometimes based on my skin colour, at other times based on pity or solidarity about being a South African. Yet, I did not really understand the issues in South Africa well enough to articulate them in a way that connected me to the struggles of my 1976 counterparts. I was an authentic South African, but not really because I had never experienced apartheid or racism the way my parents talked about their own experiences.

I belonged somewhere provided I accepted being 'othered', or light-skinned or politically conscious. I belonged everywhere because I connected to so many places that defined me, but ultimately I always felt as though I was a political, cultural and spiritual outcast. I did not choose to go into exile. I did not even have a choice of where I would live. Yet, I had to create a web of complex relationships, often with hostile host societies in places that I had to call home. I was under pressure to integrate smoothly without causing too much havoc, but, at the same time, retain my parent's socio-cultural particularities which to some extent deprived me of a sense of belonging. My definition of 'sense of belonging' means validating the importance of my cultural life, expression and experiences. If they are multiple, how am I defined? This was a question that vexed me for a long time.

At university in America, I was a constant target for the black sister sororities. I thought it was because I was intelligent. This was so until I coerced my reluctant dark-skinned friend, Linda, to go to the membership orientation day with me. We were met by a sea of girls who I would have never been caught dead talking to on any given day. They were the type that dressed well enough to catch the eye of our basketball players. That was not my scene. As if that were not enough, Linda decided to storm out of the room. When I finally caught up with her, she warned me, in no uncertain terms, never again to take her to some light-skin-girl convention. 'I will throw you into the butter section of the grocery store where all light skin girls like you think you are special,' she added. I was taken aback. Shocked and humiliated at being 'othered'. My light-skin experience had never been 'special', I shouted back at her. All my life, I explained, I had been treated with either contempt or as different because I was light-skinned. Men wanted to marry me because I could give them light-skinned babies.

Whites thought I was not white enough. Political activists in the black power movement thought I was not authentic enough to be a real South African because I was not truly 'black'. This was a paradox for me. At one level I was light and beautiful, yet, not ethically authentic.

In 1989, I decided to end the exile I had not chosen, and ventured into South Africa after twenty-five years of being away from what I had been told was home. I needed to end my purely nostalgic connection with this home. I latched passionately onto the cause of liberation of South Africa as a way of finding my identity. This took me back to Soweto and the Transkei where my parents come from. Having left the country at a young age, I did not fully appreciate the nuanced social norms that would make my relatives, whom I knew only through photographs, treat me as a guest and not as a South African. To my dismay, the sentimental idea that I would come 'home' and settle among my people and be part of the liberation struggle was no longer viable. I was a foreigner in my own country. I could not relate or share in the experiences, culture and norms of the country of my birth. I realised that my life needed all the worlds I had lived in to survive. The realities of my homeland had been fragments of sentiment that did not give me the sufficient comfort of belonging.

It is not always comfortable to be 'othered'. Yet, it is these identities that have challenged my social memberships, my old concepts of self. Being 'othered' has added layers of a rich social diversity and cultural multiplicity which has allowed me to enjoy the making of me in many nations, nationhoods and nationalisms. Exile may have taken away the meaning of belonging to a particular nation, such as South Africa. Yet I think I am a more whole person despite the 'othering', exclusion and even stigmatising. The moulding of my 'othering' in exile has defined and secured my own positive identity that transcends race, geography, ethnicity, economics and ideology. My shades of toffee, caramel and butterscotch are an affirmation of the many layers that make up who I am.

I gave it all

Rajes Pillay

Rajes Pillay was born in Pietermaritzburg, KwaZulu-Natal, although she grew up in the 1950s in Kimberley, Northern Cape, at a time of heightened resistance to apartheid education. She completed her secondary schooling in England and returned to South Africa where, in 1966, she became an activist in the Natal Indian Congress. She undertook tertiary studies at the University of Natal, following which she worked as a bank clerk at the New Republic Bank. She was dismissed for union activities and went on to work as a social worker for the South African Council of Churches, giving support to ex-Robben islanders and prisoner's families. She was regularly harassed by the South African police and had her passport withdrawn. In 1978 she fled into exile in Swaziland where she worked for the African National Congress. She remained in exile for fourteen years. Currently, she lives in retirement at Reservoir Hills, Durban.

My story deals with my childhood and my journey through life as a young person in my teens when the armed struggle was undertaken. My journey led me to seek for truth and justice and the African National Congress (ANC) was the only vehicle that could achieve this for me.

The new generation is entirely different. This is the digital age; all schools are open; the buses and transport systems are open to all; intermixing and interracial marriages are now recognised. The defence force is open to all who want to join it – not just for whites as in the past. Gone are the sign boards painted 'Whites only' – a visible proof of the alienation for the black majority in the country of their birth. To quote Nelson Mandela on his inauguration as the first black president, 'Never will there be a time repeated when man exploits man again'.

This contribution is a memoir of one who went through the apartheid era and strove for equality and dignity for all races in South Africa. It is a contribution for the new generation who will take their place among all other nationalities on the world stage.

Prelude to exile

In 1966, I was a student at the University of Natal. I became the secretary to the Student Representative Council (SRC) and served in this capacity from 1966 to 1969. The SRC included Paul David, Ben Ngubane, Steven Biko and Rogers Ragavan.

Those years were bleak for activists. Most of the ANC leaders were banned, under house arrest or serving sentences on Robben Island. Any activity opposing the government was slated as being 'communist'.

Student organisations were particularly targeted by the Special Branch. The campuses were fully infiltrated by the security police and their agents. Those who headed student organisations could well expect visits from the Special Branch. I had first-hand experience of this.

Paul David was a fellow colleague. He invited me to meet his sister, Phyllis Naidoo. She was under house arrest and banned. She had three young children – Sadhan, Saradh and Sukthi – and her husband was serving a five-year sentence on Robben Island.

Phyllis's flat was always full of activists, and other politicos such as A.K.M. Docrat, Poomoney Moodley, Judson Khuzwayo, Shadrack Maphumulo and Jacob Zuma, among others. Despite the banning order (which forbade visitors to the home of a banned person), others who frequented her place included Mewa Ramgobin, George Sewpersad, Tim Naidoo, M.J. Naidoo, Rabi Bhagwandeen as well as several youth members of the Natal Indian Congress.

Our activism included protest meetings held at Kajee Hall (convened by Fatima Meer), activists in the Black Consciousness Movement (such as Saths Cooper and Strini Moodley), arranging concerts, shows and film shows as part of fund-raising for the cause.

I was appointed as publicity officer for the Theatre Council of Natal. This was an organisation formed to politicise a mixed audience on the cultural front through plays and musical items. We invited the Inanda Seminary choir to perform at one of our concerts that was held at the Goodwill Lounge.

I also participated in sending Diwali parcels to Robben Island which we thought would cheer up the inmates. According to Natoo Babenia (ex-Robben islander), the authorities finally stopped these parcels getting to prisoners after several prisoners told the wardens that they had converted to Hinduism.

According to the speeches and writings of O.R. Tambo, 1978 was a particularly bleak period for the ANC inside the country. The organisational structures of the ANC inside the country were so weak that the ANC relied on the Indian congresses to organise mass meetings and funeral services on their behalf. Rick Turner's and Monty Naicker's funerals were cases in point. Funerals were occasions when fiery anti-apartheid speeches could be made, an avenue for mass mobilisation.

By 1977, several islanders had been released. Among those whom I met were Sunny Singh, Indris Naidoo, Mac Maharaj, Sunny Venketrathnam and Ebrahim Ismail, as well as George Naicker. It was rewarding to talk to them because they presented a realistic view of the degree of oppression inside the country. They related stories of their prison experiences and told of the Special Branch torture methods to which they had been subjected.

The Black Consciousness Movement was started in the 1970s and several of its activists were detained for their political activities. They had organised a rally at Curries Fountain to celebrate Mozambique's independence in 1975. These celebrations were organised countrywide among black communities (that is, Africans, Indians and coloureds). Mapetla Mohapi, Saths Cooper, Strini Moodley were detained; Mapetla Mohapi died in detention.

While all this was going on, Judson Khuzwayo was released from Robben Island. He was released at about the same time as Jacob Zuma. I met both of them at Phyllis Naidoo's office. Around 1979, I was recruited into the ANC underground by Judson. He never persuaded me to undertake any serious underground activity at that stage. I made him aware of the fact that I was a fieldworker for the South African Council of Churches, along with Father Mabaso. As fieldworker, I could interact with ex-prisoners and their families, a useful cover for my political activities. I asked Judson to give me the names of families who would need assistance. He promised to give them to me, but never came forward with any results.

In 1977, Sunny Singh, Phyllis Naidoo, Mac Maharaj and Judson Khuzwayo suddenly disappeared. This event marked the tentative beginnings of my life as an underground activist. It was obvious that what one could not achieve legally had to be done illegally – such were the circumstances inside the country. This was not new. All political activity during periods of repression took on an underground hue.

We could not get books on other revolutions to study. Foreign publications on the independence of Angola, Mozambique, Kenya, and Vietnam were difficult to obtain. Frequently, they were listed as banned literature and it was an offence to be found in possession of these books. Writings by Lenin and Marx, though housed at the city hall library, were banned to black persons. A.K.M. Docrat broke this ban. He ordered books through Premier Bookstore and sold them privately as well. He was banned for fifteen years. His house arrest only allowed him four hours a day to see to his business interests. To keep my links with ANC friends, I kept in touch with Phyllis Naidoo, who, it became known, had fled first to Swaziland and then Lesotho.

Into exile
The year was 1978. I was working at Game Stores, which was then situated in Smith Street, Durban. A letter arrived for me via my work address, but with a Swaziland stamp. The letter was from Judson. In it he advised me that he was sending me a

courier who needed help obtaining material he wanted in Durban. The courier finally arrived, a well-built woman, who gave me a letter addressed to 'Scarecrow' (Judson's name for me). I thanked her for the letter and took her home with me. My mother was astonished, but kindly offered supper. We slept in my bedroom that night. The following day, I dropped her at the airport and told her to tell Judson that I would do my best to carry out what he had requested.

The letter requested some topographical maps of Durban. I did not know what a topographical map was, so I purchased some street maps of Durban, and several layout maps, showing the townships of the different areas in Durban. I did not have to wait long. Two weeks later, the same woman returned. I hid the maps in a large artist's carry-all, rolled up and disguised in a tin. This time the courier wanted to go to Clermont and asked if I could drive her there. I refused, saying that I would stand out as an Indian in an African township, so I took her to the bus stop and dropped her off, admonishing her to wear a *doek* (head scarf), as most of the Zulu women did. She was surprised, but complied. The following day I dropped her outside the departure lounge at the airport.

The requests now came thick and fast. I decided that we had to find an easier way to communicate. To this end, I enlisted the help of Daisy whom I knew from Phyllis Naidoo's place. We recruited a courier (a student from the University of Zululand) and hid material under the carpets in my car. I got petrol money to send him to Swaziland with the booty in the car. He drove all the way there. On his return, he reported that he had made contact with Judson and that he was now required to carry out tasks which he could not discuss with me. I was sent money to pass on to base ANC operatives.

I knew that I would not last long. As it turned out, the ANC subsequently sent a nurse to see me. She knew my private home address, my telephone number and where I worked. She also knew my real name. Should she have been arrested, it was a sure thing that she would reveal my identity to the Special Branch. I then received a message from Cecil (the courier Daisy and I had recruited to travel between Durban and Swaziland) that I should think of leaving or expect to be arrested as the nurse had indeed turned out to be an *impimpi* (informer).

Two weeks later, a young man arrived at my desk at work. He used Judson's code name and said that he had been sent to get me out of the country. The decision to leave or stay was mine, and I decided to leave. I had, in the course of my escape, to wait a fortnight before we found a suitable means of transport out of the country. We arrived at the Swaziland border and walked from Nomahasha to Manzini – a small town in the centre of Swaziland. We walked for twelve hours without stopping and my bones were sore and weary after the long walk. I was taken to Judson (here known as Mthethwa) and was warmly welcomed by his wife, Beauty. She gave us something to eat and then we went to find somewhere to live. We found shelter at St Joseph's Mission in Mzimpofu for about a month before the ANC claimed me as a member. The chief representative at the time was one Patrick Nyawose. He took me through the steps of registering me as a refugee, under the aegis of the ANC.

Procedure for registration

All refugees arriving in Swaziland had to report to the local police station. They had to go through an interview with the head of the police who listened to their stories and then decided whether they could stay in Swaziland or not. The intervention of the diplomatic mission of the ANC was crucial. There were about three interviews – I think that this was aimed at preventing bandits from streaming into the country.

Finally, the chief of police advised me that, since I was Indian, I would not fit into African society. He advised me to seek accommodation with two Indians who were staying at St Joseph's Mission. I was to share my life with these two other refugees for the next fourteen years. Needless to say, we were cynical about the security arrangements of the Swazi police. Swaziland was still economically dependent on South Africa. As such, it shared a common customs union with South Africa. In the final analysis, Swaziland could not exert herself as a wholly independent entity; South African pressure on it could force the police to act against the ANC. This was borne out by several raids on refugee houses in the years that followed. As Indians, we were to some extent exempt; we were seen as separate entities from the other refugees with whom we interacted.

Also resident in Swaziland were refugees who had left South Africa in the 1960s. They were now married to Swazi women, or employed in some profession or another (for instance Reggie Mhlongo, Graham Morodi, someone known as the 'Lion of the East', Aaron Madida, John Nkadimeng, Stanley Mabizela, Patrick Nyawose, Joe Mkhwanazi and others). Women included Alzina Zondi, Beauty Khuzwayo and someone called Joyce. It was not surprising that most of the local people knew the ANC members quite well and were fully aware of what conditions they faced in exile.

I was granted refugee asylum for a period of one year. If, through their security apparatus, the Swazis found out that a certain refugee was a threat to the security of their country, that refugee could be declared a prohibited immigrant and would be dispatched to some other country where there was an ANC presence (such as Zambia or Tanzania). Phyllis Naidoo was deported in such a manner.

The two main sources of power in Swaziland were the monarchy, headed by King Sobhuza II, and the church. An influential person in church circles was Bishop Zwane who had influence with the king and with the Swazi chief of police. Many worshipped the bishop as a saviour, including the refugees who came flooding into Swaziland in 1980.

Most of the ANC refugees received good treatment – a place to sleep, applications for United Nations High Commissioner for Refugees (UNHCR) scholarships, some measure of protection from the South African incursions by the South Africa Defence Force (SADF), jobs (where available), and food and clothing. They were totally dependent on the ANC. An invaluable source of diplomatic persuasion came from Moses Mabhida who frequently came to Swaziland and who had developed a relationship with the Swazi authorities. Of course, it goes without saying that the influence of the ANC was strengthened by the largely personal influence of O.R. Tambo himself.

I felt very much at home here; the Swazis were kind, loving people. Also, I valued the influence of the church – especially the Roman Catholic and Protestant missions that preached brotherhood and solidarity. The attitude of the local people was one of accommodation, for which we refugees were grateful.

Friends in the church

Bishop Zwane was a diminutive man. However, his stature was deceptive – he wielded enormous power in the Kingdom of Swaziland. He exerted his influence with the Roman Catholic church, the government and the monarchy with a steely determination. I was a foreigner in Swaziland and decided that the only way I could make contact with the local people was to find a job so that I could integrate properly. Unfortunately, I had no academic qualifications that would have allowed me to get a teaching job. Government service was reserved for Swazi nationals only.

Accordingly, I conveyed my desire to Ivan with whom I was sharing a house at Mzimpofu. He conveyed my request to Patrick Nyawose and the matter was reported to the chief representative (John Nkadimeng, at the time). It was Bishop Zwane's recommendation that led to me being appointed as refugee counsellor in a project managed by the UNHCR. The UNHCR collaborated closely with the Swaziland Council of Churches on projects connected with refugees. Bishop Zwane was in touch with the High Commission in Geneva.

The Swaziland Council of Churches sought to unify all church organisations into the refugee programme: the Protestant mission, local African churches and the Roman Catholic mission (headed by Bishop Zwane). Other church organisations who participated were the Mennonites, an agency from America. The meetings were held once a month. As refugee counsellor, it was my duty to oversee the passage of refugees fleeing the country, particularly those in the Pan-Africanist Congress (PAC). Travel tickets were bought using money from the Catholic Bishops' Fund for mostly Portuguese refugees, who sought to repatriate to Portugal.

My other duties included the housing of refugees who came flooding in from South African townships, as well as the Mozambican National Resistance (MNR) movement refugees fleeing the newly liberated Mozambique. To accommodate all those who did not have homes, a house was built with bunk beds for all refugees (ANC, PAC and MNR). The refugees were not happy with this arrangement; some left and found accommodation in the rural areas. Others fled the country and illegally jumped the fence into the eastern Transvaal, South Africa, where they sought training from the SADF (these were particularly the MNR refugees). Some PAC refugees went to the council office, where they were given R40 for subsistence, collected R40 from the UNHCR, and then travelled to Botswana. All those caught entering the country illegally were arrested and put into prison. They could either claim asylum or be deported to their country of origin. This applied to all newcomers to the Kingdom of Swaziland.

Several refugees lived their whole lives this way, jumping from one country to another. Bishop Zwane was well aware of this dilemma. He was critical of the degree of commitment the church was showing to refugees and argued that the homeless should at least be fed and clothed according to God's word. Accordingly, any complimentary cinema tickets the church received, he would distribute among the refugees. He frequently took newly arrived refugees and housed them in the bishop's quarters, much to the annoyance of the other church elders. Also, he exhorted all Swazis to support refugees and give them food and shelter. Needless to say, his influence in commanding support for refugees was fervently supported by all the nuns and priests from the Roman Catholic mission.

When I was appointed, he invited me to his quarters in Manzini and asked me to share lunch with him. He said, 'I know that your way of cooking is different; I will show you how we eat'. He dished out *pap* (soft cornmeal) onto a wooden dish, with some roasted meat and poured some wine. We ate together, while we conversed. The food was delicious.

Among my fellow colleagues at the office was an ex-teacher called Gugu, a very motherly, proud woman. She kept telling me that she was a Dlamini – related to the king. She became my good friend and introduced me to a nun whom we called Florence. Then there was Mrs Ntuli who did the typing at the office. We began the day with a short prayer every morning. The secretary general of the refugee service was one querulous being call Harold Wenger. He had been accepted by the church council from the Mennonite mission in America.

Other friends I made through the church office were Felicia at Ephesus House, Michael Broadbent (a volunteer from England), some members of the International Voluntary Service, Ed and Laureen Morrow from the South African mission, several priests from Germany and representatives from the local African church missions. A close friend of the bishop's was a priest called Father Skhakane – a polite and kindly man. We got to know the church personalities quite well. There was a Bishop Mkhabela, Father Mdiniso (whose brother headed the police) and Father Ciconne at the Mzimpofu mission. The churches had spread throughout the country – and priests came from the rural areas to consult with the bishop, who was always warm and accommodating.

One big occasion was an international conference called to discuss fertility and the host country was Swaziland. Translators, foreign cars, diplomatic personnel came pouring into Manzini and Mbabane. The conference proceedings went on for two weeks. Bishop Zwane attended the closing session. No one really knows what happened later that night. He was found dead in his car, with no signs of murder except for a thin trickle of blood coming from his forehead. A little known fact was that he had paid so much for the repatriation of the Portuguese refugees from his Bishops' Fund – he died virtually bankrupt.

The whole country mourned. All businesses, government offices and schools were closed for the day of the funeral. Everyone came pouring into the funeral – refugees, farmers, businessmen, diplomatic personnel. A solemn service was held at the cathedral. Voices rose in loud unison as his favourite hymn, Psalm 11, was sung. The rafters rang with sound. His body was incarcerated at the Roman Catholic church in a vault. He was worshipped by all those who knew him. His memory will live within us forever.

The United Nations High Commissioner for Refugees

When I arrived in Swaziland, I had to report to the police first, then apply for refugee status from the UNHCR. The decision to grant refugee status was not automatic as the remits of the Swazi police and the UNHCR were different. The UNHCR could agree to give refugee status, but this did not mean that the Swazis were bound by this decision. The Swazis could declare someone a prohibited immigrant if they felt they were dangerous and the UNHCR could not interfere.

Considering the rapid influx of refugees, I decided to look at the rules governing refugee status. According to the Geneva Convention (to which Swaziland was a signatory), all refugees who had nowhere else to go were to be steadily incorporated into Swazi society. However, from the Swazi side, no refugee, no matter how long he or she was resident in Swaziland, could qualify for Swazi citizenship. Thus, an exiled South African who could be married to a Swazi woman remained a refugee; marriage did not give him the right to claim citizenship. Further, there was the added difficulty that the Swazi government had to be approached in the cases where there were applications for government jobs, such as teachers. A job in the police service and direct representation in the Swazi government was prohibited. A refugee could start a business (frequently projects funded by the UNHCR) but, if declared a prohibited immigrant, he or she could not claim compensation for all the years of toil. If deported, the Swazi government could take over the business.

It must be noted that the spirit of the Geneva Convention was not followed to the letter. There were vast areas of conflict over the legal application of the convention.

I pointed this out to Mr Sabiti (then representative of the UNHCR) and he immediately called the head office in Geneva to attend to the matter. Their response was that they had to abide by the rules and regulations of the government or else they had to face closure themselves. That was that.

The security that UNHCR registration offered (on paper at least), seemed inviolable – but several incidents in the years that followed showed that there was no such security. Incidents such as the SADF incursions into Swaziland with impunity, which resulted in kidnaps and assassinations, the theft (four times or more) of refugee files from the UNHCR offices (which carried photographs and real names), all pointed to the fact that the UNHCR was powerless to exert any pressure on the South African government. Furthermore, in 1979, South Africa was not a member of the United Nations. Due to its apartheid policies, it had pariah status. A refugee was thus left to his or her own devices to survive and seek support and protection from other agencies such as the church and personal friends among the Swazi and expatriate communities.

The police were aware of the presence of unregistered refugees. Frequently, they would call up all refugees and count the number present in the country. Some secret police were sympathetic and would turn a blind eye to the presence of these refugees. There were members of the PAC still around, as were SADF Security Force members (such as Eugene de Kock). Swaziland was a maelstrom of refugees from all corners of Africa, including Portugal (MNR), Kenya and Uganda. Countries which gained independence took back their citizens (as in Zimbabwe, Kenya and the Congo) so that, gradually, there were fewer and fewer refugees around.

The UNHCR grants for refugee women were only increased after a demonstration in front of their offices. In 1982, the rate was raised from R40 a month to R80. Truth to tell, the ANC's logistics department gave out food rations and basic foodstuffs to all refugee families, which was funded by the UNHCR.

Around 1985, after the signing of the Nkomati Accord, after which ANC personnel were deported from Mozambique, the Swazis decided that, given the violence emanating from the black areas in South Africa, there would soon be an explosion in Swaziland as well. The last thing they wanted was a spillover onto their territory. There was probably pressure from the South African government as well. The Swazi government targets were those who were identified as members of military wings of liberation movements.

Some shootouts did occur between the Swazis and the military wing of the ANC. Many lost their lives – and this infuriated the Swazi community as they lost personnel as well. Depending on the violence monitor, according to the SABC news broadcasts, every time there was an explosion in South Africa, the ANC was blamed. A series of raids on the refugee community present in the country would follow. Thus, in 1982, the Swazi authorities deported the ANC chief representative and cleared out refugees thought to be dangerous. Men and women who had been resident in the country from 1960 were rounded up and told they were being deported. The UNHCR funded the travel grants to Zambia where the ANC headquarters was situated. From there they would have to find their way to other sympathetic countries.

By 1985, the situation in Swaziland had become intolerable. There were increasing raids by the SADF into the country. Most of the remaining refugees surviving illegally were afraid for their lives, as indeed were we. We all retreated to Zambia in 1985.

The exodus was not only from Swaziland. Given the 'total onslaught strategy' of the apartheid government, refugees from Botswana, Lesotho and Mozambique all converged on Lusaka; some several hundreds were sitting in Zambia. Some went to Tanzania, others to Kenya or Uganda. No one knew what the road forward would be.

Several serious bombing attacks in the neighbouring states took place in the 1980s. Lusaka was hit by bombings of ANC people and property. In Mozambique Albie Sachs was injured in a car bomb. There were other attacks on high-profile activists in Europe.

SADF attacks

While I was still employed at the Swaziland Council of Churches as refugee counsellor, I was sent by the office to Two Sticks, a small township near Manzini. While in the office, we all heard a big bang. The secretary general got news that there had been a bombing in the township. He sent me there to investigate.

I drove to the spot and was told that two houses had been bombed from the air. The victim was a Swazi child, the daughter of Marwick Dlamini. Marwick pointed out the place where the house used to be. There was no structure. Everything around looked like sea sand. Marwick picked up a shred of cloth from the dust and identified it as the remnants of the dress his daughter was wearing when he last saw her. The SADF had mistaken his house for that of one where South African refugees were staying. Marwick looked at the scene without emotion, saying simply that he would never see his daughter again.

The blast from the bomb had reached another house where South African refugees were sleeping. One refugee shot through the roof of the building; when he was found, he had lost one of his legs. No fuss was made of this incident – just a stoical silence and a short report in the Swazi *Times*.

Another person affected was Zweli, the brother of Siphiwe Nyanda. He had been sharing a small house with a fellow refugee called Cyril (aka 'Fear'). They had returned home with their girlfriends and entered the house, and were ambushed. According to Cyril, he ran away by jumping through the window, his girlfriend in tow. Zweli tried to save his girlfriend by pushing her through the window. She escaped, but Zweli was shot in the back. Those who escaped raised the alarm through Stanley Mabizela (the new chief representative of the ANC). Zweli's body was found in the bathroom, riddled with bullets. The women's organisation was called in to clear up the mess.

Cyril moved into another house. Years later, the ANC claimed that Cyril was a plant. He died in ANC detention in Zambia.

A funeral was arranged through the auspices of the Protestant churches. All ANC members invited friends and supporters to the funeral. Siphiwe could not attend as he claimed that he could be targeted. He sent a letter which was read out at the funeral service. For the first time, after a long silence, the ANC was reactivating itself by mobilising its membership. The funeral service was addressed by George Manare, an old Umkhonto we Sizwe (MK) operative, who was now in retirement in one of the suburbs of Manzini. He came out strongly in a speech against the apartheid regime.

If anything, the function brought the plight of refugees to the attention of all who were present. This included the Lutheran mission, Ed and Laureen Morrow, Father Michael Broadbent, several Swazi dignitaries and the South African refugee community at large. We ended by singing 'Nkosi Sikelel' iAfrika' (God bless Africa) with clenched fists.

The Matola raid

Krish Rabilal came from Merebank in Durban. He joined MK as an operative and subsequently fled the country. He was closely associated with Mduduzi Guma, a lawyer from Durban who had also fled the country in about 1979. Both lived in Swaziland. In about 1981, they went to Mozambique where they were housed on the outskirts of Maputo, in a township called Matola. They had gone to Maputo to attend a conference. The delegates included Krish Rabilal, Mduduzi Guma, William Khanyile and several others. They were all armed in case of an attack.

At about midnight, there was a knock on the door. One of them looked out of the window and saw a van which they believed belonged to FRELIMO, the Mozambican resistance organisation. They thought they were among comrades, so they opened the door. It turned out to be an ambush. Several SADF members, disguised in the FRELIMO van, with blackened faces, stormed the house and opened fire. Twenty-two people in the house died. The sole survivor, who jumped out of the two-storey house and hid in the toilet outside, waited until it was safe and then made his way back to Maputo to relate the story to the ANC. The funeral was widely publicised internationally. The whole of the ANC community, friends and comrades attended the funeral. The incident became known as the Matola raid.

Abduction

Joe was my husband Ivan's brother. For security reasons, they decided to live separately. Joe remained on St Joseph's Mission, while Ivan and I moved out. Joe was a registered refugee and taught at the mission school. We were warned by Nzima (Patrick Nyawose) that the SADF was around. We were told to be vigilant. We went to warn Joe, but he merely laughed the whole thing off and said that he was small fry. The SADF was after the big fish. As was the custom, we did not sleep at our home, but went to a friend's place to spend the night.

At about 6 a.m. the next morning, Judson arrived. He took Ivan aside and closed the door. When they came out, both looked pale and careworn. I asked them what the matter was. Finally, reluctantly, they told me that Joe had been kidnapped from the mission. The whole incident had been witnessed by a fellow Swazi colleague, David.

David himself was devastated, half-afraid of what he had witnessed for the first time, and also angry that he could not save his friend. According to David, two refugees from MNR, the South African-backed Mozambican resistance movement, had come to his house on the mission and asked to see Joe. Joe had come out and pretended that he was not Joe Pillay, but a friend. The two kidnappers had insisted on visiting Joe's house. Joe left David's place and made his way to his own cottage. But before he could reach there, they grabbed him, forced him into a car and drove out at a terrific speed.

In the scuffle, a passport fell to the ground, which was found by David. It carried the stamp of South African immigration. Their complicity could be proved. He brought the passport to Ivan, who, with Nzima, went to the Swazi police and reported the matter. After the kidnap, David slept at our small outhouse in Manzini. He swore that he could not rest until he caught the kidnappers. As it happened, David recognised the car parked in one of the houses in our neighbourhood. He identified, from a distance, the two kidnappers. He immediately went the Swazi police and reported the matter. The abductors were arrested.

In the meantime, we got protest action going with our friends and contacts. The UNHCR pledged support, but wanted to know what they could do. Amnesty International expats sent out the information for radio broadcast on 'Voice of America'. The South African black journalists' forum publicised the incident in the Sunday papers and the *Post*. The radio broadcasts inside the country blared the news as well.

Our diplomatic mission, using the Swazi authorities, conveyed that they would return the kidnapper to South Africa, provided that Joe was returned to Swaziland (an exchange). This was accomplished by their dumping Joe in the middle of nowhere in Swaziland at about midnight. Joe said they had not even been checked through the border post, but just drove in.

They had tortured Joe. He had been taken to Vlakplaas, where he was interrogated by a former ANC operative who had stayed at his house. The operative was subsequently arrested while on some mission inside the country. He had turned into an askari and had tried to persuade Joe to give information on Ivan and myself, assuring Joe that he would be looked after by the SADF. Joe refused to budge and was tortured with beatings and exposure to freezing cold weather while being moved from place to place. They broke his ribs in the process.

As published by the Truth and Reconciliation Commission, the whole episode had been delegated by the SADF top brass to Dirk Coetzee. The security apparatus of the SADF had planned a quiet abduction, but the whole affair turned into an international incident. Coetzee was severely reprimanded by his superiors. He then decided to blow the whistle on Security Branch activities, in return for amnesty. Coetzee applied for membership of the ANC in exile. I think he was granted this.

Actually, abductions were commonplace in Swaziland. A school teacher, who lived on the border between Mozambique and Swaziland, had been abducted from there in the late sixties. It was a way of life.

Car bomb

By late 1982, school boycotts inside South Africa had escalated. Again the external mission of the ANC was accused of causing the havoc. Trade union activity deepened the resistance. Jabu and Patrick Nyawose were trade unionists. During an emergency period, they decided to vacate their house, which was in a suburb of Manzini, at night and slept in another township nearby.

The following morning, on their way back home, they entered their car and started it. The car had been booby-trapped. Both died, with one of their kids in the car as well. As with most bombings, there was no trace of any human remains afterwards. Only the shell of the car remained. As was becoming ritual, an ANC funeral was arranged.

Raid

Thabiso was an ANC refugee living in Mbabane. He had a girlfriend who was Swazi and visited him often. Given the conditions of instability, as is evident from the stories above, we all operated in completely tight compartments. No other person, except the commander, knew about the details of our existence. We were organised in cells. This did not mean that we did not care about each other. We all existed side by side, but what we were actually doing was held as secret.

Thabiso was arrested with another friend called Nyameko by forty policemen who raided their house in the early hours of the morning. Thabiso was deported while his girlfriend was taken into custody. She was pregnant. In detention, she was tortured and pistol-whipped by the head of the Swazi Security Branch. She miscarried as a result. Thereafter, the head of police started making overtures to the girlfriend, but she saw this as an attempt to get information out of her. This incident incensed members of the ANC and Swazi women alike. We whispered in huddles about the injustice of it all.

Then the police head was inexplicably shot. He died, and the Swazi authorities accused the ANC of using their country for armed warfare. What followed was the deportation of all ANC refugees from Swaziland. Some decided to stay there illegally.

Mawelawela

Around 1981, all ANC refugees were arrested and taken to Mawelawela camp in Matsapha. By this time, Judson Khuzwayo had been re-deployed to Lesotho, and then from there to Zimbabwe. The elders in the community included Shadrack Maphumulo (who took over from Judson) and Johannes Mkhwanazi. Ivan and I got away because the Swazi authorities never understood anything about the ANC alliance with the Indian congresses. To save our skins, we pretended that we were selling fruit and vegetables for a living. Since they were hard-pressed to prove a link between us and the ANC, they left us alone in the main. It was only years later that the Swazi Security Branch accused us of doing administrative work for the ANC, and on this charge requested that we leave the area. They were good enough to tip us off that the South African authorities were becoming interested in us, and that this was not good for our safety.

The activities at Mawelawela camp proved troublesome for the Swazis. The prisoners started to demand food from the UNHCR and would redistribute what was received to the prison warders and other guards. Apparently, this softened the attitude of the guards towards them. Planes were seen hovering over the camp, but it was never established whether these planes came from South Africa or the Swazi Air Force. After two months, the prisoners started walking out of Mawelawela camp. The guards did not stop them.

Pressures on the exile community

ANC buildings were often targeted for raids and attacks. The office in Maputo was bombed. We were now living in Manzini illegally, in an outhouse rented from a local businessman. We claimed to be social refugees. We kept leaving the Manzini area and hiding in the countryside. We were ably assisted by a Swazi national, whom we referred to as Baba Nzimande. His background was dubious, but he was faithful to the ANC. He gave us information on the status of the locals.

Our neighbours were also ANC refugees, hiding from the police. One day they gave us photographs of a girlfriend of one of the members. She had been severely tortured by the Swazi police for giving shelter to ANC members. Her body was bruised purple from the beatings. We gave the photographs to Amnesty International.

The Swazi radio started broadcasting that Swazi nationals should be on the lookout for persons occupying houses who did not leave for work in the mornings, but moved about after dark. In addition to this, pamphlets were dropped by plane onto the streets, giving instructions on how to recognise ANC refugees – they were wanted by the police and dangerous. Roadblocks cut off entry to Mbabane and Manzini, as well as the border areas. They were determined to trap us wherever we were. Ivan's photograph was published alongside other ANC persons, 'Wanted Dead or Alive' on the front pages of the Swazi *Times*. I was relieved that he was not around at the time.

Over the years, we had developed a close association with the expat community, mainly the Dutch. They were invaluable support staff and gave generously of their time. They assisted us with transport, medical attention and freely let us use their outhouses for refuge. There were several of them located at the Kwaluseni campus. There was Barbra and Rens, Fred and Marianna, Wim and Trudy, Alice Armstrong. Also, there were expatriates who taught at the church school in Manzini. We called them the Aarons (Michael and June). Then there was Malcolm and Marissa (Marissa was connected to the Black Sash) and also Laureen and Ed Morrow. During the state of emergency, these friends helped to hide, feed and clothe us. They were not suspected of having ANC connections, and so they were safe.

Jacob Zuma was sent to Swaziland to try to improve Swazi-ANC relations. He was scorned, with the Swazis categorically stating that they did not know Zuma, but knew Moses Mabhida. They would not talk to anyone else but Mabhida. Zuma left.

After several weeks in rural areas, we crept back to Manzini, and shifted house for the umpteenth time. We had worked out a regime where we would move overnight, covering our tracks as far as possible.

By 1984, back in South Africa, things were moving very fast. The United Democratic Front had been formed and resistance was growing from strength to strength. This also had its ramification for us. Refugees were no longer safe; assassinations were becoming common.

As mentioned before, Shadrack took over from Judson Khuzwayo (Mthethwa). We were leaving Swaziland, and so passed all materials and functions to him. We had hidden together, travelled together and had many experiences together, which made the relationship very special. We warned him that the Boers (white nationalist rulers in South Africa) would not leave him alone. They would be out to get him, as they knew he was based in Swaziland. Moreover, Eugene de Kock had his operatives among the Swazis as well. No one knew who they were, but they would be the eyes and ears of their commanders.

During Shadrack's tenure, Tambo's aide, Bongani, was kidnapped from Swaziland. As we had found Bongani accommodation through our contacts, we were directly implicated. Apparently, Shadrack had been in touch with a Security Branch policeman in South Africa who had passed him information from SADF files. The policeman was arrested but managed to escape to Swaziland, where Shadrack gave him shelter. However, at the same time, Tambo's aide, Bongani, was kidnapped from Swaziland by the SADF and was subsequently shot dead in South Africa.

Then there was the capture of an operative, known as Glory Sedibe (code-named 'September'), who had been captured by the Boers. He turned under torture and was used to track down refugees still living in Swaziland. Since he knew most of them quite well, he led his captors directly to their targets.

September was involved again in 1985 when two members of the ANC National Executive Committee came to Swaziland to try to reach a truce with the Swazis. They were not welcome and were shot at the Matsapha Airport as they were disembarking. One was Paul Dikeledi. He was married to a beautiful Mozambican woman called Carla. They had two children. September pointed out the house to the SADF operatives, who entered the house, assaulted Carla, broke furniture and attacked her – and then left. Mercifully, they did not kill her.

At about the same time, Shadrack was assassinated in Swaziland. He was returning home and the assassins followed him. Shadrack knew he was being followed, so he ran into his flat, shut the door and hid his children under the bed. He was shot through the closed door, and his body carted away. The children's mother returned home from work to find blood stains on the floor and the children severely traumatised. The case was referred to The Hague War Crimes Tribunal, where Shadrack's wife, Khumbuzile Phungula (Maphumulo), testified.

The family returned home after the ban had been lifted on the ANC. Unfortunately, Khumbuzile could not find ready employment, and the special pension she received was too meagre to cover the upkeep of a flat and her children. She died of stress. Her children are being looked after by friends, but still have a hard time. They cannot go to school as they have no money for fees and are working instead. The youngest got very sick and died in 2009. With the disbanding of MK, there is no care or comfort for these children, or families who have returned from exile. They have been abandoned like so many others who returned home to the emptiness of their personal lives.

Epilogue

When we retreated to Zambia, we were told that it would be inadvisable for us to return to Swaziland. We should look for another avenue of occupation, but re-employment in the frontline states was out of the question. After spending over ten years in exile, I did not welcome this news. Was I now to languish in the rear states unemployed?

The sanctions imposed on apartheid South Africa were another hurdle. In some ways, it was a carry-over from the sanctions imposed on South Africa in the late 1960s and 1970s. There were developments in England, with the hawkish Thatcher government replaced by a less right-wing Conservative government led by John Major. Would this change in British politics affect us favourably?

Then in 1985 or 1986, a business delegation from South Africa came to Zambia to consult with the ANC. Talks were held with all the ANC leaders. A breakthrough was something both parties were seeking. Then came the Mandela visit. We all assembled at the stadium in Lusaka, euphoric in our reception of a man whom we all regarded as the unquestionable leader of the movement. The mood of the gathering was ecstatic.

Mandela read out his speech. In it he stated that the time for negotiations had come and that this had to be the priority for the movement. There was a dead silence as he read his speech. I am sure that many MK members were shocked at this sharp departure from all that the exile community had been engaged in for over ten years.

I was sent back home for medical treatment on an emergency travel certificate. An ANC doctor had diagnosed my condition as schizophrenia. They recommended that treatment could only be received in South Africa. There were no medical facilities to treat this condition in Zambia.

It was a big wrench to part from Ivan and the other close colleagues whom I had known for almost a decade. The future was terribly uncertain. However, after Mandela's visit, one thing had became clear: for better or for worse, we all had to return home. The ban on ANC cadres was lifted.

The reaction of the SADF to returning exiles showed that they, too, were confused. A report in the Sunday papers carried a story of a complaint by one of the high-ranking officers of the army. 'What are we going to do now?' he asked. 'First these people are your enemies, and we were told to shoot them; now they are not your enemy and we must look after them.'

In the same vein, there was a cartoon in one of the dailies. It showed Adriaan Vlok inviting a fleeing black figure carrying an AK-47, to join the police force. The caption read, 'Please join the Vlok'.

On a personal note, I now found myself living in two worlds. One was within the ANC, where we had accepted the leadership without question. Was I now to return and be regarded as a separate entity in South Africa? To some extent, the exile existence resulted in some form of assimilation. We were 'Africanised' in exile. Our customs, habits had changed as we adapted to exile conditions. How would this be received in South Africa?

I was fortunate enough to be escorted back home by my brother – the only family I had now. My mother-in-law also came to fetch me. Somehow, I could not respond to their overtures. I was too tied up with the assassinations and kidnappings which we had witnessed (and luckily escaped).

I had to be urgently hospitalised. At St George's Hospital there were many patients suffering from some mental condition or another. They were all victims of social violence (particularly those who came from the African townships). We started talking among ourselves and the women related that safety in the townships could no longer be taken for granted. The police force was nowhere to be found to restore law and order. One patient added, 'They only come when everyone else has left'.

Finding a job or some means of survival was difficult. Prospective employers wanted to know what I had been doing for ten years in exile. There was no straight reply to this question. My husband could not take the strain either. We were living on the old-age pension his mother received. Life was hard and unpredictable. Ivan and I grew apart. We finally separated in 1994.

My brother found me a flat, and patiently tended to me, administering the medication given to me at the hospital. He remarked that I was different from the person he had known. Only after my mother died did I move into my own flat with money that was a combination of a legacy from my mother's will and the payout I received on being demobbed.

I demobbed because I was not going to serve in the SADF (especially since I knew what they were). The demob centre was Waterkloof Air Base, where tents had been erected to accommodate us. We travelled all night by bus to get there. Shadrack's wife and I shared a tent, and we demobbed together. There were many exiles assembled there. I kissed one of the young activists I knew from Swaziland goodbye. The reaction of the soldier on duty was '*My Here God*!' (Good God!).

Although I would not admit it at the time, my medical condition was severe. I could see and hear things that were not there. I could hear voices and imagined that attention was being focused on me. I was being followed and so on. It has taken fifteen years to regain my sanity. I still suffer from over-reaction to small things, such as forgetting where I have put my handbag. This is a backlash from the pick-pocketing and the break-ins we had to undergo while still in exile. Fortunately, my family stood by me. In exile, as a woman, there was little I could look forward to in the form of personal attention or comfort from the men with whom we had served. My friends had been the Dutch people who had been working in Swaziland.

Sixteen years down the road, we are still looking for answers. The xenophobic attacks on foreigners (Zimbabweans, Nigerians, Ghanaians, Congolese and others) are a stark difference from the hospitality we received from them in their countries while in exile. That camaraderie is not present in South Africa.

Frequently, I have heard several acquaintances boast that they had been the sole driving force of the revolution. This is inexact and untrue. The path to liberation was governed by several aspects – not least the international situation (our support from other countries and the extent to which they could extend a helping hand), the internal situation and the fast-changing scenario, when both these aspects combined.

I am happy that at least schools, restaurants, public places, parks and gardens are now open to all, irrespective of colour. I recall boarding a bus to the centre of town in 1994. An African man sitting on the bus shifted in his seat uncomfortably when I sat next to him. He asked, 'Are you sure you don't mind?'

Of course, the current crime statistics are disappointing. South African is now one of the most crime-ridden countries in the world. It does not make me proud when *dagga* (marijuana) is smuggled from here through Heathrow Airport. The rape statistics do not impress me as a member of the female population.

The education policy is currently under review – but, given the world recession and the falling pass rate of matriculants, urgent action is needed from the government.

There is yet another dream. I would like to see South Africa emerge as a world power, able to manage her economy and social affairs so well that she stands out as a shining example of progress in all avenues – such as education, sport, business affairs and as a tourist destination. We can only achieve this if, in the spirit of combined action as used during the liberation struggle, we all stand together to realise this dream.

This is not such an impossibility, as most pessimists predict. After all, there were other countries that recovered from the Second World War period and in ten years achieved stature in the international arena. Think of India, Japan, Malaysia and other such countries. Indeed, the Vietnamese and other socialist countries have fast adapted to re-structuring their economies to deal with the advent of a new era. We need to be aware of this and push in the same direction.

This may well take many years, but the outcome of free interaction with all races of the world will surely be a vastly different experience than that of living under apartheid. Our youth need to be guided by far-sighted leaders who will surely leave their legacies to a proud new generation.

Retelling the flight into exile
Elizabeth Trew

Elizabeth Trew was born in Cape Town in 1942. She left South Africa in 1965 after her husband, Tony, was imprisoned for involvement in sabotage activities of the African Resistance Movement. They lived in exile in England for twenty-seven years where Elizabeth taught English as an additional language to immigrants and refugees who had fled political repression and economic deprivation in poor or oppressive countries. They returned to Johannesburg in 1991 with the unbanning of political organisations. Back home, Elizabeth continued to teach English and obtained a master's degree in English education from the University of the Witwatersrand. She became a volunteer counsellor at People Opposing Women Abuse and still serves on the editorial board of POWA's women's writing project. Now retired in Cape Town, she helps at Siviwe, a girls' shelter, and is a keen and regular hiker on Table Mountain. Her poetry has been published in literary journals and poetry magazines in England and South Africa.

The messenger
Mind the sprinklers spinning
inside the scorched garden.
Go up the steps. As her guard-dogs
leap out unbolted they kiss,
nearly knocking you over

Go reach out a greeting,
go down the dark passage,
her big shaded home
going mindful of love between
mother and son banished, barred

Attend, go beside as the messenger
bringing shiny bags full of news.
As her hand presses lightly, retelling

the flight into exile, leafing
through cuttings and snapshots curled yellow

Pink flowers sway browning
beneath her barred sill,
raw meat hangs on hooks
above creamy pitchers of milk
inside the cool kitchen

The roast lies on starched cloth

Going out the steps linger,
they tear the flecked path.
Go touch her as her hand burns her blue necklace.
Go take her picture by the palm tree he planted.
Go with love, go.

Princess vlei
Here opening the valley
the eye of a princess
her fertile tear hemmed in a watershed

Here tasting salt bending
daughter-streams drink

Here her bruised mouth
where the stubbled marsh grows

Here held among bullrush
his torn body floats

Here from her throat bending
daughter-streams drink

Here milk and blood mingle

Here her smoke drifts,
kissing wattle and willow

Here waiting still
is the voice of the watermaid,
maker of smoke, and dew

Homecoming

I turn my web on London grass
and walk through cones of primrose light
by sheds of water opening the drowned canal.
I find you in the river's bow
stringing flags to welcome me.
On the bridge you pass me by on roller blades
turning shoes with tiny keys.
On the stairs you brush my coat with lemon stars.
Sipping every voice of you
I drench my boots with snowdrop lids,
let my litmus lift and turn the wheel
across our world, my leaving you.

My exiled days return to you,
nudge my certain landing rush
towards your open cosmos eye
through gold-reef doorways city deep.
Under the bridge I touch your scars and broken lips.
On the hill my trumpet vines
reveal the ruby blare of you.
I tap the mourning earth
replace my roots,
line my river paths with river feet
the spirit flow of you,
return my bedrock dance to you,
my coming home.

Holding pattern

I turn towards you on my landing path
and drive towards the city's heart.
Across the bridge a ferris wheel
is birthed beside the flowing Thames –
the bolted hub holds rays of steel,

the contours cradle window seats.
London's eye looks down and winks at me.

Once more I visit out of season,
lay my web on crescent grass,
growing paths in search of you.
I walk through cones of primrose light
by sheds of water opening the drowned canal.
I find you in the river's bow
stringing flags to welcome me.
On the bridge you pass me by on roller blades,
turning shoes with tiny keys.
I catch an echo of your laugh
down woodland rise by redbrick yard.
On the stairs you brush my coat with lemon stars.
Sipping every voice of you
I drench my boots with snowdrop lids,
let my litmus lift and turn
the wheel across our worlds,
my leaving you.

The prisoner
A prisoner opens a smuggled, battered book
written by a girl concealed in her country,
a girl marked by a yellow star in hiding,
writing to herself at an angle of the stairs
in a dark house, with words shining through the dark.
Quiet and still her breath mists the window crack
above yellow-starred people moving in the street.

Day 235: *I make my own stars patient and calm.*
Day 613: *I long to move freely under the stars.*

Monday evening, 8 November 1943:
I see eight of us hidden inside a piece of blue sky
surrounded by gathering darkness closing in
squeezing us more tightly
until we make our own star which cannot be crushed yet.

He collects the girl's days, writing her words
small on a paper scrap, which he rolls up tight
and hides on himself to be smuggled to others
until the bloom of her words fills each cell.

(*The Diary of Anne Frank* was passed around on Robben Island.)

The language class

Leaves are falling from the trees. Swallows have begun flying south for their summer
in Africa. In her room above a wine shop, Rhona gathers papers and books to teach
her last language classes of the year. She looks out at the grey morning. Despite
having lived in exile for more than a decade she still longs for the warmth of home.
At least the end of year party at the Language Centre will brighten these dark, cold
days of winter, when the blackbirds are silent.

Abdul speaks English to Rhona and when he speaks for Narinda at the doctor's.
His English flows like a smooth river. Hers is hard and unfriendly, like the people she
meets: the old lady who sat behind her on the bus spitting: 'Horrible! Horrible!' in her
ear, and the boy's block of ice which struck like fire on her back. Then she remembers
the good people, when she was the centre of attention, a firebird in her brightest sari
and flashing all her gold for the mothers and children at the playgroup.

'You are beautiful!' they had said. She still thinks of the small boy staring up at
her, surprise and wonder on his face.

Now Narinder needs to speak English for herself because Abdul is sick and grey.
He stares out with sad eyes, always in the house complaining of headaches.

'Before, I was handsome and strong, the boxer of Sylhet! I carried heavy bunches
of bananas on my shoulders. A mahout working in the forest with my elephant,' he
tells Rhona.

Once, she and Abdul went to London zoo with the Learning Centre. She loved
the Indian elephant, the way he uncurled and stretched his trunk towards her, although
Abdul felt sad to see his beloved animal pacing back and forth in the enclosure.

'Can you not see how homesick he is?'

Narinder spent yesterday making cards to give to Rhona and Tariq, a new student
in Advanced Level. She cut out patterns from scraps of material which she glued
with sequins and squares of silver foil onto coloured card. Her young daughters
helped write the messages.

Her sari glitters under her winter coat which hides her gold neck chain and red
bangles. Gold-leaf earrings shine in the room laden with smells of incense, spices
and cooking. She takes the cards propped against her sewing machine, calls goodbye
to Abdul, who watches her walk down the road in the drizzling rain to the party.

Juanita slices egg, cheese, tomato and lettuce to fill the sandwiches she sells at the college. Warmth from a batch of empanadas in the oven sends out their savoury aroma into the kitchen. These are soon ready to take to the Learning Centre. She keeps some aside for Tariq.

The family were in hiding for a year in Chile, sleeping wherever it felt safe – once in a disused henhouse – before escaping to seek political asylum in England. Juanita and Pedro were put in Rhona's reception class for survival English to learn the signs of the city – Exit, Entrance, Stop, Go – to navigate their way round the streets and to use the underground. Keen to learn, Juanita never misses a class, but Pedro stays in the cold house where he sinks in despair or seethes with anger.

'No English! No learn English! Kill Pinochet!' He marches inside the house in his dog-tooth overcoat, pausing now and again to draw a finger slowly across his throat.

'Feel the vibration of your vocal cords,' Rhona tells the class. 'Let the sound explode under the tongue and push it out your lips.' Juanita finds the new stresses and rhythms so different from Spanish. Her English sounds more like Spanish, so Rhona has also given her special sounds to work on.

Juan, their eldest boy, has begun stealing from school, even from friends. The principal has called the family together and given them a warning.

'I understand . . . but the fact is that we cannot tolerate stealing from anyone. Juan must be punished, or he must leave.' The principal's words burn in Juanita's ears. They listen to her in silence.

Juanita wheels out her bicycle, carefully places the boxes of empanadas and sandwiches on the carrier, singing a familiar jazz chant:

Sally speaks Spanish but not very well.
When she speaks Spanish you can't really tell
what language she's speaking or trying to speak.
The first time I heard her I thought it was Greek.

Balancing her small body between the wheels, her dark plait down her back, she rides off to the party.

Siddique stays with an English family while studying at the Learning Centre before he leaves for college in the north of England. This is his first winter.

'I am freezing right down to my bones!' he shivers. He wears all his clothes – thin, summery layers of the beautiful shirts his mother packed, and two linen jackets.

'Please let me wash your clothes!' begs Mrs Whitehouse after the second week. 'Please let me run a hot bath for you – to get you warm.' But Siddique knows only about showers and refuses to bath in dirty water.

'I presume he'll wear overalls or something when he starts car maintenance at the centre,' Mr Whitehouse says to his wife.

'So you're going to learn car maintenance from a woman!?' laughs Mr Whitehouse loudly to Siddique. Siddique is unsure if this is a statement or a question as the Englishman's voice rises at the end of his sentence. He must check with Rhona.

The Whitehouse family have grown fond of their delightful, young lodger who plays and laughs with the children.

'Did I tell you that Timmy actually managed to tie Siddique to a chair without him knowing? We all had a good chortle over that!' laughs Joan Whitehouse to her husband.

'Children are treasures, the flowers of life,' Siddique tells Mrs Whitehouse.

'He does look miserably cold,' she remarks to her husband. 'We must really buy him some winter things, dear. Make him decent. He looks like the dog's breakfast in those clothes.'

'You may wash this shirt,' Siddique says shyly, handing Mrs Whitehouse his best shirt which he'll wrap later in cloth from Sudan and give to Tariq at the party.

Nhung walks through the market on her way to class. She enjoys looking at the displays of fruit and vegetables, which shine through the gloomy day. She pauses to read the labels: oranges from Israel; plantains, bananas from Jamaica; mangoes from India; sweet pepper, chilli from Portugal; pomegranates from Brazil; figs from Turkey. Cape apples and grapes. Rhona says she won't buy South African until her country changes. Nhung sees Binh buying vegetables for her restaurant and greets her warmly. Binh, a successful woman, single and independent, cooks for the rich and famous. 'Sting and Mick Jagger love my Thai cooking,' she says proudly.

'And David Dimbleby came to the kitchen to congratulate me after Lady Weymouth's dinner party,' she tells Nhung.

Nhung and Binh were among the first 'boat people' who came over from Vietnam.

'One hundred and ninety people in a small sailing boat with no room to lie down. So we slept sitting up. The boat nearly turned over once, but everyone started chanting to the Buddha, and behold, twenty minutes later, a wind came up and carried us on,' Nhung tells the class.

Shy, soft-spoken and hard-working, Nhung has progressed steadily from Level 2 to Advanced. Writing is easier than speaking. Her writing is interesting and complex: 'My small country has been like a battlefield for a long time. Today in the world, many communist countries have changed and are still changing into democracy. We hope Vietnam will follow in their footsteps so our people will become free and have peace, a neutral nation,' she writes.

But speaking is another matter. Her syllables rattle like sharp stones in her mouth.

'Listen to the music, the flow of English music,' Rhona tells all her learners. 'Find the stress and let it swing.'

Nhung's family are settled in their new country. Her daughters won scholarships to go on to tertiary, while Peter, her only son, struggles with depression. Nhung spends her free time alone reading English books. The girls and Nam, her hard-working husband, are either out or busy. Peter usually stays alone in his room.

She has baked a cake for the party and wonders what to give Tariq. Perhaps an English book. He was a teacher in his country. She would like to raise her voice and lift her face to look him in the eye, but this is not done by a Vietnamese woman.

Tariq cannot sleep. He slips out of his refugee hostel to walk the maze of cold, dark streets, the narrow passages and alleys of the city. He hears cries and whispers coming from its deep recesses, his nightmare of pain returning. His heart beats in his chest, feeling like a trapped, fluttering bird. On his way he meets a fox – a wild thing coming to scavenge in the city. He glances at the full moon appearing between passing cloud.

Tariq has found the Learning Centre after his sleepless night walking. He comes unannounced and, for the first time, into Rhona's class. He has dark rings under intense dark eyes.

'I have a story of love and darkness,' he tells the class.

'Men with hatred in their hearts, who have made terrible laws against the women of my country. Their religion is a shameful thing. I loved a woman. Our love was deep and good – a bird of liberty and peace. It was a beautiful thing. They destroyed it because we broke their laws. But it was *she* who was punished. It was a terrible thing. Terrible! They dug a deep hole. They dragged her. They buried her up to her neck in the ground. They took stones and threw them at her head. They stoned her to death! They forced me to watch.' His voice comes in short bursts which rise and fall to a crescendo of grief. He buries his face in his hands.

Tariq's story stuns everyone in the class to silence. Nhung sheds a tear. Rhona discovers that Tariq's birthday falls on the day of the party. She tells Nhung. Word spreads.

All the winter leaves have fallen. The Learning Centre hums and buzzes inside with sounds of the end of year party. Rhona notes that everyone has arrived: Shantini from Sri Lanka, Mangkoru from Thailand, Lee Lee from Malaysia, Zhu Qi from China, Amin and Sabat from Iran, Carlina from Phillipines . . . no Tariq.

Voices from the three classes rise in a confluence of sounds and fill the hall decorated with bunches of coloured balloons and streamers. Paper cups of orange squash are handed round as well as plates of cakes and crisps.

'We are like the United Nations!' exclaims Siddique to Banza, Maconda and Dinganga from the Congo. Rhona puts on some music, hearing also the keys and tunes of language learnt, all the drills, rhythms and tones, and silent letters of the year. Narinder lets new words play on her tongue on the brink of sound. Everyone glances at the door, waiting for Tariq.

Tariq arrives, overwhelmed, at his surprise party. Everyone gathers round to cheer and sing and watch him open presents and cards. He bends to kiss each gift then turns to face the crowded room.

'Dear friends, thank you from my heart. I send salaams – as many as the stars, and birds flying' [line by Abbas Ibn al-Ahnof].

Postscript

I am Rhona in the story, and 'The language class' is based on my experiences of teaching English language in parts of England and London. Many of my students were refugees and immigrants who had fled political repression and economic deprivation in poor or oppressive countries. I became deeply aware of the injustice across our skewed, unequal world, hearing first-hand accounts of dictatorship, war and economic hardship in their countries. Behind each individual there were whole societies in pain. The Learning Centre provided a welcoming centre and refuge for those torn apart from family, friends and country. Learners became good friends who helped each other in the bewilderment of learning a new language and starting afresh in another country, one in which they were not always welcomed. I learnt much from the experiences, which my students shared with me.

Tariq became a volunteer translator and teacher, helping victims of torture. Some oppressive regimes have fallen. Juanita and her family were free to return to Chile. Nhung was allowed to visit family she thought she would never see again in Vietnam. And Tony and I were able to return to South Africa in 1991 after twenty-seven years in exile. Despite this causing a split in our family (my sons remain in England), I am overjoyed to be home and to be part of building a new, democratic country.

My recollections of exile

AnnMarie Wolpe

AnnMarie Wolpe was born in 1930 into a middle-class Jewish family of Lithuanian origin. A graduate of the University of the Witwatersrand, she met Harold Wolpe whom she married in 1955. Their lives were inextricably linked to the fight against the apartheid government. Harold escaped from jail in 1963 following the Rivonia arrests and the family landed up in exile in England. After their move to Bradford, Yorkshire, AnnMarie started working at the university there as a research assistant. This led her to a life in academic work and her involvement in the women's movement. In 1991, she and Harold were able to return to the country where they both worked at the University of the Western Cape. Harold died in 1996 and AnnMarie continued working for the Department of Education chairing a task team on gender equity. She is now retired in Cape Town, although she remains active in the Harold Wolpe Memorial Trust.

I had a perfectly uneventful upbringing in a conventional middle-class, secular Jewish family. My father had come to South Africa as a baby. His parents were from Lithuania and his mother travelled with the children by ox-wagon to Pretoria. I never knew what my grandfather did. He was long since dead before I was born, as was my grandmother. My father was a lawyer who tried his hand at all sorts of businesses, most of which failed miserably. My mother's mother had also travelled to South Africa with her two daughters after a twelve-year break while her husband battled to earn enough money to bring her and her children out from Moscow. My mother was born after her parents' reunion, but never really knew her father as he died when she was only two. My mother was farmed out to various families as her mother was too poor and never learnt to speak English.

I was born in 1930, the last of three children in a grand home in Parktown, Johannesburg. We were constantly on the move, to Cape Town, back to Johannesburg, from one house to another depending on my father's financial status. I knew nothing really of the politics of the country. We had servants who were all African. We lived in very comfortable houses and nothing impinged on our lives as children.

At the end of my schooling I went to the University of the Witwatersrand in Johannesburg where I got a loan to pay my way through the four-year course. It was there that I became politicised. It was an exciting period to study, directly after the

Second World War when the university had a lot of mature students who had gained access through the concessions and very generous grants had been given to ex-servicemen.

Indeed, this is how Joe Slovo, later to become one of the key leaders of Umkhonto we Sizwe (MK), the military wing of the African National Congress (ANC), was able to become a lawyer. During my third year at the university, the National Party came into power. The student body was very active in anti-apartheid work. Lunchtime lectures were held on various oppositional views and which I always attended. It was a period in which I first met Africans as equals, as well as Harold Wolpe whom I would marry seven years later.

Most of my friends from that period chose to live overseas after graduation where they felt freer and could pursue their academic careers. I did what so many had done and went to London after working for a year as a social worker. I remained there for two years, and was joined by Harold in my second year there.

We both returned to South Africa, Harold to begin work as an advocate, me as an assistant to Helen Joseph in the Transvaal Clothing Industry's Medical Aid Society. Helen was one of the founders of the Federation of South African Women, a multiracial organisation. She was also one of the leaders who led 50 000 women to the Union Buildings, the official seat of government in Pretoria, to protest against women having to carry the dreaded Pass books. She was one of the accused in the first Treason Trial, which began in 1957 and went on for several years. I learnt a great deal from her.

In 1955 Harold and I got married at a time when the atmosphere of repression in the country was gaining force. More and more legislation to destroy or prevent any protest was being introduced. The Communist Party was banned; people were banned; removals of people from their homes took place. The anti-apartheid government was strengthening its power base.

Harold was a member of the Young Communist League and the South African Communist Party (SACP) until his death. He never lost his commitment to the struggle against apartheid. He continued going to meetings, even when the party went underground. I never joined it for a number of reasons, one of which related to our having a young family. I reckoned that one of us would have to be around for the sake of the children. Harold had started out his professional life as a barrister of the high courts, but never enjoyed appearing in the high courts. So when my brother, Jimmy Kantor, offered Harold a partnership in his law practice, Harold jumped at it. From then on he became one of the main lawyers who defended people who had been arrested on some charge of breaking apartheid laws.

On 21 March 1960, following demonstrations against the Pass laws, the police shot and killed sixty-nine people, including eight women and ten children, in Sharpeville in what was then the Transvaal province. About 180 people were wounded. Tensions were high throughout the country and the government responded by declaring a state of emergency. There were mass arrests of suspected protestors of all racial groups. Harold was arrested in the second week of the emergency. He and other white prisoners from Johannesburg were transferred to Pretoria Central Prison where they were held for the next three months.

During this period I was a courier. I was asked on the morning following Harold's arrest to go and warn the Bernsteins of the arrests, but they had already been arrested. Both of them were members of the Communist Party, Hilda having been the only member of the Johannesburg City Council who was a communist, and Rusty, a practising architect. He was to be one of the Rivonia trialists. Luckily, he was acquitted and the family escaped from South Africa to live in exile.

The government denied there was a hunger strike and Harold managed to smuggle out a note from prison to prove it. I took it to the Johannesburg *Rand Daily Mail*. I did not know at the time that this constituted an offence for which I could be imprisoned for three years.

The situation in the country deteriorated following the state of emergency as the security police became more efficient and more professional. They began to recruit university graduates. They learnt about techniques of torture. Their transformation was becoming obvious. Every move by the opponents of apartheid was met with violent reactions on the part of the government.

Eventually a decision was taken by the various organisations to engage in armed struggle. Passive resistance was to be a thing of the past. This proved to be a far-reaching decision which would only end finally in 1994 when the first democratic government would be elected. And Harold was very much a part of this movement of armed resistance. Just how involved he was I did not know initially.

It was Nelson Mandela who first told me of this armed struggle decision after a celebratory luncheon following the end of Ramadan, which was hosted by Ahmed Kathrada each year. A group of activists would gather there even though I doubt that the majority were Muslims. So the founding of the armed movement MK occurred.

For reasons of security, Harold never told me how much he was involved in MK. He did so for my protection. But his silence broke down after the abortive planting of the first lot of bombs in central Johannesburg. The night they were supposed to go off they failed to do so. Harold divulged to me his part in that. He, too, had planted a bomb that never detonated. I cannot recall my emotions on hearing this, but I am sure that I felt a great relief at the fact that the bombs had not exploded.

It was not long after that I learnt about the existence of MK headquarters. Our close friends, Arthur and Hazel Goldreich, had suddenly moved to live on a farm called Liliesleaf, in an outlying suburb of Rivonia in Johannesburg. For all intents and purposes, they had wanted to live a more rural life. I could never understand initially why they had done so, little knowing that the Communist Party had purchased the farm and that Harold had arranged for the payment to be made through the offices of my brother's legal practice, and that Jimmy had signed the cheque for the purchase of the farm.

This was the headquarters of the underground movement where meetings were held, plans were drawn up for mounting the armed struggle, leaflets would be produced, and broadcasts would be made from a radio station. In addition, leaders who had already gone underground such as Walter Sisulu and Govan Mbeki were living there, dressed as farm workers! Not only had Harold been involved in the purchase of the house and farm, but he went there several times a week at night to carry on the underground activities. He became adept at fixing the Roneo machine which carried out the duplication of leaflets for the struggle. He worked on documents for MK and, indeed, one of his handwritten documents was used in evidence against him in the famous Rivonia Trial that followed the arrests of the top leadership at Liliesleaf on 11 July 1963. Harold was cited as a co-conspirator.

I never questioned Harold's commitment to the movement. After Sharpeville, it was clear to me that sooner or later the government would come down quite hard on those people who were known and who continued activities geared towards causing the breakdown of the apartheid government. It was not going to allow people to continue in clandestine activities. It was a question of time. By then I had had two daughters and then became pregnant with our third child.

At first I thought I should have an abortion, but at the last minute I could not go through with it. As the months went by I became more and more anxious about the likelihood, as far as I could see, of Harold being arrested and placed in solitary confinement. I urged Harold to agree for our family to leave the country. We were obviously on the list of named people. We would be visited in the early hours of the morning by members of the Special Branch looking for documents. Harold was very well known to the security police, particularly through his handling of political cases brought to court. He was named and banned. There had to be only one slip and he would land in jail.

Harold finally said we should consult with Bram Fischer in order to make a decision. He was one of the most honourable men I have ever known, a person of the highest integrity. He was a senior barrister in the country and highly respected in that field. As an Afrikaner, he could not accept the apartheid government's role in the country. He was also a member of the Communist Party, and as such was vilified by the Afrikaner press at the time. I expressed my doubts about the wisdom of remaining in the country. His response was quite clear. 'We need people like you,' he said definitively. 'And, if and when there is trouble, the movement will look after you and the children, AnnMarie,' Bram promised me.

Reluctantly I was convinced and gave up the thought of leaving South Africa. To prepare myself, I thought that I would try to find a job, something that would be difficult if and when Harold was arrested. I thought it unlikely that my social work qualifications would see me through a difficult period. Social work jobs were semi-governmental and as such they would never employ a wife of a prisoner. So I decided to learn to touch-type efficiently. With such a qualification and a university degree, I reasoned that that would at least provide me with a minimal skill for employment.

I was not the only one who thought about this. Ruth Slovo (First) also did. She was Joe Slovo's wife, an activist, a member of the Communist Party and editor of *New Age*, a Communist Party newspaper, which was continually banned and re-emerged under different names. The two of us took lessons privately.

By 1963, the laws enabling the police to hold a person for ninety days in solitary confinement had been enacted. Not only this, but it could be extended indefinitely. It was a frightening prospect, combined with the knowledge that the secret police were prepared and ready to torture suspects. By now a number of leading activists had gone underground. Mandela had already been arrested and imprisoned the year earlier. The attempts by Joe Slovo and Harold to organise Mandela's escape from jail during his trial had failed.

When our son, Nicholas, was born Harold was engaged at that time with trying to gain access to two young Indians, Mosie Moolla and Abdullah Jasset, who were the first victims of torture. They were part of the underground movement and had been arrested under the ninety-day law.

Joe Slovo left the country for MK training when Nicholas was just over six weeks old. It was the night that we had said farewell to Joe that Nicholas became ill. By the following morning he was in a coma. He was rushed to hospital where he battled for his life, small though he was. And for the next four weeks we spent every day in hospital. Every possible technique was used to overcome the life-threatening pneumonia, including a tracheotomy and putting tubes into each lobe of his lungs, and another in his head for a drip. The dedication of the surgeon and the one nursing sister all contributed to his survival. He began to recover after three weeks. In the meantime, my father died quite unexpectedly.

Nicholas's illness was one of the most terrifying periods in my life. This tiny little boy did not smile or react to anything around him except the vibration of the bottles that were draining the pus out of his lungs day and night.

Once it became apparent that Nicholas was going to live, the surgeon was keen to get him out of hospital as soon as possible. It was decided he could return home even though he still had a tube in his one lung. To prepare myself for his return and also for a chance to spend a little time with our daughters whom we had more or less ignored during this period, I joined my mother at the farm owned by her sister and sister's families in Rustenburg, seventy-odd miles from Johannesburg.

The morning after I had arrived, my mother came to my cousin's house in a state of agitation and amazement. 'We heard on the radio this morning that the house in which Hazel and Arthur live in Rivonia was raided by the police yesterday and they and others were all arrested. What do you think of that?'

I could not tell her what I really thought. My immediate reaction was one of despair. Clearly this was the end of the road for Harold. Given his role in purchasing Liliesleaf, he would be arrested in the very near future. I gave no indication of my feeling of panic and had to wait to hear from Harold. He telephoned from a tickey box (public pay phone) after an hour and told me very briefly that he would have to leave the country as soon as possible. There was too much evidence of his presence at the house; not only were his fingerprints everywhere, but so were documents in his handwriting and, of course, the legal documents on the purchase of the farm. He said he would contact me again when we each could collect our thoughts.

I could not divulge this to my mother, my cousin and her husband. He was of German extraction and sympathetic to the nationalist government, certainly no friend of the resistance movement. And everything was in a state of disarray among members of MK connected with Liliesleaf. Harold came to visit me at the farm to discuss what to do. Everyone was lying low. People in the movement were horrified. The arrests would have a devastating effect on the resistance movement. We could expect no help from anyone. There was no escape group operating. No structures to deal with such an emergency.

It was up to us to find some solution and the only one was for Harold to leave the country, but how? He came for the evening and stayed overnight to discuss the matter with me. By this time, we had to tell Polly and Mike, my cousin and her husband, that Harold had to leave. Mike came up with a suggestion that he was due to take some Norwegian visitors for a picnic and that he would drive Harold close to the border and – *voilà*! – everything would be quite simple and straightforward. He could simply walk across the border and, with the help of a compass, make his way to a village and safety. Harold returned a day or two later to Rustenburg with a compass and some money, ready to leave, his beard shaved off and his hair died a golden colour. We were city-dwellers and didn't even think of his having a bottle of water with him and some protection against the cold of the nights. There was a feeling of panic and a need for him to disappear out of the country. We didn't think beyond his crossing the border and getting out of South Africa. We were totally and utterly naive.

Except it all went horribly wrong. Mike appeared to have had difficulty in finding a place where they would stop and picnic. Suddenly he drove into one farm area and there was a police border control. Their car was stopped. They were all asked their names and Harold, in a moment of panic, gave a false name, something that he had told clients of his never, ever to do. That was it. Within a matter of hours, some Special Branch members from Johannesburg arrived to see who this mysterious Mr Berman was. And there was the well-known lawyer, Harold Wolpe. The police were ecstatic. He was arrested and taken back to Johannesburg.

Meanwhile, back at the farm, nightfall came and no sign of Mike. It was clear to me that something had gone radically wrong. Early the following morning we were awakened by two visiting policemen to the news that Harold had been arrested and taken to Johannesburg and Mike, too, had gone to jail, but had been released. It was tense in the farmhouse. Nobody seemed to want to talk to me.

I packed the children in the car and drove back to Johannesburg. At home, the woman who helped in the house and the young gardener told me how they had been harassed and searched by the Special Branch. They also shouted at them for working for such bad people as we were.

I was allowed to take food and clean clothing for Harold every night when he was in Marshall Square prison, a holding prison in the heart of Johannesburg. Things took a strange turn. One night, I was escorted up past the warder on duty and taken to see Harold, even though he was supposedly in solitary confinement. This was quite bizarre. And then we established means of communicating through messages, and I learnt that Harold, Arthur and the two young Indians who had been tortured and were still in Marshall Square were planning to escape and I was to play a key role in all this.

After a few weeks the escape did occur in the early hours of a Sunday morning and, within a few hours, I and one of the wives of the young Indians who had been tortured were both taken to Greys, the building in the heart of Johannesburg which housed the Special Branch division of the police for interrogation. She was released quite early, but I was interrogated for some ten hours by different police, each of whom used a different tactic on me.

One was friendly, the other one paternal, all trying to get me tell where Harold and Arthur were. Then two men came in, two of the most frightening people I have encountered. One was a man whose surname was Swanepoel. I never learnt the name of the other one. They were both in a blind rage and could barely constrain themselves from manhandling me. They had their hands round my neck as though they wanted to strangle me, or shook me in the chair.

They yelled and swore at me. Swanepoel, I learnt later, was one of the worst torturers of suspected victims. He and his colleague were inarticulate, violent men. I was lucky that they had not yet tortured any white women. They did terrify me and I warned the next interrogator that if they let those two men in again I would simply jump out of the window. As I said that I knew I would not do so because of my children but, from then on, for the rest of the time I was interrogated, someone always sat next to the window.

If they had tortured me I don't know whether I would have broken down or not and divulged any information that could lead the police to finding the escapees. Later that night, I was taken to Marshall Square and dumped in a huge cell in which I was the only occupant. Strangely, the next night I was released. My brother came to fetch me, took me to his house that night and called the press. The following morning there was a front page headline about the escape and my claim that I had been threatened but not hit by the police and that a policeman had been arrested (the man who had helped the men to escape).

Things went from bad to worse for me. The only bright event was Nicholas coming out of hospital and now beginning to behave like a baby. He began to smile and gurgle and laugh. But I really only managed to see him at night when he would wake for his feed.

The following three weeks were a nightmare. The police were only interested in capturing the two white men. In those days there was the firm belief that the young Indians were incapable of carrying out anything as daring as this, simply because they were not white. I was hassled by anonymous phone calls wishing Nicholas dead and shouting at me.

People were too scared to come near me and I felt really isolated. My mother had gone to Durban to be close to my sister. And even more catastrophic, my brother, Jimmy Kantor, was also arrested and charged with the other detainees caught at Rivonia. Jimmy was a brilliant criminal lawyer and a humanitarian, but he never engaged in any political work. I thought if Jimmy, who had clients among the police as well as many top businessmen, was arrested I could never be safe. My safety net had disappeared, and I felt I would be the next one to be arrested. There was no knowing what would happen to me.

The search for the two white men dominated the news for the next week or more. Then the news broke that Harold and Arthur had mysteriously arrived in Botswana by plane from Swaziland, dressed as priests. The government used every method to get them back into the country but failed. The two fugitives eventually found their way to Dar es Salaam where they were given heroes' welcomes.

There was great relief when I knew they were safe. But in the meantime I was feeling more and more fraught. A journalist friend of mine warned me that there were rumours that I would be re-arrested. In the end I decided that the only thing I could do was to leave the country without the children.

To begin with I thought of being smuggled onto a boat by a customs official who was known to take bribes. In the end, this failed and I returned to Johannesburg. By now my state of anxiety was acute. Joel Joffe, a friend of Jimmy's and a brilliant lawyer, agreed to wind up Jimmy's office and I was able to consult him. He applied to the security police to allow me to leave the country legally. After they conferred for a day, Joel phoned me at five that afternoon and told me I could – immediately. That was impossible. But I left the following evening without the children, including the baby, and flew out from Johannesburg to London.

And so began a life in exile which was to last twenty-eight years. I arrived in London with a small suitcase of clothing and a hundred pounds that my boss had given me when she came to say goodbye. I was numbed by all that had happened over the past few weeks. From May to August had been one long run of major disasters and fear.

Once in London I was totally dependent on a few friends. The future looked bleak. My immediate concern was about the children and my brother. I knew that it would not be long before Harold would arrive in the country. It was really a matter of days, I think, before Harold and Arthur arrived. It was not clear whether they would be given asylum or not. I went to meet them at the airport, armed with the phone number of a sympathetic member of the British parliament if there was any difficulty with their being allowed to land.

Their escape made headlines in the British and American press and no doubt also the European press. The escape of these two young white men from the apartheid jail and the repressive government had captured the world's imagination. It is probably this that was the reason there was no trouble in allowing them in, even though there was a Tory government in place.

To begin with, the first year in London was extremely difficult except for the freedom I felt. We were free from police surveillance, free from the threat of imprisonment and free from the threat of police interrogations. We had no money but were given a small grant from the movement.

In the first three months we moved ten times until I found a flat we could rent. It was relatively cheap in those days and we had somewhere permanent to live. Our house in Johannesburg had finally been sold and that paid for our goods to be shipped to the country. Within a month our two daughters were given permission by the government to travel and came unaccompanied by plane. I got them into the nearest government school. Nicholas was brought to us in late January 1964. He was then nine months old.

Within days of arriving in London, Harold and Arthur were both engaged in political activities. They gave talks all over the country as well as in Europe on behalf of the ANC and the SACP. They set out to counter the propaganda spread by the South African government that they were terrorists, hell-bent on destroying South Africa and the white community. They presented the struggle as a movement that had come to adopt a more aggressive role only after all attempts at peaceful resistance and hopes of achieving equality had been irretrievably denied by the apartheid government.

I experienced extreme loneliness and isolation because I was alone most of the time with the children. In those early years there were enormous problems to face. On one occasion when Harold was out of the country for a month I saw nobody. It was tough. I never really felt English and remained always an outsider to a certain extent. Nor, for that matter, were my children, especially the girls who always felt ashamed of having been South African-born, of being associated with the racism of the country.

Living on charity resulted in my traipsing from shop to shop to find the cheapest possible foods, literally to save pennies. I examined prices on shelves closely. I never bought a more expensive item if it could be avoided, a habit I still have. One learnt to be resourceful, although in those early days I don't recall whether there were charity shops from which one could buy really good, but cheap, second-hand clothes. It was far more difficult keeping house in a climate in which there was a great deal of cold, few really bright sunny days, constant rainfall, and the endless noise and traffic and pace of life in London. I learnt how to furnish our homes with second-hand furniture bought from junk shops.

After a year of working for the movement, Harold had to decide whether he would work full time for the movement or not. If he did, he probably would have to live somewhere in Africa. He decided against doing this largely, I think, for family reasons.

He was really lucky as he was offered a fellowship, which he took up at the London School of Economics, a progressive university. He had a year to study and to work as a sociologist.

The first job Harold was able to get after he had completed that year was in adult education in Kent in 1966. This meant we had to move to a little town called Sevenoaks, south of London. We knew no one there and I would sometimes amuse myself by driving in the country in the morning with baby Nicholas as company. I was lonely again. Harold was closeted in his study all day, working hard at preparing his courses, and would go out in the evenings to give his classes.

We then moved to Yorkshire in the north when Harold got a job at the University of Bradford in 1968. I really thought at that time I would not survive this move. The experience of loneliness became intensified and I would suffer black depression. I had no friends initially and no family on whom I could rely and Yorkshire was very different and far from London. It was a little like moving into a foreign country. And it was starting all over again – to find the contacts for everyday living.

I did hate being there to begin with. The white sky, the dry stone walls of the houses, the countryside in which I could see no beauty, the Yorkshire accent and words that were foreign. It was also a lot colder than London. All these elements conspired to make life a misery. Sheila and Vic, Harold's colleagues from the university, were my only outside contact, but they tended to talk shop all the time. The language of sociologists was foreign to me although I had done a year's course in it, but that was a number of years back. When Sheila and Vic came for supper I would prepare the meal and then afterwards sit and listen to their conversation, not understanding what they were talking about. It might have been a foreign language. I would sit and knit furiously. This went on for many months.

Then, suddenly a job came up in the sociology department in which Harold worked and his boss thought that I should apply. It was a job as a researcher in a unit

for Yugoslav studies. I had done some research as an undergraduate. I had conducted
a survey to establish the rate of tuberculosis among garment workers when I worked
for Helen Joseph in South Africa. I had also conducted some interviews for a major
study in Kent.

It was a reference I had from the professor to whom I reported my findings that
stood me in good stead. Partly, also, there was a huge education expansion in the
country at the time and a shortage of graduates, which may have accounted for my
getting the job. But I am convinced to this day that the head of sociology wanted to
strengthen her position in the university and having a researcher in her department
would increase her strength. The politics of academia are fascinating.

Miraculously, I got the job although I had only a B.A. Honours degree and had
not worked ever as a sociologist, and knew absolutely nothing about Yugoslavia. Not
only that, it meant I had to learn Serbo Croat which is a Slav language and ever so
complicated. I am not good at languages in any event, but to learn a complex one out
of a book is no easy job.

At the time, the women's movement was sweeping through Europe and America.
Women from all walks of life were becoming conscious of the burdens of their lives,
especially those women who worked not only in their homes but outside as well.
There was a major change in which women began to recognise that housework was a
form of work in its own right. Consequently, housework itself can and should be
valued every bit as much as paid work outside the home, just as men's paid work is
regarded. But this was not the case (and still is not to this day). If one were to calculate
the worth of housework, husbands would never be able to pay their wives for what
they do in the home.

This differed so from the beliefs held by both men and women that men's roles
were entirely to support the family and women were to see to the maintenance of
family life through their work in the home. Women's housework was simply a reflection
of that belief that that was what women did. Men could relax once the working day
was over and they returned home. Then, if women did go out to work, they still had
to cook, clean, see to the needs of the family irrespective of anything else. This
realisation slowly dawned on me because like most women I was brought up to believe
that women's main goals in life were housewives. Whether she worked outside the
home was immaterial.

Once I started working and studying outside the home the feeling of isolation
and loneliness was reduced. I was finally beginning to enjoy life again. We had moved
into a house. We had a dog and a swing for the children. We could go for walks in the
extraordinary countryside with hills that dipped, and we climbed hills that were marked
off by dry stone walls. I began to see the beauty and majesty of our surroundings.
Our lives were assuming a normality that so many people took for granted. We were
quite free from fear.

After three years we moved back to London. This time it was because I got a job at what was to become Middlesex Polytechnic and Harold at another Polytechnic. After several years there he took a lectureship at Essex University where he remained until our return to South Africa. I similarly remained working at Middlesex Polytechnic.

This was a period during which my own work developed greatly. It was both academic and in the women's movement. In academic terms, I first held a research post and then after 1974 was appointed to the teaching staff. I began writing articles and the first book in which I was co-editor was published in 1978. The book was called *Feminism and Materialism* and even circulated on Robben Island!

Academic work enabled me to be more available for the children than a conventional nine-to-five job. But the work was demanding and far from simple and straightforward. And there was no back-up help as one would have in one's own country with friends and family around. I realised more and more just how disadvantaged women were not only in the United Kingdom but worldwide. I focused my research on understanding how the education system discriminated against girls and women. Initially, the work I did was regarded by most of my male colleagues as an easy option and created difficulties for myself and other women in our institutions who were conscious of this work. Few of our male colleagues realised just how sophisticated and advanced our feminist studies had become.

Within two years of being back in London, I was fully involved in the women's movement – the socialist side of it – which, in itself, was extremely interesting and challenging. I was a member of the Women's Research and Resources Centre, and a founder member of a journal, *Feminist Review*, which is still operating in the United Kingdom. This influenced and affected my life overall.

There is no doubt though that I benefited hugely from the facilities of living in the United Kingdom with all its social services and, particularly, the health service and the intellectual stimuli that determined the trajectory of my life.

All the while, we obviously were in touch with South African matters, Harold far more so than me, particularly with his connection with the Solomon Mahlangu School in Tanzania. Solomon Mahlangu, an MK operative, was hanged on 6 April 1979 for the Goch Street shooting in Johannesburg on 13 June 1977, where two people died. After he was hanged there was a worldwide outcry and it was decided to create a school in his name to cater for the youth who had left South Africa.

Harold was the chairperson of the committee that worked closely with the school, devising syllabi and so on, which used to meet in our house. I was never invited to work on that committee and I only discovered years later that this was so because I was involved in feminist work.

Unfortunately, the ANC was not sympathetic to the women's movement at all, even after there had been a breakthrough in 1988 with Oliver Tambo recognising the role women played. There still was a feeling that the women's movement would prove a distraction from the real struggle issues in South Africa. When it became possible to become a member of the ANC, I did so and, towards the end of our stay in England, I chaired the Welfare Committee of our London office.

Harold never wavered from his commitment to the movement and did whatever he could to assist. It was through his academic writing, in particular, that his influence would be felt by the movement in South Africa. All his analyses and writing were geared to an understanding of the South African socio-economic conditions. His writing, although banned in South Africa, nevertheless circulated even among the prisoners on Robben Island and among the young intellectuals as well. And he would feed his ideas into the movement in London. In particular he would discuss strategies and policies for the movement at length with Joe Slovo.

From the mid-1970s onwards, the situation in South Africa was horrendous. We probably had far better coverage of all the travesties of justice through the medium of good BBC television than people in the country itself. It was going from bad to worse. There was no point in pining for South Africa. We could not return even if we wanted to. When my mother was ill and dying, I could not even get a guarantee of a safe passage and was advised not to attempt to visit the country.

Things began to change significantly from the mid-1980s. There were definite signs of the apartheid government beginning to crumble. Harold participated in clandestine meetings both in England and overseas. Things were moving very fast, too. And then suddenly the ANC, the Communist Party and other organisations were unbanned in 1990. The possibility of returning to South Africa was realised with the release of Nelson Mandela. It was not long before Harold and I were recruited by Jakes Gerwel to work at the University of the Western Cape.

After twenty-eight years of living in England, I had become entirely acclimatised to our life in London. Our children were all adult and life was becoming distinctly easier for me. The thought of returning, however, did not fill me with joy. I began to dread it. I did not want to give up everything all over again. All my friends were now firmly in England. My life's work was very much focused on conditions in that country. Although I had reached official retiring age, I did not anticipate giving up my work and studies on women's social status. The decision was clear. Harold would return in any event. He said if I did not want to come back then I could remain on in England. In the end, of course, I did return.

At that time there was distinct antagonism towards white women feminists in South Africa. And apart from this, I anticipated coming back to a society in which racism was rife and not only racism as blacks experienced it, but racism that whites were likely to experience from blacks, quite understandably. I did think that being a white feminist would not bode well for me even though I had developed quite a thick skin about the antagonism towards feminism. I had experienced a great deal of antipathy from my male colleagues at Middlesex. The thought of having to go through all that again was very daunting.

To begin with, my expectations about finding life difficult here were unhappily realised. I went through, yet again, a period of extreme loneliness and isolation. My sister lived in the Wilderness, five hours' drive from Cape Town, and I could not see her that often. Strangely, it was like reliving the early life in London. I found the work at the university enormously difficult for a variety of reasons, although nevertheless interesting. I did minimal teaching at the University of the Western Cape, but found the modes of teaching very different from the English system where students had to read texts and study on their own. The bulk of my work though was research and this was intriguing.

We had returned in 1991 and, in early January 1996, Harold died. This left a dreadful void. To begin with, I was fortunately engaged by the national Department of Education about six months after his death to chair a task team on gender equity for girls and women in education. This eased the period of grief and did help to make me feel more accepted in South Africa. After the publication of that report, I was employed by the Department of Education as well as foreign donors for short periods. I was deeply involved in the founding and development of a trust that was established after Harold's death and which continues to this day. The fundamental aim of the Harold Wolpe Memorial Trust is to promote informed discussion and debate in the country. Liliesleaf Farm on 4 Broadacres Drive in Rivonia has been developed into an interpretative centre.

It is now nineteen years since I returned to the country. All three of my children have also returned. When we came back, I no longer had friends from our earlier days. We came to Cape Town where we knew very few people.

Overall, I have benefited enormously because of my class and race. My parents were middle class and white. I had a university degree the equivalent of a B.A. Honours and had travelled overseas on two occasions. I can truly say that I have been really one of the lucky people in terms of the chances I have been given, especially the opportunity of studying and making a small contribution to the rights of women while in England.

Now, having my immediate family close by, living in one of the most beautiful cities in the world has made a huge difference. And perhaps, most importantly, I have lived to see South Africa emerge from darkness into a democracy. I feel well and truly settled here having participated as fully as I could in the reconstruction of a new society in the field of my area of specialisation, which is the educational system. And I do love this country. There is no doubt we have a long way to go and there is so much to be done in terms of achieving the aims of the struggle. We are beset with innumerable problems, but we shall get there in the end.

Abbreviations

ANC	African National Congress
APDUSA	African People's Democratic Union of South Africa
APLA	Azania People's Liberation Army
BCC	Botswana Christian Council
BCM	Black Consciousness Movement
CPSA	Communist Party of South Africa
LM	Lourenzo Marques
MAWU	Metal and Allied Workers Union
MK	Umkhonto we Sizwe
MNR	Mozambican National Resistance
NUMSA	National Union of Metalworkers
OAU	Organisation of African Unity
PAC	Pan-Africanist Congress
SACP	South African Communist Party
SADF	South African Defence Force
SASO	South African Students' Organisation
SOMAFCO	Solomon Mahlangu Freedom College
SRC	Student Representative Council
SWAPO	South West Africa People's Organisation
UNHCR	United Nations High Commissioner for Refugees
WCC	World Council of Churches
YWCA	Young Women's Christian Association
ZANU-PF	Zimbabwe African National Union – Patriotic Front